THE TASTE OF COURAGE

The drama, the humor, the horror, and sometimes the tenderness of men and women confronting their greatest ordeal speak through this absorbing narrative of World War II, told in eyewitness accounts by soldiers, housewives and journalists in the many countries involved.

Volume III: The Tide Turns is the story of the first Allied victories of the war, victories which followed endless defeats. In Russia, the Wehrmacht suffered its first major setback, when the German 6th Army, commanded by von Paulus, was first held, then smashed, at Stalingrad. In North Africa, Montgomery and the British 8th Army defeated the hitherto invincible Afrika Korps at El Alamein. At sea, the victorious Japanese Navy was stopped at Midway. The Allied Air Forces were carrying the bombing war to Germany. For the time, it seemed that the Allies had a real chance of victory . . .

THE TASTE OF COURAGE
THE WAR, 1939-1945
VOLUME III: THE TIDE TURNS

Edited by DESMOND FLOWER and JAMES REEVES

A BERKLEY MEDALLION BOOK
published by
BERKLEY PUBLISHING CORPORATION

ACKNOWLEDGMENTS

Grateful acknowledgment is made to the following for permission to reprint selections included in this book:

Brandt & Brandt
  I Was There by Admiral William D. Leahy. Published by McGraw-Hill Book Co.
  Admiral Halsey's Story by William F. Halsey and Joseph Bryan. Published by McGraw-Hill Book Co.
  Hitler and His Admirals by Anthony Martienssen. Copyright 1949 by Anthony Martienssen.
  Defeat in the West by Milton Shulman. Copyright 1948 by Milton Shulman.
Cassell & Co. Ltd.
  Sunk by Mochitsura Hashimoto. Copyright 1954 by Henry Holt & Co., Inc.
Constable & Co. Ltd.
  Retreat, Hell! by William Camp. Copyright 1943 by William Martin Camp. Published by Appleton-Century-Crofts, Inc.
Curtis Brown, Ltd.
  Still Digging by Mortimer Wheeler. Copyright © 1955 by Eric Robert Mortimer Wheeler. Published by E.P. Dutton & Co.
  The Green Beret by Hilary St. George Saunders. Reprinted by permission of the author's estate.
  The Spirit in the Cage by Peter Churchill.
The John Day Company
  The Invisible Flag by Peter Bamm.
Dodd, Mead & Company
  Going to the Wars by John Verney. Copyright © 1955 by John Verney.

TO THE

30,000,000

DEAD

INTRODUCTION

THIS is a documentary conspectus of the worst war in history, beginning at the German invasion of Poland on 1 September 1939 and ending with the last Japanese surrenders in September and October 1945. But it is not a history of the war: that has been written—by Sir Winston Churchill and by other historians, official and unofficial. This book could not have been written by one man, for it is an attempt to put together a chronicle of how it actually felt to be alive twenty years ago; to see, to hear, to smell, to feel the war at first hand. As service men and women, politicians and diplomats, workers in the resistance movements and victims of aggression, as men and women in civil occupations, and even as children, millions were aware of the war as a world-wide cataclysm hanging over the whole of life. Some, comparatively few but still numerous, wrote down their experience of that part of the war in which they were immediately involved; this book is a mosaic of such records. The contributors are world leaders, soldiers, sailors and airmen, journalists, firemen, hospital staff, factory workers, peasants—anyone who has written down in the spirit of an eye-witness or a participant his impressions of some aspect of war experience, of greater or lesser significance.

What must impress the reader of these pages is the vastness of the war: its totality, the extent to which it penetrated like an evil contagion into every corner of the inhabited world. As Marshal Pétain, the misguided master of Vichy, remarked at one stage—"Now for the first time the whole world is at war." In these pages will be found the views and feelings of housewives in London, Berlin, Moscow and Tokyo: their problems, joys and sorrows are much the same. Here, too, we present the views of British and Germans facing one another at El Alamein, of Russians and Germans creeping forward through the frozen ruins of Stalingrad, of Americans and Japanese inching through a sodden Pacific jungle. All these, and many more, were men and women committed the world over to a problem from which none could escape once the politicians had decreed that the shooting should begin. This second World War produced heroism comparable with anything which had gone before, cowardice, inefficiency, brilliance, greatness, and a dedication to one object—on whichever side it might be—of more people than have ever before been involved in a single, terrifying catastrophe.

One of us responsible for this volume was concerned in 1937 with the production of a similar book describing the first World War: it was called *Vain Glory*. In our present task we find a difference. About the second World War there was little either vain or glorious. It was a bitter, sordid affair—for even the horrors of Passchendaele had an heroic dignity which cannot be equalled. It was not in vain, since it was begun to remove the evil men of Nuremberg, and in that at least it succeeded. But, to the surprise of those who found themselves involved in it, it developed into a display of hard-hitting brutality—sparing neither men, women, nor children—which only the mythical depredations of Genghis Khan may have challenged.

If there is ever a third world war, it will no doubt be a very clean job of destruction started at a range of thousands of miles by technicians suitably protected below ground and pressing a knob. But when the first scientific flurry is over, the destruction will be so great that it will be left to the surviving men, women and children to stick it out and somehow try to get the mess through to a conclusion.

In compiling this book we have paid our respects to military prowess—the actions of the professional soldiers who have triumphed with all the skill to which their lives have been devoted; but the victims of any war are the people: people in uniform, people out of uniform, people fighting, and people fleeing. There will be nowhere to flee next time, so this book offers a record of what may be the last of its kind: for better or for worse.

D. F.   J. R.
Headley, Hants   Chalfont St. Giles, Bucks

CONTENTS

MAPS

ACKNOWLEDGMENTS

WE wish to express our gratitude to the individuals, libraries, and other bodies listed below, all of whom have been of the greatest possible assistance in the preparation of this book. The authors and publishers of the extracts used are acknowledged in full between pages 367 and 371.

> The American Embassy Library
> The Guildhall Library
> The Imperial War Museum Library
> The Information Bureau, Chatham House
> The Book Information Bureau, National Book
>   League
> The Walter Hines Page Memorial Library
> The War Office Library
> Mr. J. A. Williams

We would also like to thank the many publishers and literary agents who have lent us new books in typescript, proof, or bound copy form, a kindness which has allowed the inclusion of much recently published material. We also wish to thank Mr. T. R. Nicholson for his great editorial help in the closing stages of the preparation of the book for the printer, Mrs. Herta Ryder, who throughout has kept under her control the vast amount of material which accumulated, and Mr. Antony Brett-James for his assistance in checking proofs.

D F.   J. R.

NOTE

The contributions to this book are chosen from documentary sources. In one or two cases, where no eye-witness account is available, a reliable historian has been drawn upon for the record. Fiction has only been used when the Editors are satisfied that the writer was present at and witnessed the events which he has woven into his narrative. The war and its ramifications were so great and so many that some aspects have not been mentioned in these pages. To those on all sides whose work has not been recognized, we offer our apologies and hope that they will find some satisfaction in the overall picture of the vast struggle.

D. F.   J. R.

IDENTIFICATION
OF EXTRACTS

IN order to discover the source of any extract, the reader should note the number of the page on which it begins and its heading and first words, and then refer to the section entitled *Key to the Sources of Extracts* (pages 361 to 366). There, following the page number and brief identification of the passage, will be found a key number. Reference to this key number in the following section, entitled *Sources* (pages 367 to 371), will reveal the title, author, publisher and publication date of the work drawn upon.

The italicized passages between extracts have been interpolated by the Editors to provide a consecutive narrative.

Signatures: A very few extracts are not signed. These are the small minority of completely impersonal passages written by historians, inserted, when of a sufficiently high standard, for lack of first-hand material. Of the signed extracts, a few are anonymous; for example, "British gunner". In these cases the Editors have been unable to ascertain the writer's identity, or else the writer has wished to remain anonymous. In some cases the signatures of servicemen do not include ranks. These are omitted either because the appropriate rank could not be ascertained, or because it was thought more effective to omit them. Where a rank is given, it changes appropriately in the cases of the most famous men, and in other cases remains the same throughout, the rank likely to sound most familiar or natural to the reader being given. These are broad principles, but individual circumstances may have had to dictate some exceptions, at the expense of rules of consistency.

... THERE is a great danger in this war. But if we are among those that get back, we shall have nothing to tell. I have had adventures—pioneering mail lines; flying the Andes; being forced down among rebellious Arabs in the Sahara. But war is not a true adventure. It is a mere *ersatz*. Where ties are established, where problems are set, where creation is stimulated—there you have adventure. But there is no adventure in heads-or-tails, in betting that the toss will come out life or death. War is not an adventure. It is a disease. It is like typhus.

Antoine de Saint-Exupéry

If it be Life that awaits, I shall live forever unconquered:
If Death, I shall die at last strong in my pride and free.

Scottish National Memorial

1

COMBINED OPERATIONS

The idea of forming small, permanent, specialized units of highly trained and highly skilled troops working on independent missions while supported by naval and air units was a British one, born naturally of her peculiar strategic situation and needs in the days of defeat in 1940. It originated in the mind of Lieutenant-Colonel Dudley Clarke, R.A., early in June. The prototypes for the force had been the hurriedly raised Independent Companies used to delay the Germans in Norway. The plan fitted in well with Winston Churchill's desire to hit back at the Germans, even in defeat, and was accepted.

The Commandos are Born

WE are greatly concerned—and it is certainly wise to be so—with the dangers of the German landing in England in spite of our possessing the command of the seas and having very strong defence by fighters in the air. Every creek, every beach, every harbor has become to us a source of anxiety. Besides this the parachutists may sweep

over and take Liverpool or Ireland, and so forth. All this
mood is very good if it engenders energy. But if it is so
easy for the Germans to invade us, in spite of sea-power,
some may feel inclined to ask the question, why should it
be thought impossible for us to do anything of the same
kind to them? The completely defensive habit of mind
which has ruined the French must not be allowed to ruin
all our initiative. It is of the highest consequence to keep
the largest numbers of German forces all along the coasts
of the countries they have conquered, and we should
immediately set to work to organize raiding forces on
these coasts where the populations are friendly.

Winston Churchill, 4 June 1940

We have got to get out of our minds the idea that the
Channel ports and all the country between them are
enemy territory. What arrangements are being made for
good agents in Denmark, Holland, Belgium and along the
French coast? Enterprises must be prepared, with
specially-trained troops of the hunter class, who can
develop a reign of terror down these coasts, first of all on
the "butcher and bolt" policy; but later on, or perhaps
as soon as we are organized, we could surprise Calais or
Boulogne, kill and capture the Hun garrison, and hold the
place until all the preparations to reduce it by siege or
heavy storm have been made, and then away. The passive
resistance war, in which we have acquitted ourselves so
well, must come to an end.

Winston Churchill, 6 June 1940

Utmost care was taken in selecting the men required for
these irregular operations. There were failures, as in all
walks of life, but most of those chosen were well-chosen.
Their view of their work was well summed up by one of
their number, who died young with a D.S.O., M.C. and
bar:

Of course, it is absolutely terrific; it is the greatest job
in the Army that one could possibly get, and it is a job

that, if properly carried out, can be of enormous value . . . no red tape, no paper work . . . just pure operations, the success of which depends principally on oneself and the men one has oneself picked to do the job with you . . . it's revolutionary.

Geoffrey Appleyard

The Technique of Staying Alive

Keep the sun behind you; you can control your own shadow and merge it with the others. . . . Fruit trees harbour many birds which set up a noise if disturbed. Steady shuffling through grass does not worry them but the slightest tinkle of metal causes a flurry. . . . Cattle not milked recently will lick your face and moo. The only solution is to lie on your back and milk the damn things. . . . We killed several Germans because they always went to the same latrine and we noticed it. . . . The sniper has to work long, long hours to kill one German. . . . Dirty your hands and face with burnt cork, graphite, soot, or lamp black, but do *not* use earth. . . . An antidote for sneezing is to press the upper lip against the base of the nose. . . . Do not wear gum boots; they go "plop plop".

Within three weeks of their formation, the Commandos' first raid was mounted. It was not a success; nor was the second, on Guernsey another three weeks later. In a sense, both served their purpose: the Commandos were learning fast.

The crews of the speedboats were R.N.V.R. volunteers of a most cheerful and happy-go-lucky disposition. The first thing we found as we left the destroyer was that they had forgotten to adjust their compasses which were many degrees wrong, so we had to take a chance and guess at our landing place. By great good luck we happened to strike the right one and make our landing approximately on time.

The time ashore was uneventful. The barracks we

visted proved to be unoccupied so we were unable to make prisoners. We collected a certain amount of information from residents at Guernsey, most of whom were too frightened to talk properly, not being able to believe it was British soldiers and thinking it was some trick of the Gestapo to get information from them. The trouble started when we returned to the beach and tried to get off to the speedboats. A heavy swell had got up and the speedboats could not come nearer than about fifty yards, so we all had to swim for it, as the one small dinghy in use soon capsized and was smashed on the rocks. Three men, who had stated in their interviews that they could swim, proved to be non-swimmers and had to be left behind. This was one of our early lessons, and swimming instruction was pushed on pretty hard when we got back.

At this critical moment the Germans also came to life and started machine-gunning, fortunately not very accurately. We all had an exhausting swim through the surf, but bar the three non-swimmers all eventually got to the speedboats. One of these then broke down, and aboard the other the crew were not very good at making up their minds what to do. Even the engine-room attendant emerged from the engine-room to take part in a discussion with the captain and give his advice. We finally got underway, making about two knots, with one boat towing the other.

By this time we were nearly an hour late for the rendezvous with the destroyer, and as we emerged from Telegraph Bay we could just see her disappearing at high speed. We managed to attract her attention with a torch and the captain very gallantly returned to pick us up, thereby leaving himself open to probable air attack the whole way back to England, as the dawn was just about breaking.

We got on board the destroyer and by a miracle avoided all air attacks and returned to Dartmouth, having achieved very little, but learnt a good deal.

                                                      Major Durnford-Slater

Churchill is not Satisfied: 25 August 1940

I hear that the whole position of the Commandos is being questioned. They have been told "no more recruiting" and that their future is in the melting pot. . . . For every reason therefore we must develop the storm troop or Commando idea. I have asked for five thousand parachutists, and we must also have at least ten thousand of these small "band of brothers" who will be capable of lightning war.

Winston Churchill

The Lofoten Raid

Some months of inaction followed the initial failures. Then on 4 March 1941 a combined operation was launched against the Lofoten Islands off the coast of Norway by Commandos and naval forces.

Tuesday 5.15 (scribbled in boat):

It is just light enough to write. We are packed sardine-wise and half asleep, being embarked in more than enough time. It is calm and clear twilight. In spite of the latitude, season of the year and early morning hour, I don't need gloves, though in an open boat at sea!

. . . . We are beginning to move in earnest. I can see nothing except a saxe-blue sky, a gull, and occasionally the mastheads of the man-of-war leading us.

Some spray coming in which *is* cold!

. . . . Whole silhouette of man-of-war. She is slowing down and we are passing her. I have seldom seen anything so dramatic and beautiful—every spar and rope clean-cut against the blue, every man standing rigid and motionless at his gun or instrument.

On land, Svolvaer:

Bang-banging everywhere. Presumably demolition, plus (?) men-o'-war sinking German trawlers.

A perfectly lovely morning. Beautiful little mountain

peaks, pink in sunlight, round a rather picturesque little town.

8 a.m. (for address, see reverse side of page):
Guarding half-wrecked office.

Sapper has put one charge of explosive on safe and made a hole in it. But safe still resists and he has gone for more H.E. We don't want sappers so much as burglars!

No Germans this side of water. Must be dead or captured t'other side, because crowd is parading with Norwegian flag, cheering, etc.

10 a.m.:
Safe open. Little of interest. £5 worth of notes and coppers—to be returned to firm. Fine blaze in adjoining factory and yard.

We have captured one German soldier, a nasty-looking little twerp in a green uniform; he is smiling sheepishly and seems rather pleased to be captured. Officer has taken camera from him and is photographing fire.

Large crowd of Norsk children collecting. Much fraternization.

It *has* been very tame. Little danger now unless from air, or torpedo on return.

12 noon:
Back on S.S. *Domino* with many recruits for Norsk Army and Navy in England, one or two hundred prisoners, mainly sailors, but one flying officer and some soldiers. All objectives achieved. One casualty on our side—an officer has wounded himself with his own revolver. So it has been a mere tea-party for us, and all the heroics look a little silly.

4 p.m.:
All, or nearly all, is over. Norway is invisible to the left (PORT!). The last of the Lofotens sliding past on the right (STARBOARD!), looking like gigantic fairy icebergs in the evening sun.

. . . I must tell you that all my *arrière-pensées* about blowing up Norwegian cod liver oil factories prove unjustified. It appears that:

(i) The cod liver oil is not required for babies, but for making nitrogenous explosives, and so bombs.

(ii) The unemployment problem I feared is cancelled by the number of young men we are taking away from Svolvaer as volunteers for Norwegian Army, Navy and Merchant Services. Also, I was assured that the labour in the factory was more or less German-enforced, and that the men will be glad to go back to their own fishing. This is especially so in view of (iii), and (iii) is rather funny.

(iii) One of my jobs was to search the office for papers. I found very few of the slightest possible use. I found one or two referring to last week and then nothing between that and 1936. I naturally concluded that someone had got wind of our coming and hidden or removed the last five years' papers—though I couldn't quite make out why. I am now told that the factory closed down for lack of business in 1936: that the Nazi government ordered its re-opening for munition purposes: that last winter was spent in re-conditioning and repairing: that it re-opened yesterday. So we can say to Hitler, "Open a factory in the Lofotens on Monday, and we'll blow it up for you on Tuesday."

I was very glad of the little Norwegian I was able to learn (on top of my muddled and half-forgotten Swedish) during the voyage out. It enabled me to discover exactly what was going on, when I otherwise could not have known. It enabled me to help a lot of people, particularly a poor woman with a baby whom we had to get out of bed, and out of her home, in case the fire from the factory explosion spread. She was wife to the caretaker in the wooden office-warehouse I was responsible for, and she seemed sure we wanted to take her and her baby outside in order to bayonet them in the snow. She was the only Svolvaerian I saw who showed the slightest fear of us. I had to roar: *"For din egen Sikkerhet!"* at her about four times, and her husband and friends had to repeat it (in a

rather better accent) before she began to look less
terrified and prepare to come away. We helped her
husband carry out most of their furniture, clothes, etc., in
case of accidents, and make a dump of them at a safe
distance from the burning factory. Incidentally, the fire
didn't spread to their warehouse-office-home, so they'll be
spending the afternoon carrying them all back again.

My bad Norwegian also enabled me to discover that
some piles of timber which *were* beginning to burn were
not for German consumption, and so to start our men and
the crowd of Norwegian spectators on successful salvage.
It meant I could help a little (a very little!) in the
recruiting: most of this was going on in the main town
t'other side of the harbour which I was itching to cross all
the morning. It finally enabled me, as our boats pushed
off at midday, to shout: *"Til vi komme tilbakke!*—Till we
come back!"—to the crowd on the quay.

Evan John

Vaagso: 27 December 1941

*This raid on Norway, directed against military
installations, shipping and other targets, was much more
seriously contested, but was equally successful.*

As night fell, on Boxing Day, the ships sailed again for
Vaagso, Admiral Tovey covering our approach with the
major units of the Atlantic Fleet, including his flagship,
King George V. The submarine *Tuna* had preceded us and
was lying off the entrance to Vaagsfjord to act as a
navigational beacon on our way in. H.M.S. *Kenya* led our
particular convoy, flying the flag of Admiral Burrough.
She was followed by the destroyer H.M.S. *Chiddingfold*;
then came the *Charles* and *Leopold* carrying the troops
with the destroyers *Onslow, Offa* and *Oribi* following
close behind.

We were called at 4 a.m. I had often read in
descriptions of naval battles that the sailors wore clean
underclothes so as to minimize the risk of infection from

wounds, so I put on a clean vest and pair of pants and told all the others to do the same. I took great trouble to check up on every item of my equipment. On this operation I carried a Colt .45 pistol with three spare magazines. All these magazines were discharged by the end of the day, but I never again went into action carrying a pistol only, as these weapons do not give confidence when opposed to a man with a rifle. We had a good breakfast at 5 a.m. and carried with us a small compact haversack ration. In my case, and in nearly all other cases, this ration was untouched when we returned to the ship at 3 p.m. The excitement was too great to allow time off for eating.

Off Vaagsfjord at 7 a.m. we picked up the *Tuna* as planned. The surge of excitement which was running through our ship had erased all thought of seasickness. We entered the fjord, a spectacular passage between great, snow-covered hills. We were to land at first light, ten minutes to nine. The *Prince Charles* and *Prince Leopold* pulled into a small bay. The troops filed into the landing craft and these were lowered to the cold waters of the fjord. Then *Kenya,* two hundred yards behind us, opened the bombardment of Maaloy Island where the Germans manned a coast defence battery. We started the run-in in our landing craft.

About a hundred yards from our landing place, I fired ten red Verey light signals. This told the ships to stop firing and the aircraft to come in with their smoke bombs. As I leaped from the leading landing craft three Hampden bombers passed over me at zero feet with a roar. As they did so they loosed their bombs, which seemed to flash and then mushroom like miniature atom explosions. Some of the phosphorus came back in a great flaming sheet. Next thing I knew both my sleeves were on fire. Fortunately I wore leather gloves and beat the flames out before they could eat through my four layers of clothing to the skin. The beaching had been made, dry, against snow-covered rocks which rose thirty or forty feet in an almost sheer wall. For the moment, we were unopposed and hidden from the enemy by smoke.

Unfortunately, however, one of the Hampdens was hit by anti-aircraft fire as she came in. Out of control, she dropped a bomb on an incoming landing craft. Bursting, the phosphorus inflicted terrible burns amongst the men. The craft, too, burst into flames. Grenades, explosives, and small arms ammunition were detonated in a mad mixture of battle noises. We pushed the emptied craft out to sea where it could do us no harm, and Sam Corry, our big, efficiently calm Irish doctor, taking charge of the casualties, sent them back to the *Prince Charles*. The rest of us turned to the battle.

Major Durnford-Slater

The Capture of Maaloy Island

The Germans on the island had been caught unprepared. They were following their usual routine: the gunners were being roused by a loud-voiced N.C.O.; the officer commanding (Butziger, by name) was shaving; his batman, whose turn it was that morning to man the telephone connecting headquarters with the look-out post, was cleaning his officer's boots on the table beside the instrument. So busily engaged was he upon this task that he allowed the telephone bell to ring, and did not trouble to pick up the receiver. The German gunners thus received no warning. Outside the barracks on the island of Maaloy there was a naval signalling station established on the highest point. The signaller on duty received a message flashed by lamp telling of the advent of our forces. He ran down to the small bay on the north side of the island, leapt into a boat and rowed as fast as he could to the headquarters of the German Naval Commandant on the main island of Vaagso. Here he delivered the warning, but when asked whether he had warned the army gunners on Maaloy, he replied, "Oh no, sir, it is a military battery, and this is a naval signal." The Germans are a most methodical people.

Hilary St. George Saunders

Street Battle

Vaagso is built on one narrow street, three-quarters of a mile long, which runs parallel to, and about fifty yards from, the fjord. Behind the street, which was lined with unpainted wooden buildings, nearly sheer rocks rose to several hundred feet. I heard Johnny Giles yell, "Come on", and saw him disappear with his 3 Troop into the smoke.

That was the last I saw of Johnny. Fifteen minutes later he was dead, killed in an assault on the back of a house. He and his men had shot three Germans who had been firing on them from the house, then rushed it. They went through the rooms and as Johnny entered the last room a fourth German jumped in front of him and shot him.

At about the time Johnny met his death I went into a large oil factory near our landing beach. I was looking for Johann Gotteberg, who had been named to us as the chairman of the local quislings and was the owner of this factory. Meanwhile Bill Bradley prepared the factory for demolition. I saw a middle-aged man who seemed to be attending the machinery with extraordinary concentration, considering the circumstances.

"Who is that man?" I asked my Norwegian guide, a native of Vaagso.

"That is Gotteberg, the owner."

I had him arrested. A few minutes later he had a first-class view of his factory being blown up.

Algy Forrester went off like a rocket with his 4 Troop down the street of the town, leaving a trail of dead Germans behind him. The troop had just lost Arthur Komrower, who had suffered severe leg and back injuries when he was pinned between a landing craft and a rock. The third officer of 4 Troop was Bill Lloyd, who, with Algy, had developed the technique of landing on rough and rocky shores. Bill hardly got going before he was shot, clean through the neck. That was the end of him for this operation.

Algy waded in, shouting and cheering his men, throwing

grenades into each house as they came to it and firing
from the hip with his tommy gun. He looked wild and
dangerous. I shouldn't have liked to have been a German
in his path. He had absolutely no fear. He led an assault
against the German headquarters, in the Ulvesund Hotel,
and was about to toss a grenade in when one of the
enemy, firing through the front door, shot him. As he fell
he landed on his own grenade, which exploded a second
later. This rough landing at Vaagso was the first time we
had put into operational practice the system he and Bill
Lloyd had developed. For Algy it was also the last.

Other casualties in Algy's troop were heavy. Captain
Martin Linge, my Norwegian friend, had also been
attached to No. 4. When the attack was briefly held up
after Algy's death, he kept things moving, but only for a
few minutes. He was killed in exactly the same way as
Forrester, shot as he tried to force open a door. I had
spoken to Martin just as he left the beach.

"This is good, Colonel," he had said, laughing. "We'll
have a party at the Mayfair to celebrate when we get
back."

He was a very gallant and fearless ally and would have
made an ideal Commando soldier.

The Germans had a tank in a garage near the Ulvesund
Hotel, about a hundred and fifty yards up the street, a fact
of which we were aware through our Intelligence. The
tank was an old one, but if it were brought out on to the
street it could wreak havoc amongst us with its gun. After
Martin Linge's death, Sergeant Cork and Johnnie Dowling
of 1 Troop managed to reach the tank, still in the garage,
and blow it up. Unfortunately Cork used too heavy a
charge and didn't get away quickly enough. He was caught
in the explosion and died of wounds. Johnny was
untouched. Corporal "Knocker" White was left in
command of Forrester's troop. He performed the job so
gallantly that he was to earn a Distinguished Conduct
Medal for it.

From our out-of-doors, snow-covered headquarters

near the landing place, I could see everything that took place on Maaloy. 5 and 6 Troops, only fifty yards from the beach when the naval barrage lifted, were up the slopes of the island like a flash. I saw them advancing through the smoke in perfect extended order. Jack Churchill, who had played them in with his bagpipes, was leading them with considerable dash. On landing, Peter Young saw a German running back to man his gun position. "I was able to shoot him," Peter told me later. Ten minutes after this, Young reached the company office on Maaloy. One of the German company clerks made the literally fatal mistake of trying to wrest Peter's rifle from him. Small pockets of resistance were quickly cleaned up and many prisoners were taken, including two Norwegian women of easy virtue who had been consoling the German soldiers.

The fighting in the town was still very hot and heavy, however, and I had Charlie Head, my Signals Officer for this raid, send a message to the headquarters ship asking for the floating reserve, and another to Jack Churchill on Maaloy asking if he, too, could help. Jack promptly sent 6 Troop under Peter Young: and Charles Haydon ordered the floating reserve to the far end of Vaagso. We were now attacking on two fronts.

Back in the main street, where our attack had been stalled, Peter Young with 6 Troop got things moving again. I left the Adjutant to control our headquarters and joined him. It was very noisy: there were the different sounds from the various calibres of small arms; artillery exchanges between *Kenya* and a coast defence battery somewhere down the fjord; anti-aircraft fire from the ships against the attacking Messerschmitts; the demolitions; and the crackling roar of flames. I heard one signaller complaining how difficult it was to receive messages.

"This is bloody awful! A man can hardly hear himself think!"

Our opposition was much stiffer than I had expected. It

was not until later that I learned that about fifty men from an exceptionally good German unit were spending Christmas leave at Vaagso.

As I tried to catch up with Peter Young I saw him and George Herbert throwing grenades through windows and doors. They appeared to be enjoying themselves. I finally joined them in a timber yard which had only one entrance off the main street. Part of our plan had been to dump many sacks of grenades near the landing place. Our Administrative Officer had organized a gang of loyal Norwegian civilians who followed close behind the leading troops, carrying these sacks, and offering the troops replenishments of grenades as often as they were needed.

Suddenly, in a strange interval when artillery and demolitions seemed to pause for their wind, there was an eerie, unexpected stillness. Half of 6 Troop were clustered in the timber yard. A single rifle shot rang out and a man fell dead beside me. I thought the shot had come from a house, about twenty yards away, on the other side of the small yard. We all started firing furiously at the windows of the house. I emptied my revolver, feeling strangely helpless, for there was only one exit to the yard and unless we did something quickly it seemed certain the sniper would pick us all off, one by one. Another shot came from the house and another man fell dead. I think this was the first time in warfare that I truly felt fear. I didn't like it.

We crouched behind a pile of timber. The sniper fired whenever one of us moved. Soon he picked off a third of our number. He was shooting right down at us from a first floor window.

There was a shed just behind our cover and George Herbert disappeared into it. "Captain Young," he called, "I've found a tin of petrol!"

"Put some in a bucket, Sergeant," Peter called back. "When you've done that we'll all stand up and give you covering fire while you toss it into the house."

Herbert obeyed, and the others followed the petrol up by lobbing grenades through the windows. There was a great burst of flame. Very soon the wooden house was burned to the ground, a funeral pyre for the sniper. I wasn't sorry to leave that timber yard.

It was just about then that Lieutenant Denis O'Flaherty was wounded. He had been leading assault after assault on enemy-held houses and was leading an attack on the steamship wharf when a sniper, concealed in a warehouse, hit him in the eye. The bullet came out through his throat. O'Flaherty, a brave soldier, had been wounded twice before. This most serious wound was to cost him eight major operations and two years in hospital. He lost his eye but never his spirit. Later, still fighting for Britain, he was decorated by the Americans for gallantry in Korea.

After the affair of the timber yard, when the attack got moving down the main street again, a door on the fjord side of the street suddenly opened and a German lobbed out a grenade. It rolled between my feet and stopped. I was standing on a corner and instinctively took a tremendous dive for shelter round the edge of the building. I landed on my face, just in time to hear the grenade go off. I escaped with a couple of small bits of the grenade in my palm, but my orderly was badly wounded.

About thirty seconds later, the same door opened and the German who had tossed the grenade came out with his hands up and expressing his earnest desire to surrender. I was prepared to accept this, but one of my men thought otherwise. He advanced on the German. "Nein! Nein!" the German yelled, a small man, yellow and scared.

Our man was so angry that he shot the German dead, through the stomach. This, of course, is one of the tricky problems in warfare. Can a man throw a death-dealing grenade one second and surrender the next? I hardly think he can expect much mercy.

Then I saw Bob Clement organizing an attack on another building farther down the street. With Lance-Sergeant Culling, he led the way. As they approached the front door a German threw a percussion grenade at Culling's face, killing him instantly. Clement kept a brisk fire going into the building and called for Sergeant Ramsey and the mortar detachment, posting men all around to prevent any German from escaping. Ramsey got a direct hit on the roof with his third round and then pumped several dozen mortar bombs through the hole. The place was soon blazing. On my way back, when the flames had died down, I counted twelve German corpses inside.

This incident was to end the most severe phase of the fighting.

Major Durnford-Slater

The Attempt on Rommel

Commando operations in the Mediterranean were under the directon of Colonel R. E. Laycock. There were many expeditions, of which the best-known was the attempt to catch Rommel at what was thought to be his headquarters behind the lines in North Africa.

The attack had been planned for midnight, 17/18 November 1941, so as to coincide with the opening of General Auchinleck's offensive against Rommel. Six hours before, the Commando soldiers "fell in with almost parade-ground precision" for the final stage of the operation. They moved off, leaving behind them one man who had run a nail from the sole of his boot into his foot, to guard the spare rations. "It was pouring with rain, and we were most of the way walking ankle deep in mud. It was not long before we were wet to the skin." So bad were the conditions that they were soon compelled to move in single file "to avoid knocking one another over as we slipped and staggered through the mud" and the streaming darkness. About 22.30 hours they reached the bottom of the escarpment, rested a short while, and then began to climb its two hundred and fifty feet of muddy turf and rock. Half-way up, their passage "roused a watchdog and a stream of light issued from the door of a hut . . . a hundred yards on our flank. As we crouched motionless, hardly breathing, we heard a man shouting at the dog. Finally the door closed."

At the top of the escarpment they found a muddy track which the guides had told them would lead them straight to the back of Rommel's headquarters. Here Cook departed with his detachment to find a pylon from which the telephone wires ran, and which he was to blow up. This task he successfully accomplished, but was captured on his way back to join Laycock, and spent the rest of the war a prisoner in Italy.

. . . . The men formed up for the assault, moving to the places assigned to them in the plan drawn up by Keyes. Then Keyes, with Campbell and Sergeant Terry, pushed through a hedge into the garden of the house and went round the corner "on to a gravel sweep before a flight of steps, at the top of which were glass-topped doors". Tommy-gun in hand, Keyes ran up the steps and Campbell pushed open the door.

"Just inside we were confronted by a German, an officer I think, in steel helmet and overcoat.

"Geoffrey at once closed with him, covering him with his tommy-gun. The man seized the muzzle of Geoffrey's gun and tired to wrest it from him. Before I or Terry could get round behind him he retreated, still holding on to Geoffrey, to a position with his back to the wall and his either side protected by the first and second pair of doors at the entrance. Geoffrey could not draw his knife and neither I nor Terry could get round Geoffrey as the doors were in the way, so I shot the man with my .38 revolver which I knew would make less noise than Geoffrey's Tommy-gun. Geoffrey then gave the order to use tommy-guns and grenades, since we had to presume that my revolver shot had been heard. We found ourselves, when we had time to look round, in a large hall with a stone floor and stone stairway leading to the upper stories, and with a number of doors opening out of the hall. The hall was very dimly lit. We heard a man in heavy boots clattering down the stairs, though we could not see him or he us as he was hidden by a right-angle turn in the stairway. As he came to the turn and his feet came in sight, Sergeant Terry fired a burst with his tommy-gun.

The man turned and fled away upstairs.

"Meanwhile Geoffrey had opened one door and we looked in and saw it (the room) was empty. Geoffrey pointed to a light shining from the crack under the next door and then flung it open. It opened towards him and inside were about ten Germans in steel helmets, some sitting and some standing. Geoffrey fired two or three rounds with his Colt .45 automatic, and I said, 'Wait, I'll throw a grenade in.' He slammed the door shut and held it while I got a pin out of a grenade. I said 'Right', and Geoffrey opened the door and I threw in the grenade which I saw roll to the middle of the room. Before Geoffrey (who said 'Well done' as he saw the grenade go in) could shut the door, the Germans fired. A bullet struck Geoffrey just over his heart and he fell unconscious at the feet of myself and Terry. I shut the door and immediately afterwards the grenade burst with a shattering explosion. This was followed by complete silence and we could see that the light in the room had gone out. I decided Geoffrey had to be moved in case there was further fighting in the building, so between us Sergeant Terry and I carried him outside and laid him on the grass verge by the side of the steps leading up to the front door. He must have died as we were carrying him outside, for when I felt his heart it had ceased to beat."

Campbell returned to the hall of the building, and then went round to its back, but while he was approaching it one of the Commando soldiers posted at the back entrance mistook him for a German and shot him through the leg, thus making it impossible for him to return to the beach. The men offered to carry Campbell back across the twenty-five miles, but he refused. They left him lying there, withdrawing under the command of Sergeant Terry. Campbell was presently found and taken by the Germans to hospital. Geoffrey Keyes they also took away and buried with military honours in the cemetery close by, the chaplain of the garrison church at Potsdam performing the ceremony. He was posthumously awarded the Victoria Cross.

General Rommel was not at the house attacked, and it is now known that he had never used it. Our Intelligence was faulty. The house was the headquarters of the German and Italian supply services. Nor, as was thought at the time, was Rommel in Rome attending a birthday celebration; he was close to the front line, then about to be attacked by General Auchinleck.

The raiders, with Sergeant Terry in charge, made their way, not without difficulty, back to Laycock who was awaiting them in the wadi; and then, still hoping, though in vain, that Cook and his men would arrive, sat down to wait the return of the *Torbay*. She arrived off the coast after dark on the 20th and flashed a message in Morse, which Laycock was able to read, saying that the sea was too rough and that she would return on the following night. She then moved off after successfully floating ashore a rubber dinghy containing food and water. This was thankfully received. The party prepared to spend the remainder of the night and the next day ashore, and to pray for better weather.

. . . . The Germans were by now maintaining a sustained fire, and about two o'clock in the afternoon it became evident that it would be impossible to hold the beach against such superior forces. When the enemy were no more than two hundred yards from the caves, Laycock ordered the detachment to split up into small parties, dash across the open and seek the cover of the hills inland. There they could either try to get in touch with H.M.S. *Talisman*, which they knew would be lying off an alternative beach that night, or they could hide in the wadis which abounded and await our forces. Lieutenant Pryor, who was grievously wounded, was left behind with a medical orderly to surrender. He eventually did so and was taken off to captivity on the back of a mule watched "by a lovely great red-backed shrike sitting on a juniper bush".

After the party had scattered, Laycock found himself with Sergeant Terry. They crossed half a mile of open country, being continually sniped, but neither of them was hit. Once in the shelter of the Jebel, which offered the

excellent cover of thick scrub, they set out together to join
the Eighth Army. After the first few days they made
friends with various members of the local Senussi tribes,
who helped them and hid them each night in the wadis
which the enemy were known to have searched during the
day. "Neither of us," records Laycock, "could speak
Arabic, and our conversation was mostly carried on by
means of broken Italian and by making signs to each other.
For instance, a Senussi holding up his five fingers, pointing
at us and then drawing his forefinger across his throat,
meant that five of our original raiding party had been
murdered by the Arabs and handed over to the Germans.
Our greatest problem," he continues, "was the lack of
food, and though never desperate we were forced to subsist
for periods, which never exceeded two and half consecutive
days, on berries only, and we became appreciably weak
from want of nourishment. At other times we fed well on
goat and Arab bread, but developed a marked craving for
sugar. Water never presented a serious proposition as it
rained practically continuously."

One evening they were making a thin stew out of some
goat and bones—mostly bones—which they had flavoured
with wild garlic picked by Laycock. As they were about to
eat it a friendly Arab arrived, gave one loud sniff, and
overturned the pot. He subsequently explained to the
enraged and hungry pair that the garlic would have
destroyed their sight. They ate all that goat, returning to
dig up the lungs and entrails which they had buried.

Eventually the colonel and the sergeant joined the
British forces at Cyrene, forty-one days after they had
originally set out. "On joining them we fell upon the
marmalade offered to us and polished off a pot each."
They were the only members of the party to reach Cyrene.

St. Nazaire

*On 27-28 March 1942, a combined Commando,
Navy and R.A.F. raid was made on the port of St. Nazaire
in order to render unserviceable the only dry dock on the*

*Atlantic seaboard capable of holding the German
battleship* Tirpitz. *The following account was broadcast
anonymously in June 1945.*

I was taken prisoner in the raid on St. Nazaire in March
1942. I was commanding a small party in the landing craft
immediately astern of the destroyer *Campbeltown*. None
of us expected to be taken prisoner. We thought we would
all get away with it, blow up the docks, and return safely
to England without a casualty. The raid was a success all
right, but it didn't turn out quite like that; on the whole we
were pretty lucky. Right up to the last moment it looked
as if the raid was going to catch the Germans off their
guard.

The sea journey took two days and a night and a half.
We sailed from Falmouth. We didn't make straight for the
French coast. We set a course way out into the Atlantic,
so that if we were spotted the Germans might think we
were only a submarine sweep. It was very calm, that was
one blessing. No German aircraft came over, and I don't
think we were sighted, so at evening on the second day we
were feeling pretty optimistic.

We turned in towards the mouth of the river Loire from
the south, and took up our assault formation. The
destroyer *Campbeltown* was leading. She was an old
destroyer converted for this job and she was followed by
two flotillas of motor launches. She was stiff with
explosive, five tons of it. It was her job to charge the gates
of the St. Nazaire dry dock, about six miles up the river,
and then she was to blow herself sky-high, and the dock
gates were to go up with her. I was in the leading M.L. of
the starboard flotilla. I saw our colonel and the naval
commander go up and down the line of little ships in the
M.G.B. They hailed us and wished us luck before taking
their stations. The escorting destroyers left us, night fell,
and soon we saw a light winking at us out of the darkness.
The submarine *Sturgeon* had been waiting off the river
mouth to give the direction. It was her light we saw.
Commander Ryder, V.C., had led the whole convoy and the

navigation of Lieutenant Green, his navigating officer, had been so accurate that we met the submarine exactly at the time scheduled. Everything was going very well. She signalled good-bye, good luck and then vanished.

Now we made straight for the entrance to the river Loire. Suddenly two white fringes, like very low clouds, emerged out of the dark ahead, to port and starboard. We went in between them. They were the surf on the French coast, the two banks of the Loire, and I realized now that we had reached the river.

Gradually the river narrowed. We could hear the thud of the R.A.F. bombing and could see the flash of the ack-ack batteries replying on shore. At first, they didn't pay any attention to us and we began to think we were going to get away with it. We were pretty lucky with the tide. The operation had been put forward a night to make the most of the good weather and the tide would have been better for us the night after. I could see the *Campbeltown* outlined just ahead of me, and as far as I could tell she was going along O.K. Her commander told me afterwards that he felt her jar and in fact she touched the bottom twice going up the river. She just cleared, by a few inches, and went in very steadily with the two flotillas of little ships aft to port and starboard. They were unarmoured and we had come the whole way from England in them, that was a good four hundred miles. The searchlights caught us first. They swung across the black river from both banks and picked us up one by one. Then the coastal batteries opened up—at first uncertainly. After a few minutes everything opened up, and they let us have it. We knew we were for it then. Two searchlights were like the ones at Plymouth Harbor. We had rehearsed the operation there a week before and we never thought it would be quite like that. The *Campbeltown* looked as if she was flood-lit for a naval review. I could see her clearly, just ahead. The troops were lying down at their action stations. Commander Beattie—he received the V.C. for his ship's crew and for his own conduct in this action—Commander Beattie was on the bridge. I could see the shells all over the place, bouncing off every part of the old destroyer. I don't know how she wasn't sunk or crippled: everything in the harbour was focused on her.

Pretty quickly the searchlight began to pick up the little ships. They swept over my own M.L., and then settled on it. For the last few minutes before we landed, almost the whole convoy was floodlit. The coastal batteries began to bracket us. Shells were rustling overhead and plopping into the water. Many shells and machine-gun bullets went straight through the ships, from side to side, killing men assembled below deck. We could see the docks now, our objective, and we could see the outline of jetties and warehouses which we had memorized day after day from maps and air photographs. All of us knew the place by heart. The *Campbeltown* changed course for the last time, and I saw her turn towards the dry dock.

This was the big moment. She put on speed. She was flying the White Ensign as she went in! She opened up with everything she had and charged the boom and the huge dock gates at eighteen knots, head on, with a German battery blazing at point-blank range across her decks. The troops were lying down, firing back with their Brens; the deck was stripped and they hadn't much cover. There was a mass of flame and smoke and gunfire. She went slap into the dock gates, we saw it happen, and lay there dead centre. The gates were thirty-five feet thick and the *Campbeltown* went in with such power that she didn't stick till her bridge was level with them. The *Tirpitz* would think twice now about coming out into the Atlantic to attack our convoys. The battle of the Atlantic wasn't going too well for the Allies then, and we had been told that our attack on St. Nazaire was not just a raid but an important part of Allied strategy. The destroyer had done her job. She crashed the dock at 1.33 a.m., that was three minutes after the time laid down in our orders. At 1.45 the troops were off. At 1.50 the scuttling charges were set off. At two o'clock she was abandoned and seen to be sinking. The five tons of explosive was concreted in and due to go off some hours later. The troops poured over the sides and knocked out the coastal battery alongside the dock. Another party blew up the pumping station and the station operating the dock gate. There were many wounded on board the doomed *Campbeltown,* and we got them all ashore.

The M.L.s carrying other troops to minor objectives came in behind. The M.T.B. torpedoed the lock gates at the entrance to the U-boat basin and completely scuppered them. Our troops smashed up many installations and killed a good many Germans, but the shore batteries gave us a bad time. We saw ships manoeuvring right under their noses to get into position to knock them out. Our petrol tanks were very vulnerable and many blew up. Just as my M.L. was coming alongside I felt the whole ship shudder. The tanks were hit, she was ablaze and adrift and her steering had gone. No, I didn't know it at the time. The naval commander said "Jump", so I jumped, swam a bit, and was pulled ashore. Some men were blown into the water and got ashore and reached their objectives. Others I never saw again. Many of our men were last seen in blazing wrecks or swimming away from drifts of burning oil. Some reached shore, but others were too badly wounded.

Our colonel, Colonel Newman, managed to get ashore with what was left of his headquarters. The little area of the dock we had to knock out was under heavy fire. The Germans were pretty hysterical at first. Except in the strong battery positions, many ran away, thinking it was the invasion. Many of our men were in action for the first time. It may seem strange to you, but we had been training so long—and often with live ammunition—that honestly, it was hard to believe, in spite of what was happening, that we were on enemy coast. So curious things occurred. One man was clearing a house, for example. A German knocked heads with him as he opened the door; first he apologized, then he remembered himself and shot the German.

Most of us knew that the main task of the operation

had been achieved, because we could see the destroyer jammed in the dry dock. And we were pretty clear by now that we weren't going to get back to England. When we collected on the Old Mole for our withdrawal and looked back along the river, the water seemed to be on fire. Ships were sinking in flames and streams of fire were pouring from every side. Troops were on rafts, far out in the river, and we heard some of them singing. There was nothing left, nothing to take us home. I don't know how we ever expected that there could be. The coastal batteries were still blazing away, and managed, among other things, to sink one of their own flak ships; and some German destroyers had got out of the dock into the river.

On shore the Germans had been strongly reinforced. They began to close in on us. The colonel organized a small perimeter to hold off the Germans. In this perimeter he issued orders to fight our way through the town into open country. He led the first party himself, crossing the bridge from the docks to the town under heavy fire, and fighting up the streets. He carried out this operation entirely on his own initiative and this helped to bewilder the Germans—they had brought in several armoured vehicles and they still thought it was an invasion. Another party got through a series of German posts using German phrases we had learnt on training. Some of the ships which came in last did not land. The troops in these ships were disappointed because they had not landed. One of them got several hours clear on the way home. A German destroyer caught up with it and came alongside it in the early morning. The Germans asked if the British commander of the M.L. wanted to surrender. They asked him in perfect English, through the megaphone. As soon as the troops heard it they opened up, although their ship hadn't a chance, using their Brens against the destroyer with her guns. The destroyer replied, but they refused to surrender. The ship was sunk in the end and many of them were killed.

Most of us on shore were caught in the morning hiding in cellars and boiler rooms, waiting for a chance to get away next night. About 10.30 in the morning we heard the hell of an explosion. The Germans panicked, windows all over the town were smashed, and a huge pillar of flame shot up from the dry dock. The explosive in the *Campbeltown* had gone off, and the huge dock gates and the two merchant ships inside had gone for six. So that was that. It was no good for a year after at least. Some Germans were nosing about aboard the destroyer the moment she went up and went up with her. We were told that some of our lads had taken them aboard, but we never knew which of them had done this. I suppose we shall never know their names.

I suppose we shall never know what happened to many of the men who had been training with us for so long. They'd been expecting something of this kind and hoping for it for many months. We were a very small force, not more than two hundred and eighty soldiers and three hundred and fifty navy personnel, though the Germans said there were several thousands. Those of us who have survived were very lucky. We have come home now and we would like to pay some tribute to the ones who have not survived. I don't know if we can do better than the French people did, a few days after the raid, and perhaps the families of the men who were killed would like to know what happened.

Many of the French had fought with us on the night and gone on fighting afterwards. Somehow they got to hear of the time when our dead were going to be buried. A huge crowd collected at the hospital to make a procession and the Germans cancelled the funeral service. They tried to keep the new time secret, but the French found out again, and there were many hundreds of them at the cemetery. It was a military funeral, with full honours. The French broke right through the German cordon of guards and heaped flowers on the graves of the men who had been killed. They gave money and food which they really couldn't afford to those of us who were there, and we shall never forget the risk they took. It was thanks to their help that five of our men managed to get to the Spanish frontier and so home by way of Gibraltar. The rest of us were taken into Germany, and while there we found out that the raid had succeeded. Admiral Mountbatten had told us that the loss of all the ships did not matter so long as the dock was smashed, and smashed it was.

Commando officer

DIEPPE: 19 AUGUST 1942

The raid on Dieppe was the largest single combined operation of its kind undertaken, in which the Commandos took a subsidiary but important part in support of the Canadians, who formed the great bulk of the attacking force.

Early in April 1942 the question of a raid in force on Dieppe was raised and referred to Combined Operations Headquarters. Its main object was to enable the planning staff of the Allies to learn how best to plan for that Second Front in Western Europe without which final victory could be not achieved. There was also a political motive. At that time the situation on the Eastern Front was far from good, and the Russians were clamouring for sufficient action in the West to contain in France at least forty first-line German divisions. In such circumstances, therefore, a raid on a scale much larger than any yet attempted was desirable and, the planners thought, not impracticable.

Canadians at Dieppe

Even before we put to sea some had an ominous feeling about what was ahead of them on the other side of the Channel. Nobody said anything but many were wondering how the security had been in the time since 7 July. Did the Germans know the Canadians were going to France and were they waiting? This was the question being asked in many minds.

They were puzzled, too, why the raid had been decided upon so suddenly. They would have liked more time to adjust themselves.

I shared most of their mental discomfort. For the first hour or so I ran over the plan and studied my maps and photographs and was surprised I had forgotten so much of the detail. I found misgivings growing in my mind. This seemed somewhat haphazard, compared with the serene way in which the cancelled raid was mounted.

The final Dieppe plan was altered only slightly from the one prepared for July. British Commandos were assigned to tasks on the flanks previously allotted to paratroopers.

. . . . It was one of the finest evenings of the summer. The sea was smooth, the sky was clear and there was the slightest of breezes. The ships cleared and the Royals went to dinner before making their final preparations. In the wardroom, the officers sat around the tables and dined in Navy style, as the last sunshine poured through the open portholes. We had a good meal and everyone ate hungrily, for on the way to the boats all we had had was haversack fare—a few bully-beef sandwiches.

The Royals officers were in good spirits at dinner. Looking around the table you would never have thought that they were facing the biggest test of their lives. They joked and bantered across the tables and renewed old friendships with the naval officers whom they had known in "practice Dieppe" training days.

. . . . We were about ten miles from the French coast and until now there hadn't been a hitch in the plan. The minefield was behind us. The boats filled with infantrymen were lowered as the *Emma* stopped and anchored. Nobody spoke. Silence was the strict order but as our boat, which was the largest of the landing craft and was jammed with about eighty soldiers, pushed off from the *Emma,* a veteran sailor leaned over and in a stage whisper said, "Cheerio, lads, all the best; give the bastards a walloping." Then we were drifting off into the darkness and our coxswain peered through the night to link up with the rest of our assault flotilla.

. . . . Eyes were accustomed to the darkness now and we could discern practically all our little craft; the sea was glossy with starlight.

The boats plunged along, curling up white foam at their bows and leaving a phosphorescent wake that stood out like diamonds on black velvet.

We were about seven or eight miles from Dieppe when the first alarm shook us. To our left there was a streak of tracer bullets—light blue and white dots in the night—and the angry clatter of automatic guns. This wasn't according to plan and everyone in that boat of ours tightened up like a drum. We kept our heads down behind the steel bulwark of our little craft, but it was so crowded there that even to crouch was crowding someone beside you. I sat on a cartful of 3-inch mortar bombs. More tracer bullets swept across ahead of us and some pinged off our steel sides. A big sailor by my side rigged his Lewis gun through a slit at the stern of our boat and answered with a few short bursts. A blob in the night that was an enemy ship—an armed trawler or more likely an E-boat—was less than two hundred yards away. It was firing at half a dozen craft including ours, which was in the lead at that time. From other directions came more German tracer. There might have been four ships intercepting us.

There wasn't much we could do. There isn't any armament on these assault craft to engage in a naval action against E-boats or trawlers. Our support craft didn't seem to be about at that particular time. It looked as if we were going to be cut up piecemeal by this interception; our flotilla already had been broken up from the close pattern of two columns we had held before the attack.

I blew up my lifebelt a little more. A few more blasts of tracer whistled past and then there was a great flash and a bang of gun-fire behind us. In the flash we could see one of our destroyers speeding up wide-open to our assistance. It fired a dozen rounds at the enemy ships and they turned and disappeared towards the French coast. They probably went right into Dieppe harbour and spread the word that

British landing craft were heading in.

. . . . Our coxswain tried to take us in to one section of
the beach and it proved the wrong spot. Before he
grounded he swung the craft out again and we fumbled
through the smoke to the small strip of sand which was
the Puits beach. The smoke was spotty and the last thirty
yards was in the clear. Geysers from artillery shells or
mortar bombs shot up in our path. Miraculously we
weren't hit by any of them. The din of the German ack-
ack guns and machine-guns on the cliff was so deafening
you could not hear the man next to you shout.

The men in our boat crouched low, their faces tense
and grim. They were awed by this unexpected blast of
German fire, and it was their initiation to frightful battle
noises. They gripped their weapons more tightly and
waited for the ramp of our craft to go down.

We bumped on the beach and down went the ramp and
out poured the first infantrymen. They plunged into about
two feet of water and machine-gun bullets laced into them.
Bodies piled up on the ramp. Some staggered to the beach
and fell. Bullets were splattering into the boat itself,
wounding and killing our men.

I was near the stern and to one side. Looking out the
open bow over the bodies on the ramp, I saw the slope
leading a short way up to a stone wall littered with Royals
casualties. There must have been sixty or seventy of them,
lying sprawled on the green grass and the brown earth.
They had been cut down before they had a chance to fire a
shot.

A dozen Canadians were running along the edge of the
cliff towards the stone wall. They carried their weapons
and some were firing as they ran. But some had no
helmets, some were already wounded, their uniforms torn
and bloody. One by one they were cut down and rolled
down the slope to the sea.

I don't know how long we were nosed down on that
beach. It may have been five minutes. It may have been
twenty. On no other front have I witnessed such a
carnage. It was brutal and terrible and shocked you

almost to insensibility to see the piles of dead and feel the hopelessness of the attack at this point.

There was one young lad crouching six feet away from me. He had made several vain attempts to rush down the ramp to the beach but each time a hail of fire had driven him back. He had been wounded in the arm but was determined to try again. He lunged forward and a streak of red-white tracer slashed through his stomach.

I'll never forget his anguished cry as he collapsed on the blood-soaked deck: "Christ, we gotta beat them; we gotta beat them!" He was dead in a few minutes.

. . . . For the rest of that morning one lost all sense of time and developments in the frantic events of the battle. Although the Puits landing had obviously failed and the headland to the east of Dieppe would still be held by the Germans, I felt that the main attack by three infantry battalions and the tanks had possibly fared better on the beach in front of the town.

Landing craft were moving along the coast in relays and the destroyers were going in perilously close to hit the headlands with shell-fire. I clambered from one landing craft to another to try to learn what was going on. Several times we were bombed too closely by long, black German planes that sailed right through our flak and our fighter cover.

Smoke was laid by destroyers and our planes along the sea and on the beach. Finally the landing craft in which I was at the time, with some naval ratings, touched down on the sloping pebble main beach which ran about sixty yards at that point to a high sea wall and the Esplanade, with the town beyond.

Smoke was everywhere and under its cover several of our ratings ran on to the beach and picked up two casualties by the barbed wire on the beach, lugging them back to the boat. I floundered through the loose shale to the sea-wall. There was heavy machine-gun fire down the beach towards the Casino. A group of men crouched twenty yards away under the shelter of the sea-wall.

The tobacco factory was blazing fiercely. For a moment

there was no firing. It was one of those brief lulls you get in any battle. I thought our infantry were thick in the town but the Esplanade looked far too bare and empty.

There was no beach organization as there should have been. Some dead lay by the wall and on the shale. The attack here had not gone as planned either. A string of mortar bombs whanged on the Esplanade. The naval ratings waved and I lunged back to the boat as the beach battle opened up again. In choking smoke we pulled back to the boat pool.

. . . . Then the German air force struck with its most furious attack of the day. All morning long, British and Canadian fighters kept a constant patrol over the ships and the beaches, whole squadrons twisting and curling in the blue, cloud-flecked sky. Hundreds of other planes swept far over northern France, intercepting enemy fighters and bombers long before they reached Dieppe. Reconnaisance planes kept a constant lookout on the roads from Amiens and Abbeville and Rouen where reinforcements could be expected. There were air combats going on practically all morning long. It was the greatest air show since the Battle of Britain in the fall of 1940, and the R.A.F. and R.C.A.F. had overwhelming superiority. The High Command had hoped the German air force would be lured into the sky and most of the enemy strength in western Europe came up.

. . . Bullets screeched in every direction. The whole sky and sea had gone mad with the confusion of that sudden air attack, and a dozen times I clung to the bottom of the boat expecting that this moment was the last as we were cannoned or another stick of bombs churned the sea.

Several landing craft near us blew up, hit by bombs and cannon shells. There was nothing left. They just disintegrated. These craft had been trying to make the main beach again, as we had been, to take off troops on the withdrawal.

Ross Munro, Canadian War Correspondent

On the Ships

At about that time, within a minute or two of a quarter-past one o'clock, a JU88, hard pressed by fighters of the R.A.F., jettisoned a heavy bomb in a vain attempt to escape destruction, and sank the destroyer *Berkeley* with this single chance blow. The bomb struck slightly forward of amidships, destroying the bridge and wrecking the wardroom. The boiler-room and engine-room were at once flooded, and *Berkeley* broke her back.

Wing Commander S. H. Skinner, R.A.F., Observer of Combined Operations Headquarters, had been standing on the bridge at the side of Lieutenant I. J. S. Yorke, R.N., in command of *Berkeley*. Both were killed. A third man, Lieutenant-Colonel L. B. Hillsinger, of the U.S. Army Air Corps, was blown off the bridge to the forward deck, where he sat staring in anger and consternation at the place where his right foot had been. The foot, with the shoe still on it, could be seen floating a few yards from the sinking destroyer.

The vessel was at that moment alive with furious activity, with sailors running to aid the wounded and to the rescue of others who were trapped below. Two sailors came at once to the aid of the American colonel, and his behaviour impressed itself deeply upon them, even in their urgency. The colonel continued to sit up, staring alternately at his right stump and at his missing foot wearing the shoe. Suddenly with a gesture of intense irritation he tore the shoe from his good left foot and flung it after the other into the water.

"Take the goddam pair!"

The colonel turned then to the sailors.

"New shoes," he said. "Bought them this week. First time on. What d'you know!" He seemed unaware of pain.

One of the steam gunboats had at once come to the rescue, and was swiftly alongside the sinking destroyer, while *Albrighton* stood by. There was little time to lose, and the last of the wounded were transhipped within ten minutes.

By that time surgical dressings were getting scarce, but the naval medical personnel helped by R.C.A.M.C. did their best to make the wounded comfortable. Lieutenant-Colonel Hillsinger declined all but the treatment necessary to save his life. He refused injections. He refused a bunk, and insisted on lying out on the deck of the gunboat looking up at the sky.

"I'm meant to be observing this air battle," he said.

Commandos at Dieppe

One question worried all of us in those last silent twenty minutes after the long, cramped voyage in the starlight. Would the Germans be ready for us? Thinking of it made my stomach flutter. I remembered that old R.A.F. saying, "I had kittens", and suddenly knew what it meant. But I hung, in my rising funk, on to the thought that "the other bastards" were twice as scared as me.

The sergeant, still peering ahead from the back centre seat, began a whispered running commentary:

"About five hundred yards now. . . . See the cliffs? . . . There's the crack we want. . . . Look at the Jerry tracer-bullets. Don't think they're firing at us, though. . . . A hundred yards now. . . . Fifty. . . . God, there's a bloke on the cliff!"

Our question was answered. Throwing back my head, I could just make out a figure, silhouetted for an instant in the half-light.

Anderson, beside me, gave a little jerk, screwed up his face, and said:

"Blast! I've got cramp. Hell, damn and blast! I've got cramp."

"All right," I whispered. "Take it easy. Nothing you can do. It'll pass."

That was the worst moment, as we all said afterwards. The assault craft grounded, nosed a little to port, grounded again, and stayed put.

With great self-control, Anderson sat quite still while the ramp dropped and the forward men shuffled out on to the beach. By the time our turn came, his cramp had passed.

Just ahead of us the Frenchman, who had been bobbing up and down with excitement, stepped ashore muttering, *"C'est drôle."* He had not been back since Dunkirk.

We had grounded on the shingle at full tide, a few yards from the foot of the cold-looking, unscalable, hundred-foot, overhanging chalk-white cliffs. As we blundered, bending, across the shingle to the cliff foot, a German machine-gun began to stutter from up above.

The Oerlikon guns from our support craft answered. Red-hot tracer bullets flashed past each other between cliff-top and sea, looking vicious and surprisingly slow, like the lighted matches boys flick across a room.

But for the moment we were under cover, brought in at the exact spot at exactly the appointed time—4.50 a.m.—by the sound seamanship of the Navy.

At the same moment the other half of 4 Commando, led by Lord Lovat himself, had made their landing a little farther west. They were beginning their movement across the low ground, and past the cottages and farms of Le Haut, to take the battery in the rear, while our forces, covered by mortar fire, made the frontal attack.

We found in the first few minutes that the crack in the cliffs to the left, nearest Dieppe, was so crammed full of barbed wire that we would not have time to risk it. The second crack, a little to the right, ended in an almost vertical beach staircase for holiday bathers and fishermen, about twenty feet wide between walls of chalk. Above that was a long gully, just as narrow as its bottom, running back to the woods and fields.

Had the Germans prepared their defences properly, we would not have had a chance. One platoon with a machine-gun could have held it against a fair-sized army. But the Commando leaders knew there was just a chance that the Germans would not believe anyone could be fool enough to try such a suicidal approach.

I waited at the foot of the cliff with the signallers, just round the corner from the crack. A pioneer section from

A Troop (Commandos have troops, not companies) were
at the top of the stairs, thrusting their long, pipe-like
bangalore torpedoes under the two banks of barbed wire.
They lit the fuse and dodged back under cover.

In a few seconds we heard the bang, muffled by the
cliffs, but still loud enough to make your head ring.

"And now," I thought, "the Germans will be really
roused, and that gully will be impossible."

But no. The Commando spearhead, scrambling through
the chalk rubble, the smashed concrete and the flattened
wire, and followed by the mortar platoon, were creeping
cautiously up the gully.

At that moment the howitzers fired—a dull, hollow
sound like an explosion in a quarry. The noise depressed
me for a moment. It hadn't been the perfect surprise, after
all. They might wreck our main force.

The light had grown just enough for their observers to
spot craft a fair way out to sea. I watched the splashes and
felt a little cheered. They were just spouts of water, not the
smoke and steam of hits. Perhaps we'd be in time yet.

For a few minutes, as I sat by the signallers' portable
wireless set, waiting for the spearhead troop to report
back, I could see the soaring fireworks across the Dieppe
approaches.

The naval bombardment of Dieppe, timed for twenty
minutes after our landing, had begun. The shore batteries
and all the light German guns were replying. The sky was
scored with the slow tracks of incendiary shells, and the
Dieppe basin was beginning to rumble and thud like the
explosive growling of a volcano crater.

A formation of four-cannon Hurricanes dived out of the
sky on to the cliffs above us, spitting fire at the machine-
gun posts, and at the two German flak-guns to left and
right of our position. The gun-flashes of the Hurricanes,
coming in head on, made them look as if they were being
pulled through the air by blades of flame instead of
propellers.

Boston bombers, higher up, hurried across the coast on
their way to strafe the German guns nearer Dieppe.

Commando troopers beside me waved and shouted, "Give them hell!" They were excited and pleased by their first sight of air support.

. . . . An explosion in front of us, louder and longer than anything we had heard that morning, made us crouch suddenly. It seemed to be the father and mother of all explosions, far louder than the biggest bomb I had heard in the London blitz.

We waited by the mortar battery wondering what had happineed, and ducking when the shells from a German mortar, somewhere beyond the woods, came a little too near.

Presently Major Mills Roberts, Irish Guardsman, the leader of our part of the Commando force, came back through the trees, grinning with pleasure.

"We've got their ammunition dump," he said. "Mortar-shell bang on top of it. Bloody fools!—they'd got their ammunition all in one lot. Must have been drunk with power."

"Doc. You'd better get your stretcher-bearers up the road quickly. There's a badly wounded man not far off."

A few minutes later I was running down the cliff gully again with another message to pass to England.

It read, "Battery demolished 06.50."

A. B. Austin, war correspondent

German War Diary, H.Q. C.-in-C. West: 19 August

17.40 hours: No armed Englishman remains on the Continent.

The Cost

Of the 4,963 all ranks of the Canadian Army embarked, 2,211 returned to England; 589 of these were wounded but survived, while in twenty-eight cases wounds proved mortal. No less than 1,944 Canadian officers and men, however, became prisoners of war, at least 558 of them wounded. At Dieppe, from a force of fewer than five

thousand men engaged for only nine hours, the Canadian
Army lost more prisoners than in the whole eleven months
of the later campaign in North-West Europe, or the twenty
months during which Canadians fought in Italy. Sadder
still was the loss in killed. As now computed, the total of
fatal casualties was fifty-six officers and 851 other ranks;
these include seven officers and sixty-four other ranks who
died in captivity. Canadian casualties of all categories
aggregated 3,369. Of the seven major Canadian units
engaged, only one (Les Fusiliers Mont-Royal) brought its
commanding officer back to England. Little was left of 4
Brigade, not much more of the 6th. Months of hard work
were required before 2 Division became again the fine
formation that had assaulted the beaches.

Dieppe served also to confirm the Germans in the belief
that a basic consideration in the Allies' minds at the very
outset of an invasion would be the capture of a major
port, and thus encouraged them to devote their best efforts
to developing heavy defences about such places. Thus the
Germans were, as a result of the raid, centering their
defence upon the ports when simultaneously the Allies,
also in part as a result of the raid, were increasingly
turning their attention to the possibility of invading over
open beaches without immediately gaining a major port.
The great conception of the prefabricated harbour owes
something to the lessons learned at Dieppe concerning the
difficulty of capturing a German-held port.

Hitler's Commando Order: 18 October 1942

For some time our enemies have been using, in their
warfare, methods which are outside the International
Geneva Convention. Especially brutal and treacherous is
the behaviour of the so-called Commandos, who, as is
established, are partially recruited even from freed
criminals in enemy countries. From captured orders it is
divulged that they are directed not only to shackle
prisoners, but also to kill defenceless prisoners on the spot
at the moment in which they believe that the latter, as

prisoners, represent a burden in the further pursuit of their purposes, or could otherwise be a hindrance. Finally, orders have been found in which the killing of prisoners has been demanded in principle.

I therefore order:

From now on all enemies on so-called Commando missions in Europe or Africa, challenged by German troops, even if they are to all appearances soldiers in uniform or demolition troops, whether armed or unarmed, in battle or in flight, are to be slaughtered to the last man. It does not make any difference whether they are landed from ships and aircraft for their actions, or whether they are dropped by parachute. Even if these individuals, when found, should apparently be prepared to give themselves up, no pardon is to be granted them on principle. In each individual case full information is to be sent to the O.K.W. for publication in the Report of the Military Forces.

If individual members of such Commandos, such as agents, saboteurs, etc., fall into the hands of the military forces by some other means, through the police in occupied territories, for instance, they are to be handed over immediately to the S.D. Any imprisonment under military guard, in P.W. stockades, for instance, etc., is strictly prohibited, even if this is only intended for a short time.

I will hold responsible under Military Law, for failing to carry out this order, all commanders and officers who either have neglected their duty of instructing the troops about this order, or acted against this order when it was to be executed.

This order is intended for commanders only and must not, under any circumstances, fall into enemy hands.

Adolf Hitler

THE OTHER SIDE OF THE HILL

The Commando idea suited Britain's war, in which manpower needed to be conserved and a long and vulnerable enemy-held coastline close by invited attack. The American Army faced totally different strategic problems in which raids by means of combined operations had comparatively little place, though the Rangers and other units became justly famous. Of the Axis powers, Germany was the only one to produce a comparable fighting force. This was led by Otto Skorzeny, whose most brilliant feat was the rescue of Mussolini after his arrest and imprisonment by the Italians in 1943.

Adolf Hitler to Captain Otto Skorzeny: 26 July 1943

I have a very important commission for you. Mussolini, my friend and our loyal comrade in arms, was betrayed yesterday by his king and arrested by his own countrymen. I cannot and will not leave Italy's greatest son in the lurch. To me the Duce is the incarnation of the ancient grandeur of Rome. Italy under the new government will desert us! I will keep faith with my old ally and dear friend; he must be rescued promptly or he will be handed over to the Allies.

Skorzeny lays his Plans

My own handful of Intelligence people now brought me the news—amounting to practical certainty—that Benito Mussolini was held in a mountain hotel in the Campo Imperatore (Gran Sasso *massif*) and was guarded by a Carabiniere unit.

. . . . A ground operation seemed hopeless from the start. An attack up the steep, rocky slopes would have cost us very heavy losses, apart from giving good notice to the enemy and leaving them time to conceal their prisoner. To forestall that eventuality the whole *massif* would have to be surrounded by good mountain troops. A division at least would be required. So a ground operation was ruled out.

The factor of surprise could be our only trump as it was to be feared that the prisoner's guards had orders to kill him if there was any danger of rescue. This supposition later also proved well founded. Such an order could only be frustrated by a lightning intervention.

There remained only two alternatives—parachute landings or gliders.

We pondered long over both and then decided in favour of the second. At such altitudes, and in the thin air, a parachute drop would involve too rapid a rate of descent for anyone equipped with the normal parachute only. We also feared that in this rocky region the parachutists would get scattered too widely, so that an immediate attack by a compact detachment would not be possible.

So a glider landing remained the only solution.

. . . . After this decision had been given, Radl and I worked out the details of our plan. We had to make careful calculations of the distances, make up our minds as to what arms and equipment the men should carry and, above all, prepare a large-scale plan showing the exact landing-place for each of the twelve gliders. Each glider could take ten men, i.e. a group, in addition to the pilot. Each group must know exactly what it had to do. I decided that I would go myself in the third glider so that the immediate assault by my own and the fourth group could be covered by the two groups already landed.

At the conclusion of these labours we spent a little time discussing our chances. We did not bluff ourselves that they were other than very slim. No one could really say whether Mussolini was still on the mountain and would not be spirited away elsewhere before we arrived. There was the further question whether we could overpower the guards quickly enough to prevent anyone killing him first, and we had not forgotten the warning given by the staff officers.

We must, in any event, allow for casualties in the landings. Even without any casualties we should only be

108 men and they could not all be available at the same moment. They would have to tackle a hundred and fifty Italians, who knew the ground perfectly, and could use the hotel as a fortress. In weapons the two opponents could be regarded as approximately equal, as our parachutists' tommy-guns gave us an advantage, compensating to some extent for the enemy's superiority in numbers, particularly if we had not suffered too badly at the outset.

12 September 1943

I glanced at my watch. One o'clock! I gave the signal to start. The engines began to roar and we were soon gliding along the tarmac and then rising into the air. We were off.

We slowly gained altitude in wide circles and the procession of gliders set course towards the north-east. The weather seemed almost ideal for our purpose. Vast blanks of white cloud hung lazily at about three thousand metres. If they did not disperse we should reach our target practically unobserved and drop out of the sky before anyone realized we were there.

The interior of the glider was most unpleasantly hot and stuffy. I suddenly noticed that the corporal sitting behind me was being sick and that the general in front had turned as green as his uniform. Flying obviously did not suit him; he certainly was not enjoying himself. The pilot reported our position as best he could and I carefully followed his indications on my map, noting when we passed over Tivoli. From the inside of the glider we could see little of the country. The cellophane side-windows were too thick and the gaps in the fabric (of which there were many) too narrow to give us any view. The German glider, type DFS 230, comprised a few steel members covered with canvas. We were somewhat backward in this field, I reflected, thinking enviously of an elegant aluminum frame.

We thrust through a thick bank of clouds to reach the altitude of three thousand five hundred metres which had been specified. For a short time we were in a dense grey world, seeing nothing of our surroundings, and then we emerged into bright sunshine, leaving the clouds below us. At that moment the pilot of our towing machine, a Hentschel, came through on the telephone to the commander of my glider: "Flights One and Two no longer ahead of us! Who's to take over the lead now?"

This was bad news. What had happened to them? At that time I did not know that I also had only seven machines instead of nine behind me. Two had fallen foul of a couple of bomb craters at the very start. I had a message put through: "We'll take over the lead ourselves!"

I got out my knife and slashed right and left in the fabric to make a hole big enough to give us something of a view. I changed my mind about our old-fashioned glider. At least it was made of something we could cut!

My peephole was enough to let us get our bearings when the cloud permitted. We had to be very smart in picking up bridges, roads, river bends and other geographical features on our maps. Even so, we had to correct our course from time to time. Our excursion should not fail through going astray. I did not dwell on the thought that we should be without covering fire when we landed.

It was just short of zero-hour when I recognized the valley of Aquila below us and also the leading vehicles of our own formation hastening along it. It would clearly be at the right place at the right time, though it must certainly have had its troubles, too. We must not fail it!

"Helmets on!" I shouted as the hotel, our destination, came in sight and then: "Slip the tow-ropes!" My words were followed by a sudden silence, broken only by the sound of the wind rushing past. The pilot turned in a wide circle, searching the ground—as I was doing—for the flat meadow appointed as our landing-ground. But a further, and ghastly, surprise was in store for us. It was triangular all right, but so far from being flat it was a steep, a very steep hillside! It could even have been a ski-jump.

. . . . I called out, "Crash landing! As near to the hotel as you can get!" The pilot, not hesitating for a second,

tilted the starboard wing and down we came with a rush. I
wondered for a moment whether the glider could take the
strain in the thin air, but there was little time for
speculation. With the wind shrieking in our ears we
approached our target. I saw Lieutenant Meyer release the
parachute brake, and then followed a crash and the noise
of shattering wood. I closed my eyes and stopped thinking.
One last mighty heave, and we came to rest.

The bolt of the exit hatch had been wrenched away, the
first man was out like a shot and I let myself fall sideways out of the glider, clutching my weapons. We were
within fifteen metres of the hotel! We were surrounded by
jagged rocks of all sizes, which may have nearly smashed
us up but had also acted as a brake so that we had taxied
barely twenty metres. The parachute brake now folded up
immediately behind the glider.

The first Italian sentry was standing on the edge of a
slight rise at one corner of the hotel. He seemed lost in
amazement. I had no time to bother about our Italian
passenger, though I had noticed him falling out of the
glider at my side, but rushed straight into the hotel. I was
glad that I had given the order that no one must fire a shot
before I did. It was essential that the surprise should be
complete. I could hear my men panting behind me. I
knew that they were the pick of the bunch and would
stick to me like glue and ask no explanations.

We reached the hotel. All the surprised and shocked
sentry required was a shout of *"mani in alto"* (hands up).
Passing through an open door, we spotted an Italian
soldier engaged in using a wireless set. A hasty kick sent
his chair flying from under him and a few hearty blows
from my machine-pistol wrecked his apparatus. On
finding that the room had no exit into the interior of the
hotel we hastily retraced our steps and went outside again.

We raced along the façade of the building and round
the corner, to find ourselves faced with a terrace two and
a half to three metres high. Corporal Himmel offered me
his back and I was up and over in a trice. The others
followed in a bunch.

My eyes swept the façade and lit on a well-known face at one of the windows of the first storey. It was the Duce! Now I knew that our effort had not been in vain! I yelled at him, "Away from the window!" and we rushed into the entrance hall, colliding with a lot of Italian soldiers pouring out. Two machine-guns were set up on the floor of the terrace. We jumped over them and put them out of action. The Carabinieri continued to stream out and it took a few far from gentle blows from my weapon to force a way through them. My men yelled out, *"Mani in alto."* So far no one had fired a shot.

I was now well inside the hall. I could not look round or bother about what was happening behind me. On the right was a staircase. I leaped up it three steps at a time, turned left along a corridor and flung open a door on the right. It was a happy choice. Mussolini and two Italian officers were standing in the middle of the room. I thrust them aside and made them stand with their backs to the door. In a moment my *Untersturmführer* Schwerdt appeared. He took in the situation in a glance and jostled the mightily surprised Italian officers out of the room and into the corridor. The door closed behind us.

We had succeeded in the first part of our venture. The Duce was safely in our hands. Not more than three or four minutes had passed since we arrived!

At that moment the heads of Holtzer and Benz, two of my subordinates, appeared at the window. They had not been able to force their way through the crowd in the hall and so had been compelled to join me via the lightning-conductor. There was no question of my men leaving me in the lurch. I sent them to guard the corridor.

I went to the window and saw Radl and his S.S. men running towards the hotel. Behind them crawled *Obersturmführer* Menzel, the company commander of our Friedenthal special unit and in charge of glider No. 4 behind me. His glider had grounded about a hundred metres from the hotel and he had broken his ankle on landing. The third group in glider No. 5 also arrived while I was watching.

I shouted out, "Everything's all right! Mount guard everywhere!"

I stayed a little while longer to watch gliders 6 and 7 crash-land with Lieutenant Berlepsch and his parachute company. Then before my very eyes followed a tragedy. Glider 8 must have been caught in a gust; it wobbled and then fell like a stone, landed on a rocky slope and was smashed to smithereens.

Sounds of firing could now be heard in the distance and I put my head into the corridor and shouted for the officer-in-command at the hotel. A colonel appeared from nearby and I summoned him to surrender forthwith, assuring him that any further resistance was useless. He asked me for time to consider the matter. I gave him one minute, during which Radl turned up. He had had to fight his way through and I assumed that the Italians were still holding the entrance, as no one had joined us.

The Italian colonel returned, carrying a goblet of red wine which he proffered to me with a slight bow and the words: "To the victor!"

A white bedspread, hung from the window, performed the functions of a white flag.

After giving a few orders to my men outside the hotel I was able to devote attention to Mussolini, who was standing in a corner with *Untersturmführer* Schwerdt in front of him. I introduced myself: "Duce, the Führer has sent me! You are free!"

Mussolini embraced me: "I knew my friend Adolf Hitler would not leave me in the lurch," he said.

Otto Skorzeny

The Uses of the Duce

A few hours later the Duce was in Vienna. Just before calling me the Führer had had a telephone conversation with him. He told me that the Duce was deeply shaken by developments. He informed the Führer that he was tired and sick and would first of all like to have a long sleep. On Monday he wanted to visit his family in Munich. We shall soon see whether he is still capable of large-scale political activity. The Führer thinks so. At any rate he will meet Mussolini at G.H.Q. on Tuesday.

However much I may be touched on the human side by the Duce's liberation, I am nevertheless sceptical about its political advantages. With the Duce out of the way, we had a chance to wipe the slate clean in Italy. Without any restraint, and basing our action on the grandiose treachery of the Badoglio régime, we could force a solution of all our problems regarding Italy.

To me it had seemed that, besides South Tyrol, our boundary ought to include Venetia. That will hardly be possible if the Duce re-enters politics. It will be very difficult for us even to put in our claim for South Tyrol. Under the leadership of the Duce, assuming he becomes active again, Italy will attempt to start a national rump government, towards which we shall have obligations in many respects. Both the English and ourselves could hack the Badoglio régime to pieces. A régime under the leadership of the Duce would presumably fall heir to all the rights and duties incident to the Three-Power Pact. A rather distressing prospect!

Dr. Goebbels

2

EL ALAMEIN

A STONY, waterless desert where bleak outcrops of dry
rock alternated with stretches of sand sparsely clotted with
camel-scrub beneath the pitiless African sun—such was
the Alamein front in July of 1942. Lying between the
rocky hillock of Tel el Eisa on the Mediterranean coast
and the six-hundred-foot pyramid of Qaret el Hemeimat
near the edge of the Qattara depression, it was the one
position in the whole of the Western Desert which could
not be outflanked.

General Bayerlein, Afrika Korps

*Early in August 1942, the retreat to the Alamein Line
and the state of the Eighth Army made Winston Churchill determine that changes of command must be made,
despite the resolution which General Auchinleck had
displayed in resisting the hard blows of Rommel. The new
commander of the theatre was to be General Alexander
and the new commander of the Eighth Army General
Montgomery.*

1. Your prime and main duty will be to take or destroy
at the earliest opportunity the German-Italian Army

66

commanded by Field-Marshal Rommel, together with all its supplies and establishments in Egypt and Libya.

2. You will discharge or cause to be discharged such other duties as pertain to your Command, without prejudice to the task described in paragraph 1, which must be considered paramount to His Majesty's interests.

Winston Churchill to General Alexander

The New Broom

I believe it was in the second week in August that we were visited by the Prime Minister, the C.I.G.S. (now Lord Alanbrooke) and others. I think they only spent one day in the Desert, but it was a very full one. They saw and spoke with the senior commanders and saw a number of troops. They no doubt obtained a pretty accurate "feel" of the state of the Eighth Army. Auchinleck had a long discussion with them, and went over the maps and future plans in his map lorry. Churchill was naturally eager for another offensive and wanted it soon. He was off to Moscow, and so this was important. The Commander-in-Chief would not promise anything very quickly—and how right he was. I thought perhaps he was a bit abrupt in the way he refused to be drawn over this matter. I remember noticing that the Prime Minister did not like this attitude, but he was an admirer of the "Auk" and had been lavish in his praise for the way he had pulled the November offensive out of the fire.

Either the next day or the day after Auchinleck was summoned to Cairo. He appeared, I thought, a little worried before he left, but returned full of hope and heart. We went for our usual stroll that evening, and he discussed with the greatest enthusiasm our plans. Considerable reinforcements and new equipment were promised, and it now looked as if before many weeks were over we would be in a position to assume the offensive.

The next day one of the Prime Minister's staff came up during the afternoon with a letter. I guessed what it might contain. The Commander-in-Chief was very quiet at dinner, and afterwards asked me to come for a walk. He put his arm in mine and said, "Freddie, I'm to go."

. . . . It was a hot and sultry morning, and as I drove towards Alexandria I experienced considerable excitement. I was, of course, delighted that Montgomery had been selected, but I did not expect I should remain long in office. It was only natural that he (Montgomery) would bring out his own Chief of Staff. I was looking forward to the meeting, for I knew at the very least it would be exhilarating.

I arrived at the crossroads, and had only been there five minutes when his car turned up, and after a characteristic greeting with a wave of the hand, he asked me to jump in beside him, and off we started for the Ruweisat Ridge.

Montgomery was full of spirit and looking very fit. He said, "Well, Freddie, you chaps seem to have been making a bit of a mess of things. Now what's the form?" I rather nervously tendered my paper, but he thrust it back, saying, "I don't like reading papers, tell me about it." I spent some time running through the various points, and then answered numerous questions. He then said, "I was only told I was coming out here in London forty-eight hours ago, but I have been doing a lot of thinking since. Yesterday I spent at G.H.Q., Cairo, and worked out with Harding* how I want this Army organized. You'll never win a campaign as it is at the moment."

He then went through his proposals for the future. It was extraordinary how he had spotted most of the weaknesses even before his arrival. And he gave out his ideas to a gathering of all the Headquarters Staff officers that very evening as the sun was setting below the Ruweisat Ridge. On arrival at the Headquarters—I saw at once that he didn't like the look of it—he said, "I want to speak to all the staff." I asked "When sir?" "Why, this

---

* Now Lieutenant-General Sir John Harding, who was then a D.C.G.S. at Cairo, dealing with organization, training and equipment.

evening of course," was the reply. I had to get busy, as
they had to be summoned from far and wide, but we just
got them there in time.

Major-General Sir Francis de Guingand

It was clear to me that the situation was quite unreal
and, in fact, dangerous. I decided at once to take action. I
had been ordered not to take over command of the Eighth
Army till 15 August; it was still only the 13th. I knew it
was useless to consult G.H.Q. and that I must take full
responsibility myself. I told General Ramsden he was to
return at once to his corps; he seemed surprised as he had
been placed in acting command of the Army, but he went.
I then had lunch, with the flies and in the hot sun. During lunch I did some savage thinking. After lunch I wrote a
telegram to G.H.Q. saying that I had assumed command of
Eighth Army as from 2 p.m. that day, 13 August; this was
disobedience, but there was no come-back. I then cancelled
all previous orders about withdrawal.

I issued orders that in the event of enemy attack there
would be *no* withdrawal; we would fight on the ground we
now held and if we couldn't stay there alive we would stay
there dead.

General Montgomery

The new Army Commander made himself felt at once. I
saw him first when he called, unannounced, a few days
after his arrival. He talked sharply and curtly, without any
soft words, asked some searching questions, met the
battalion commanders, and left me feeling very much
stimulated. For a long time we had heard little from Army
except querulous grumbles that the men should not go
about without their shirts on, that staff officers must
always wear the appropriate arm-bands, or things of that
sort. Now we were told that we were going to fight, there
was no question of retirement to any reserve positions or
anywhere else, and to get ahead with our preparations. To
make the intention clear our troop-carrying transport was

sent a long way back so that we could not run away if we wanted to!

Brigadier Kippenberger

Rommel's final thrust was still awaited.

Alam Halfa

My orders from Alexander were quite simple; they were to destroy Rommel and his army. I understood Rommel was expected to attack *us* shortly. If he came soon it would be tricky, if he came in a week, all right, but give us two weeks and Rommel could do what he liked; he would be seen off and then it would be our turn. But I had no intention of launching *our* attack until we were ready; when that time came we would hit Rommel for six right out of Africa.

. . . . It was soon pretty clear to me, after talking with de Guingand, that all indications pointed to an early attack by Rommel; he would make a last attempt to get to Cairo and Alexandria, and secure the Delta. It was evident that, if so, he would probably make his main effort on the south or inland flank, and would then carry out a right hook in order to get in behind the Eighth Army.

He could not leave the Army intact and pass on towards the flesh-pots of Egypt; he must first destroy the Eighth Army, after which the flesh-pots were all his for the asking.

General Montgomery

The Army Commander carried out a very detailed examination of the whole front to decide how he would fight the defensive battle. The new policy meant that a great deal of ammunition and supplies had to be moved to the forward area, so that the troops there could fight in their present positions for a long period. He appreciated at once that the Alam Halfa ridge was of vital importance, but was virtually undefended. The ridge was in rear of the Alamein Line and commanded a large area of desert, and was undoubtedly a key to the whole defensive system. Any "right hook" by Rommel must capture this feature to be successful. No troops were available within the Army, and so he asked that 44 Divisions, which had recently arrived in Egypt, should be sent up. The story of the move of this division will give an idea of the change of tempo.

Before Montgomery's arrival G.H.Q. had said that 44 Division would not be available until the end of August at the earliest. Montgomery told me one evening at 5 or 6 p.m. to phone to Cairo and say he required the Division *at once*. I got on to the staff at G.H.Q. and was told that this was quite impossible, but that they would try and get elements of the Division moving in a few days' time. I reported this to the Army Commander. He seized the phone and had a few minutes' talk to Alexander. Later that night I was rung up and told that the division would start moving that night, and it arrived up complete, I believe, in a couple of days. This insistence probably helped considerably in repelling Rommel's attack at the end of the month.

Major-General Sir Francis de Guingand

I had pondered deeply over what I had heard about armoured battles in the desert and it seemed to me that what Rommel liked was to get our armour to attack him; he then disposed of his own armour behind a screen of anti-tank guns, knocked out our tanks, and finally had the field to himself. I was determined that would not happen if Rommel decided to attack us before we were ready to launch a full-scale offensive against him. I would not allow our tanks to rush out at him; we would stand firm in the Alamein position, hold the Ruweisat and Alam Halfa Ridges securely, and let him beat up against them. We would fight a static battle and my forces would not move; his tanks would come up against our tanks dug-in in hull-down positions at the western edge of the Alam Halfa Ridge.

During the day I met on the southern flank the general commanding 7 Armoured Division, the famous Desert

Rats. We discussed the expected attack by Rommel and he said there was only one question to be decided: who would loose the armour against Rommel? He thought he himself should give the word for that to happen. I replied that no one would loose the armour; it would not be loosed and we would let Rommel bump into it for a change. This was a new idea to him and he argued about it a good deal.

When I got back to my headquarters that night the outline of my immediate plans for strengthening the Alamein position was clear in my mind. I was determined to make the position so strong that we would begin our preparations for our own great offensive and not become preoccupied by any attack that Rommel might decide to make. All information seemed to suggest that he would attack towards the end of the month in the full moon period; I wanted to begin my preparations for the battle of Alamein before then, and to continue those preparations whatever Rommel might do.

Therefore we must be strong, with our forces so "balanced" that I need never react to his thrusts or moves: strong enough to see him off without disrupting the major preparations. That was my object.

General Montgomery

Rommel attacked the Alam Halfa position during the night of 30 August; by 5 September he had been met, held and repulsed. The final thrust upon Egypt had failed. The Eighth Army was now set to its preparations for attack.

Plan and Preparation

I was watching the training carefully and it was becoming apparent to me that the Eighth Army was very untrained. The need for training had never been stressed. Most commanders had come to the fore by skill in fighting and because no better were available; many were above their ceiling, and few were good trainers. By the end of

September there were serious doubts in my mind whether the troops would be able to do what was being demanded; the plan was simple but it was too ambitious. If I was not careful, division and units would be given tasks which might end in failure because of the inadequate standard of training. The Eighth Army had suffered some eighty thousand casualties since it was formed, and little time had been spent in training the replacements.

The moment I saw what might happen I took a quick decision. On 6 October, just over two weeks before the battle was to begin, I changed the plan. My initial plan had been based on destroying Rommel's armour; the remainder of his army, the un-armoured portion, could then be dealt with at leisure. This was in accordance with the accepted military thinking of the day. I decided to reverse the process and thus alter the whole conception of how the battle was to be fought. My modified plan now was to hold off, or contain, the enemy armour while we carried out a methodical destruction of the infantry divisions holding the defensive system. These unarmoured divisions would be destroyed by means of a "crumbling" process, the enemy being attacked from the flank and rear and cut off from their supplies. These operations would be carefully organized from a series of firm bases and would be within the capabilities of my troops.

General Montgomery

Large scale rehearsals for the coming battle were carried out, and the lessons learnt gone into very carefully by the commanders. And by the end of the third week in October we began to realize that all these vast preparations were successfully reaching their conclusion. From the staff point of view there was a healthy slackening in the tempo of work, denoting that the stage was set.

Montgomery had been indefatigable, and had satisfied himself that all was in readiness. He very rightly had decided that in order to get the best out of his troops it was necessary for them to know the whole plan so that they would realize how their particular contribution fitted in with the general scheme.

On 19 and 20 October he addressed all officers down to lieutenant-colonel level in XXX, XIII and X Corps. It was a real *tour de force*. These talks were some of the best he has ever given. Clear and full of confidence. I warrant there were no doubters after he had finished. He touched on the enemy situation, stressed his weaknesses, but was certain a long "dog-fight" or "killing match" would take place for several days—"it might be ten". He then gave details of our great strength, our tanks, our guns and the enormous supplies of ammunition available. He drummed in the need never to lose the initiative, and how everyone—*everyone*—must be imbued with the burning desire to "kill Germans". "Even the padres—one per weekday and two on Sundays!" This produced a roar. He explained how the battle was to be fought, and finished by saying that he was entirely and utterly confident of the result.

The men were let into the secret on 21 and 22 October, from which date no leave was granted. And, as a result of everything, a tremendous state of enthusiasm was produced. I have never felt anything like it. Those soldiers just knew they were going to succeed.

Major-General Sir Francis de Guingand

In the open desert the possibilities of concealment were negligible, and it was impossible to disguise from the enemy the fact that the Eighth Army was preparing a major thrust. But nevertheless the army's camouflage experts were called upon for a deception plan on a vast scale—first to disguise from the enemy the full extent of the build-up of troops, weapons and stores, and second to convince him that the expected thrust was to come in the south instead of the north.

From the enemy's point of view on that morning of 22

October 1942, "Martello" must have looked precisely as
he had become accustomed to seeing it for the past few
weeks—a fairly dense concentration of thin-skinned
vehicles with nothing specially menacing about it. Down
in the south, he could see that the new pipe-line was
finished. He could put his own interpretation on the recent
dumping of thousands of tons of petrol, ammunition and
food, and on the appreciable massing of artillery at
Munassib. In the Staging Areas, astride the system of
tracks leading southwards, he could still see the whole
array of our armour and take what comfort he could from
the fact that so long as it stood there he still had some
days of grace. The blow could hardly fall for another two
days, or even three. In the north? Some new and possibly
disquieting tracks leading up to the front? Yes—but in the
absence of any appreciable increase of dumping or any
massing of guns, might not these new tracks be a clumsy
attempt to deceive? On the whole, the visible emphasis
leaned towards the south.

And in reality? All the "armour" in the Staging Areas,
the "guns", the "dumps", and the "pipe-line" in the south
were stick and string, tin and canvas. Four hundred 25-
pounders were in their barrage positions in "Cannibal 2",
ready to cast away their disguise and deluge the enemy
with fire. The petrol, ammunition, food and stores were all
in their appointed places to feed the offensive. Safely
tucked away under their sunshields, the tanks stood ready
on their jumping-off points. The full strength of the Eighth
Army was on its marks—in the north—not in two days'
time, but *now*. All was in readiness for Alamein.

Southron and I stayed with the substitution scheme
until it was complete. We had been given, in strict secrecy,
the day and the hour of zero. There was nothing more for
us to do, and so on the afternoon of 23 October we set out
with Ashman in the Chevrolet for Cairo and the office, to
catch up on the paper war. It was, I seem to remember, a
lovely day. Towards sunset we decided to camp for the
night beside the trail. We were far from any main track

and apart from distant flights of aircraft no signs of war were to be seen or heard. It was a golden evening, serene and still.

We were too tired to be elated because the job was done, or apprehensive lest it had been done to no purpose. We lolled, while Ashman made tea and a meal. A few fleecy clouds rode overhead. All round us the reddish, stone-flecked sand was dotted with tufts of scrubby vegetation encrusted with the empty shells of dead snails.

The sun went down. We smoked and talked, our faces turned to the westward, towards the front line and beyond the long, low, distant horizon. I thought of what must be going through the minds of so many thousands up there beyond the skyline. I could see them checking things over, brewing up, singing their favourite mournful song, writing their letter home. It took me back twenty-six years to another night and another place where I too had waited in a trench and wondered what it would be like when the whistles blew and the moment came to climb out and take my chance.

Night fell and the stars came out. It was deeply quiet. We watched. Then on the very stroke of zero the sky to the north-west suddenly became alive with a faint continuous flickering. The four hundred guns in "Cannibal 2" had opened the barrage.

Colonel Geoffrey Barkas

Attack

There was complete quiet all the afternoon. I strolled about and came on a party from the Scottish battalion holding the line being briefed for a patrol that night. They were completely unaware that anything particular was going to happen. Hardly anyone else was visible.

Immediately after dusk there was activity everywhere. The infantry got out of their cramped slits and made their final preparations. The cookers came up with the last meals for many of them. The tracks from the rear, Sun, Moon, Star, Bottle and Hat were lit with their distinctive

signs and the transport moved up in orderly sequence.
Exactly to the minute, the hundred first-line vehicles and
anti-tank guns of the Brigade arrived and were parked
close to headquarters. Equally punctually the heavy tanks
of the Wiltshire Yeomanry rumbled up and Peter Sykes,
their commander, reported in. John Currie called to make
sure that everything was in order. It was evident that 9
Armoured Brigade meant business. The battalion
commanders came in, all cheerful and confident, chatted a
little while and went away with more than our casual good
wishes. We all continually looked at our watches.

Brigadier Kippenberger

As the time drew near we got into our cars and drove to
a good viewpoint to see the opening of the battle. We
passed the never-ending stream of tanks and transport. All
moving with clockwork precision. This was X Corps
moving up to its starting line. The moon provided
sufficient light to drive by, but the night protected them
from the prying eyes of enemy aircraft. We had some of
our own aircraft up over the enemy's forward positions
making distracting noises. Otherwise all seemed fairly
quiet and normal. An occasional Verey light and burst of
machine-gun fire, a gun firing here and there, as would
happen any night. We looked at our watches, 21.30
hours—ten minutes to go. I could hardly wait. The
minutes ticked by, and then the whole sky was lit up, and
a roar rent the air. Over a thousand of our guns had
opened up. It was a great and heartening sight. I tried to
picture what the enemy must be thinking; did he know
what was coming? He must do now. How ready was he?
Up and down the desert, from north to south, the
twinkling of the guns could be seen in an unceasing
sequence. Within the enemy's lines we could see an
occasional deep red glow light up the western sky. Each
time this happened the XXX Corps C.C.R.A.*—Den-
nis—let out a grunt of satisfaction. Another Axis gun

* Commander Corps Royal Artillery.

position had gone up. We checked each change in the artillery plan; the pause whilst the guns switched to new targets. It was gun drill at its best. Now the infantry had started forward. We could see the periodic bursts of Bofors guns which, with their tracer shell, demarcated the direction of advance. Behind us great searchlight beams were directed towards the sky. These beacons were used to help the forward troops resect their positions, and so find out when they had reached their objectives, for few landmarks existed in this part of the desert.

Major-General Sir Francis de Guingand

At this critical moment, Rommel was in hospital in Germany: General Stumme had been left in command of the Axis forces.

Back in H.Q.—which was sited on the coast only a few miles behind the front—General Stumme heard this tornado of fire, but because of the meagre stocks of ammunition in Africa, did not authorize the artillery to open fire on the British assembly positions. This was a mistake, in my view, for it would have at least reduced the weight of the British attack. When the artillery did finally open fire it was unable to have anything like the effect it might have had earlier, for the British had by that time been able to instal themselves in the defence posts they had captured during the night. When dawn broke on 24 October, headquarters had still only received a few reports, and there was considerable obscurity about the situation. Accordingly, General Stumme decided to drive up to the front himself.

The acting Army Chief of Staff, Colonel Westphal, pressed him to take an escort vehicle and signals truck as I had always done. But he refused to take any escort apart from Colonel Buechting; he intended to go no farther than the headquarters of 90 Light Division and considered it unnecessary to take any other vehicles.

Concentric artillery fire began again in the early hours of the 24th, this time on the southern sector, where the

British soon attacked with infantry and about a hundred and sixty tanks. After overrunning our outposts they were brought to a halt in front of the main defence line.

Rommel

We did not expect any news until after the first objective had been reached at 11 p.m. I got restless and went out on to the low ridge behind which we were sheltering. There was nothing to be seen, not even the hundreds of bursting shells, through the thick dust and smoke. The moonlight was dulled. There would plainly be trouble in keeping direction and touch. Far away on our right I could hear clearly the skirling of the Highland pipes, warlike, stirring music. It was not easy to return to the A.C.V. and sit down again. The minutes passed slowly. Whenever anyone opened the door the maddening incessant clamour of the guns became deafening. A whole field regiment was firing directly over us from a few hundred yards back. The waiting group of officers and orderlies stood on the lee side to get some shelter from the uproar and concussion.

Two signallers with a set had accompanied the sappers who were to make the left gap. We had no set to spare for the other gap. At about the expected time they called to say that the sappers had started clearing the gap and were under small-arms fire. They knew nothing about the infantry except that there was fighting going on ahead.

Brigadier Kippenberger

Crisis: 25 October

I have always thought that this was when the real crisis in the battle occurred.

General Montgomery

The Army Commander went to bed in his caravan that night at his usual time—between 9.30 and 10.00 p.m. As things appeared rather uncertain, I decided to stay up and keep a close touch with the Corps. Towards 2 a.m. on the

25th it was obvious that the situation in the southern
corridor about the Miteiriya Ridge was not satisfactory.
Various reports were coming in. Congestion was
considerable in the cleared lane through the minefields,
with a lot of damage being done by enemy shelling and
mortar fire. Freyberg was personally directing operations
from his tank in this critical zone. Altogether I gained the
impression from these reports and those from liaison
officers just back, that a feeling in some quarters was
creeping in which favoured suspending the forward move,
and pulling back under cover of the ridge. I decided,
therefore, that this was an occasion when the Army
Commander must intervene, and so I called a conference
for 3.30 a.m. at our Tactical Headquarters, asking Leese
(XXX Corps) and Lumsden (X Corps) to attend. In my
long association with Montgomery I think I could count
the times I have awakened him at night on my two hands. I
went along to his caravan and woke him up. He appeared
to be sleeping peacefully in spite of a lot of attention from
the enemy air force outside. He agreed to the action I had
taken, and told me to bring the two Corps Commanders
along to his map lorry when they arrived. To my mind,
this conference should be classed as the "First Stepping
Stone".

Under the best circumstances, 3.30 a.m. is not a good
time to hold a conference. The conditions surrounding this
one called for the best qualities the Army Commander
could produce. I led the generals along the little path to
the lorry. Inside, Montgomery was seated on a stool
carefully examining a map fixed to the wall. He greeted us
all most cheerfully, motioned us to sit down, and then
asked each Corps Commander to tell his story. He listened
very quietly, only occasionally interrupting with a question.
There was a certain "atmosphere" present, and careful
handling was required. Lumsden was obviously not very
happy about the role his armour had been given. As the
situation was being described, I looked out of the lorry
door and saw the placid Mediterranean at our feet
twinkling in the moonlight. In contrast to this peaceful

scene was the constant fire of A.A. guns, the droning of aircraft overhead, and every now and again the vicious whistle and crump of a bomb nearby. A little later Montgomery spoke to the commander of 10 Armoured Division on the telephone. He heard his version of the situation, and then clearly and quickly made it very plain that there would be no alteration to his orders. The armour could and must get through. He also ordered the headquarters of this division to be moved farther forward.

Before this call had been put through there had been some discussion in the map lorry, in which the Army Commander, speaking very quietly, gave his views. I remember the reaction his words had on me. They were a tonic, and we felt not only that these orders would stand, but that there was no possible question that the plan could fail. The firm decision to make no change in the plan at that moment was a brave one, for it meant accepting considerable risks and casualties. Unless it had been made I am firmly convinced that the attack might well have fizzled out, and the full measure of success we achieved might never have been possible. The meeting broke up with no one in any doubt as to what was in the Commander's mind.

By 08.00 hours that morning the leading armoured brigade of 10 Armoured Division was reported to be two thousand yards west of the minefield area, and in touch with 1 Armoured Division to the north. In addition, we heard that the New Zealand Division and 8 Armoured Brigade were clear of the main minefields, and were advancing south-westwards in accordance with the plan. This was all very encouraging, and justified the Army Commander's confidence.

During the 25th, 15 Panzer Division carried out several counter-attacks against us, but they were all repulsed with heavy loss to the enemy. From now onwards fierce fighting took place around a feature we named "Kidney Hill". It was a small kidney-shaped contour on the map, and we had a great deal of difficulty in locating it exactly. Everyone gave it a different map reference. Eventually I

believe it was established that the ring contour denoted a
depression and not a hill! I was so exercised about this at
one period that I sent out a special survey party to
establish its position once and for all.

Major-General Sir Francis de Guingand

*In the XIII Corps sector to the south, 7 Armoured
Division got through the first minefield on the opening
night, but was stopped in front of the second. As losses
were rising, Montgomery discontinued the attack in the
south, for he wanted to preserve 7 Armoured Division for
further action elsewhere. Meanwhile the Germans were
becoming very worried.*

Rommel Returns

On the afternoon of the 24th, I was rung up on the
Semmering by Field-Marshal Keitel, who told me that the
British had been attacking at Alamein with powerful
artillery and bomber support since the previous evening.
General Stumme was missing. He asked whether I would
be well enough to return to Africa and take over
command again. I said I would. Keitel then said that he
would keep me informed of developments, and would let
me know in due course whether I was to return to my
command. I spent the next few hours in a state of acute
anxiety, until the evening, when I received a telephone call
from Hitler himself. He said that Stumme was still
missing—either captured or killed—and asked whether I
could start for Africa immediately. I was to telephone him
again before I actually took off, because he did not want
me to interrupt my treatment unless the British attack
assumed dangerous proportions. I ordered my aircraft for
seven o'clock next morning and drove immediately to
Wiener Neustadt. Finally, shortly after midnight, a call
came through from the Führer. In view of developments
at Alamein he found himself obliged to ask me to fly
back to Africa and resume my command. I took off next
morning. I knew there were no more laurels to be earned

in Africa, for I had been told in the reports I had received
from my officers that supplies had fallen far short of my
minimum demands. But just how bad the supply situation
really was I had yet to learn.

Rommel

He [Rommel] was at Panzer Gruppe Headquarters
again a couple of hours after sunset that same night.

I think he knew then that El Alamein was lost: he had
found out how short of petrol the Afrika Korps was. He
told Bayerlein that we could not win, but he made
desperate attempts to retrieve the situation. He was up
almost all night planning a counter-attack against Kidney
Ridge (Miteiriya) in the north.

Lieutenant Heinz Werner Schmidt

General von Thoma and Colonel Westphal reported to
me that evening on the course of the battle to date,
mentioning particularly that General Stumme had
forbidden the bombardment of the enemy assembly
positions on the first night of the attack, on account of the
ammunition shortage. As a result the enemy had been able
to take possession of part of our minefield and to
overcome the occupying troops with comparatively small
losses to himself. The petrol situation made any major
movement impossible and permitted only local counter-
attacks by the armour deployed behind the particular
sector which was in danger. Units of 15 Panzer Division
had counter-attacked several times on 24 and 25 October,
but had suffered frightful losses in the terrible British
artillery fire and non-stop R.A.F. bombing attacks. By the
evening of the 25th, only thirty-one of their 119 tanks
remained serviceable.

There were now only very small stocks of petrol left in
North Africa, and a crisis was threatening. I had
already—on my way through Rome—demanded the
immediate employment of all available Italian submarines
and warships for the transport of petrol and ammunition.
Our own air force was still unable to prevent the British

bombing attacks, or to shoot down any major number of British aircraft. The R.A.F.'s new fighter-bombers were particularly in evidence, as is shown by the fact that every one of the captured tanks belonging to the *Kampfstaffel* had been shot up by this new type of aircraft.

Our aim for the next few days was to throw the enemy out of our main defence line at all costs and to reoccupy our old positions, in order to avoid having a westward bulge in our front.

Rommel

The Australians Strike

By about mid-day* Montgomery realized that the "crumbling" operations by the New Zealand Division would prove very expensive and made a decision to switch the axis to an operation by 9 Australian Division—northwards. The object was to destroy the Germans in the salient, and it might also reduce the strength facing the main drive. This movement proved so successful that I have always considered it "Stepping Stone to Victory No. 2".

1 Armoured Division were ordered to fight their way westwards with the object of threatening the enemy's supply routes in the Rahman track area. They would also threaten the rear of the enemy holding the coastal salient. This attack made no appreciable progress until the night of the 26th/27th, when a brigade of the division established themselves about Kidney Hill.

The Australian attack went very well, ground being gained and very heavy casualties being inflicted on the enemy. In this area the enemy's defences were very strong, and their garrison preponderantly German. I think this area saw the most determined and savage fighting of the campaign. No quarter was given, and the Australians fought some of the finest German troops in well-prepared positions to a standstill, and by their action did a great

* 26 October (Ed.)

deal to win the battle of El Alamein. This division fought
continuously for nine days under their fine commander,
Morshead; and at the end of this period they were ready
for a well-earned rest.

Major-General Sir Francis de Guingand

Attacks were now launched on Hill 28 by elements of
15 Panzer Division, the Littorio and a Bersaglieri
battalion, supported by the concentrated fire of all the
local artillery and A.A. Unfortunately, the attack gained
ground very slowly. The British resisted desperately.
Rivers of blood were poured out over miserable strips of
land which, in normal times, not even the poorest Arab
would have bothered his head about. Tremendous British
artillery fire pounded the area of the attack. In the evening
part of the Bersaglieri battalion succeeded in occupying
the eastern and western edges of the hill. The hill itself
remained in British hands, and later became the base for
many enemy operations.

I myself observed the attack that day from the north.
Load after load of bombs cascaded down among my
troops. British strength round Hill 28 was increasing
steadily. I gave orders to the artillery to break up the
British movement north-east of Hill 28 by concentrated
fire, but we had too little ammunition to do it successfully.
During the day I brought up 90 Light Division and the
Kampfstaffel, in order to press home the attack on Hill
28. The British were continually feeding fresh forces into
their attack from Hill 28 and it was clear that they wanted
to win through to the area between El Daba and Sidi Abd
el Rahman. Late in the afternoon German and Italian
dive-bomber formations made a self-immolating attempt
to break up the British lorry columns moving towards the
north-west. Some sixty British fighters pounced on these
slow machines and forced the Italians to jettison their
bombs over their own lines, while the German pilots
pressed home their attack with very heavy losses. Never
before in Africa had we seen such a density of anti-
aircraft fire. Hundreds of British tracer shells criss-crossed

the sky and the air became an absolute inferno of fire.

British attacks supported by tanks tried again and again to break out to the west through our line south of Hill 28. Finally, in the afternoon, a thrust by a hundred and sixty tanks succeeded in wiping out an already severely mauled battalion of 164 Infantry Division and penetrated into our line towards the south-west. Violent fighting followed in which the remaining German and Italian tanks managed to force the enemy back. Tank casualties so far, counting in that day's, were sixty-one in 15 Panzer Division and fifty-six in the Littorio, all totally destroyed.

Following on their non-stop night attacks, the R.A.F. sent over formations of eighteen to twenty bombers at hourly intervals throughout the day, which not only caused considerable casualties, but also began to produce serious signs of fatigue and a sense of inferiority among our troops.

Rommel

The Decisive Phase

Montgomery has always been most careful to husband his forces, in fact ensures that he has fresh troops available for the decisive moment. This regrouping now produced the nucleus of reserves for the decisive phase of the battle. I would, therefore, call it the "Third Stepping Stone to Victory".

2 New Zealand Division was pulled out of the line into reserve. Their place was taken by a side-stepping northwards of 1 South African and 4 Indian Divisions. The New Zealanders were made first priority for all tank replacements, and they spent a day or so resting and bathing. We could see this cheerful body of men spread out along the beach from Headquarters, the horrors of the Miteiriya Ridge forgotten, preparing themselves for the ordeal ahead.

27 October was a good day on the sea, in the air, and on land. News came in that two tankers and a merchantman had been sunk near the entrance to Tobruk

harbour. The loss of these much needed supplies to the enemy, including vital petrol, no doubt had a great influence on the battle. The R.A.F. attacked with great gallantry, and their losses were very heavy. The Desert Air Force shot down at least eighteen enemy fighters during the day. On land the regrouping went smoothly ahead, and at 2 p.m. the Army Commander held a conference at his Tactical Headquarters. At this meeting the regrouping plan was given out, and also plans for the continuance of the Australian attack. XIII Corps were ordered to make final arrangements for moving 7 Armoured Division and other troops to the northern sector. During the night of the 26th/27th 21 Panzer Division moved northwards, and so these forces could be spared. In the morning we had located, by wireless direction finding, the headquarters of this German armoured division opposite Kidney Hill.

For most of the day, the two German Panzer divisions launched attacks against our Kidney Hill positions. This suited us well, and 1 Armoured Division excelled themselves. They claimed fifty enemy tanks knocked out, as well as others damaged. In addition, the R.A.F. was doing good work bombing these attacks as they formed up. Good claims of transport destroyed were made. It was an exciting day, and during the afternoon I stood by our command vehicle listening to the loudspeaker which was turned to the wireless "net" which served the forward tanks. We heard a running commentary on the fight. One could hear the fire orders being given to the tank crews and the results of their shooting. This sort of thing:

"Look out, Bob, a couple sneaking up your right flank—you should see them any moment now."

You would hear the fire order given by the tank commander as the enemy came into view. Then:

"Well done—good shooting—another brew-up."

We ticked off the numbers claimed and felt very pleased. Looking westwards there were visible signs of success. Pillars of black smoke towering into the sky showed the truth of the reports we were hearing on the radio. Then, every three-quarters of an hour, the fleet of

medium bombers would fly overhead, and drop their load
with a terrific crump on the enemy concentrations. A great
cloud of dust would rise up, interposed with black smoke
which came from vehicles hit.

After this Montgomery decided that 1 Armoured
Division needed a rest, and withdrew it into reserve. This
particular sector would, for the moment, remain a
defensive one.

Major-General Sir Francis de Guingand

28 October

Dearest Lu,

Who knows whether I'll have a chance to sit down and
write in peace in the next few days or ever again. To-day
there's still a chance.

The battle is raging. Perhaps we will still manage to be
able to stick it out, in spite of all that's against us—but it
may go wrong, and that would have very grave
consequences for the whole course of the war. For North
Africa would then fall to the British in a few days, almost
without a fight. We will do all we can to pull it off. But
the enemy's superiority is terrific and our resources very
small.

Whether I would survive a defeat lies in God's hands.
The lot of the vanquished is heavy. I'm happy in my own
conscience that I've done all I can for victory and have
not spared myself.

I realized so well in the few short weeks I was at home
what you two mean to me. My last thought is of you.

Rommel

A real hard and very bloody fight has gone on now for
eight days. It has been a terrific party and a complete
slogging match, made all the more difficult in that the
whole area is just one enormous minefield. . . . I have
managed to keep the initiative throughout, and so far
Rommel has had to dance entirely to my tune; his
counter-attack and thrusts have been handled without

difficulty up to date. I think he is now ripe for a real hard blow which may topple him off his perch. It is going in tonight and I am putting everything I can into it. . . . If we succeed it will be the end of Rommel's army.

General Montgomery to General Sir Alan Brooke,
1 November

Victory

At 1 a.m. on 2 November the divisions drawn out of the line by Montgomery were launched at the Germans around Kidney Ridge. In spite of furious resistance and counter-attacks, they burst through.

♦ 2 November

Dearest Lu,

Very heavy fighting again, not going well for us. The enemy, with his superior strength, is slowly levering us out of our position. That will mean the end. You can imagine how I feel. Air raid after air raid after air raid!

Rommel

At about midday* I returned to my command post, only just escaping by some frantic driving a carpet of bombs laid by eighteen British aircraft. At 13.30 hours an order arrived from the Führer. It read in roughly the following words:

To Field-Marshal Rommel:

In the situation in which you find yourself there can be no other thought but to stand fast and throw every gun and every man into the battle. The utmost efforts are being made to help you. Your enemy, despite his superiority, must also be at the end of his strength. It would not be the first time in history that a strong will has triumphed over the bigger battalions. As to your

* 3 November (Ed.)

troops, you can show them no other road than that to
victory or death.

                                                    Adolf Hitler

This order demanded the impossible. Even the most
devoted soldier can be killed by a bomb. In spite of our
unvarnished situation reports, it was apparently still not
realized at the Führer's H.Q. how matters really stood in
Africa. Arms, petrol and aircraft could have helped us,
but not orders. We were completely stunned, and for the
first time during the African campaign I did not know
what to do. A kind of apathy took hold of us as we issued
orders for all existing positions to be held on instructions
from the highest authority. I forced myself to this action,
as I had always demanded unconditional obedience from
others and, consequently, wished to apply the same
principle to myself. Had I known what was to come I
should have acted differently, because from that time on
we had continually to circumvent orders from the Führer
or Duce in order to save the army from destruction. But
this first instance of interference by higher authority in the
tactical conduct of the African war came as a considerable
shock.*

                                                    Rommel

4 November: Break-through—Retreat

At 2 a.m. I directed two hard punches at the "hinges"
of the final break-out area where the enemy was trying to
stop us widening the gap which we had blown. That
finished the battle.

The armoured car regiments went through as dawn was
breaking and soon the armoured divisions got clean away
into the open desert; they were now in country clear of

* *Note by Manfred Rommel:* The existence of such passages as
this caused my father to decide, in 1944, to burn that part of the
manuscript dealing with El Alamein. His death on 14 October of
that year prevented him carrying out his design.

minefields, where they could manoeuvre and operate against the enemy rear areas and retreating columns.

The armoured cars raced away to the west, being directed far afield on the enemy line of retreat.

General Montgomery

Enormous dust-clouds could be seen south and southeast of headquarters, where the desperate struggle of the small and inefficient Italian tanks of XX Corps was being played out against the hundred or so British heavy tanks which had come round their open right flank. I was later told by Major von Luck, whose battalion I had sent to close the gap between the Italians and the Afrika Korps, that the Italians, who at that time represented our strongest motorized force, fought with exemplary courage. Von Luck gave what assistance he could with his guns, but was unable to avert the fate of the Italian armoured corps. Tank after tank split asunder or burned out, while all the time a tremendous British barrage lay over the Italian infantry and artillery positions. The last signal came from the Ariete at about 15.30 hours:

"Enemy tanks penetrated south of Ariete. Ariete now encircled. Location five kilometres north-west Bir el Abd. Ariete's tanks in action."

By evening XX Italian Corps had been completely destroyed after a very gallant action. In the Ariete we lost our oldest Italian comrades, from whom we had probably always demanded more than they, with their poor armament, had been capable of performing.

A view over the battlefield from Corps H.Q. showed that strong British tank formations had also broken through the Afrika Korps and were pressing on to the west.

Thus the picture in the early afternoon was as follows: on the right of the Afrika Korps, powerful enemy armoured forces had destroyed the XX Italian Motorized Corps, and thus burst a twelve-mile hole in our front, through which strong bodies of tanks were moving to the west. As a result of this, our forces in the north were threatened with encirclement by enemy formations twenty

times their superior in tanks. 90 Light Division had
defended their line magnificently against all British
attacks, but the Afrika Korps' line had been penetrated
after a very gallant resistance by their troops. There were
no reserves, as every available man and gun had had to be
put into the line.

Rommel

*General Ritter von Thoma of the Afrika Korps threw
his own headquarters unit into the breach in a forlorn
attempt to stop the break-through.*

"Go to the El Daba command post. I shall stay here and
personally take charge of the defence of Tel el Mampsra."
I could see that Thoma was utterly disheartened and
foresaw no good. His A.D.C., Lieutenant Hartdegen,
remained with the general: he had a wireless transmitter.
The general put on his greatcoat and picked up a small
canvas bag. I wondered whether the general intended to
die. Then I left Tel el Mampsra and drove to the rear.
It was eight o'clock before the British attacked, after
approximately one hour's artillery preparation. Their main
effort was directed against Tel el Mampsra. By
committing all its forces the Afrika Corps was able to hold
attacks by two hundred British tanks.
At eleven o'clock Lieutenant Hartdegen appeared at my
command post and said:
"General von Thoma has sent me back, with the radio
transmitter. He doesn't need it any more. All our tanks,
anti-tank guns and ack-ack have been destroyed on Tel el
Mampsra. I don't know what has happened to the
general."
I immediately climbed into a small armoured
reconnaissance car and drove off eastwards. Suddenly a
hail of armour-piercing shot was whistling all about me. In
the noontime haze I could see countless black monsters
far away in front. They were Montgomery's tanks, the
10th Hussars. I jumped out of the armoured car and
beneath the burning midday sun ran as fast as I could
towards Tel el Mampsra. It was a place of death, of

burning tanks and smashed flak guns, without a living soul. But then, about two hundred yards away from the sandhole in which I was lying, I saw a man standing erect beside a burning tank, apparently impervious to the intense fire which criss-crossed about him. It was General von Thoma. The British Shermans which were closing up on Tel el Mampsra had halted in a wide half-circle. What should I do? The general would probably regard it as cowardice on my part were I not to go forward and join him. But to run through the curtain of fire which lay between General von Thoma and myself would have been to court certain death. I thought for a moment or two. Then the British Tanks began to move forward once again. There was now no fire being put down on Tel el Mampsra. Thoma stood there, rigid and motionless as a pillar of salt, with his canvas bag still in his hand. A Bren carrier was driving straight towards him, with two Shermans just behind. The British soldiers signalled to Thoma. At the same time one hundred and fifty fighting vehicles poured across Tel el Mampsra like a flood.

. . . . The Afrika Korps signals officer brought Rommel a decoded message, from the 10th Hussars to Montgomery, which our people had intercepted. It read:

"We have just captured a general named Ritter von Thoma."

The Field-Marshal took me aside, and said:

"Bayerlein, what we tried with all our might to prevent has now happened. Our front is smashed and the enemy is pouring through into our rear area. There can no longer be any question of obeying Hitler's order. We're withdrawing to the Fuka position so as to save what still can be saved.

. . . . "Bayerlein," Romel went on, "I'm putting you in command of the Afrika Korps. There's no one else to whom I can entrust it. And if it should happen later on that the Führer court-martials us for our disobedience, we'll both have to answer squarely for our decision to-day. Do your duty as best you can. All your orders to the troops carry my authority. You may say this to the senior commanders, in the event of your having any trouble with them."

"I shall do my best, sir," I replied. Then Rommel got into his armoured command vehicle, to visit the other units of his beaten army and to give the orders for the retreat.

General Bayerlein

This decision could at least be the means of saving the motorized part of the Panzer Army from destruction, although the army had already lost so much as a result of the twenty-four-hour postponement of its retreat—including practically the whole of its infantry and large numbers of tanks, vehicles and guns—that it was no longer in a position to offer effective opposition to the British advance at any point. Orders for the retreat went out at 15.30 hours, and the movement began immediately.

There was now no chance of getting order into our columns, for nothing short of a quick retreat could save us from the British air attacks which reached a climax that day. Anything that did not immediately reach the road and race off westwards was lost, for the enemy followed us up over a wide front and overran everything that came in his path.

Next morning—far too late—signals arrived from the Führer and the Commando Supremo authorizing the withdrawal of the army to the Fuka position.

Rommel

. . . . The General* was certain. He said he had told the Army Commander that the battle was over and had sent a cable to the same effect to the New Zealand Government. In the late afternoon there was a divisional conference. The General said the gap was made to all intents and purposes and next morning we would go south through it and head westwards and north to Fuka on the desert road to cut off the Germans in the north. The six Italian

* Montogomery (Ed.)

divisions in the south, without troop-carrying transport, were doomed in any case. We were to load up with eight days' water, rations, petrol for five hundred miles, the gunners with three hundred and sixty rounds per 25-pounder and two hundred rounds per medium gun. This was great news.

Brigadier Kippenberger

The Field

Below them stretched nothing but death and destruction to the very horizon. Shattered trucks, burnt and contorted tanks, blackened and tangled heaps of wreckage not to be recognized; they scattered the landscape as thickly as stars in the sky. Like dead stalks in the sand, rifles were thrust upright—a denuded forest. And each one meant a man who had been maimed or killed. Inside each wrecked tank a putrid, blackening paste on the walls was what an armour-piercing shell had left of the men who had manned it. Over the miles of wire hung at intervals the bodies of men, like a ghastly and infinite tableau. In dug-outs, pits and trenches the dead lay tangled and piled. Here and there from a heap of dead a hand reached forth as if in supplication, or a pair of eyes stared up accusingly—and would stare so until they rotted into the skull. Here was a body with the limbs torn from it or without a head; and somewhere else a head lay on its own. Ripped-apart bellies with the viscera swelling outwards like some great sea-anemone; a throat impaled by the long shard of a shell. These were details of the scene repeated again and again in every corner of the desert landscape: a great rubbish-heap of metal and human flesh. So the victors sat, gazing across the gigantic desolation.

Graves: El Alamein

Live and let live.
No matter how it ended,
These lose and, under the sky,
Lie befriended.

For foes forgive,
No matter how they hated,
By life so sold and by
Death mated.

John Pudney

It may almost be said, "Before Alamein we never had a victory. After Alamein we never had a defeat."

Winston Churchill

3

STALINGRAD

In Russia in the autumn of 1942, the decisive battle was about to be fought. On the northern flank of their advancing troops in the Caucusus, the German onslaught on Stalingrad slowed. It was not until 15 September that Army Group B reached the outskirts of the city, and there its spearhead—6 Army commanded by General Paulus—remained.

STALINGRAD lies beside the Volga and the German enemy had reached the city's centre. The Russian troops holding the ruins received orders which left no room for misunderstanding:

"You can no longer retreat across the Volga. There is only one road, the road that leads forward. Stalingrad will be saved by you, or be wiped out with you."

THE BATTLE OF ATTRITION

Our losses . . . were very heavy, especially during the first stages of the Stalingrad battle; they were then much heavier than the German losses; later, after we had dug in at Stalingrad, the German casualties began to pile up far beyond ours—not to mention the encirclement phase when the German losses became truly fantastic.

But during the first stage our losses were, of course, very heavy indeed. And yet, the people who survived acquired a tremendous experience in the technique of house-to-house fighting. Two or three men of such experience could be worth a whole platoon. They knew every drain pipe, every manhole, every shell-hole and crater in and around their particular building, they knew every brick that could serve as shelter. Among piles of rubble, which no tank could penetrate, a man would sit there, inside his manhole or crater, or hole in the floor, and, looking through his simple periscope, he would turn on his tommy-gun the moment he saw any German within firing distance. Seldom anything short of a direct hit could knock him out; he was very hard to pick out of his hole and bombing, as I said before, only tended to create new shelters.

In the nightmare of this positional warfare the nucleus of experienced men survived, in the main; it was the new people who perished most easily. . . . Snipers also played a great part in inflicting heavy losses on the Germans and in harassing them. And then there was the continuous activity—the technique of small counter-attacks—practised by the defenders of Stalingrad; they seldom gave the Germans a moment's peace. In October, and especially in November, it became hard to determine who was actually attacking—we or the Germans. The whole of Stalingrad became a seething cauldron of small attacks. In these small battles we had the initiative; in the big attacks, right through September and October, the Germans had the initiative; and the middle of October was the most terrifying period of all. From the end of October, though the Germans were showing signs of great weariness, we had a new and very serious cause of worry—the iceflows in the Volga and the river's reluctance to freeze.

General Talensky

.... On 14 October the Germans struck out; that day will go down as the bloodiest and most ferocious in the whole Battle of Stalingrad. Along a narrow front of four to five kilometres, the Germans threw in five brand-new or newly-reinforced infantry divisions, and two tank divisions, supported by masses of artillery and planes. It began in the morning with a terrible artillery and mortar barrage; and during the day there were over two thousand Luftwaffe sorties. That morning you could not hear the separate shots or explosions: the whole merged into one continuous deafening roar. At five yards you could no longer distinguish anything, so thick were the dust and the smoke. It was astonishing: in a dugout the vibration was such that a tumbler on a table would fly into a thousand bits. That day sixty-one men in my headquarters were killed. After four or five hours of this stunning barrage, the Germans started to attack with tanks and infantry, and they advanced one and a half kilometres, and finally broke through at the Tractor Plant. Our officers and soldiers did not retreat a step here, and if the Germans still advanced it was over the dead bodies of our men. But the losses the Germans had suffered during that day were so heavy that they could not maintain the power of their blow.

.... From then on till the end the two armies were left gripping each other in a deadly clutch; the front became virtually stabilized. Despite this virtual stabilization, we were ordered by the High Command in November to activize our front. It was essential that the Stalingrad group of divisions keep the Germans busy with constant attacks and divert their attention from the flanks. The rest of the story is known.

General Chuikov, G.O.C. 62 Army

The Germans

All our attempts to get the better of the Balka* held by

* Dry river bed (Ed.)

the enemy had so far been in vain. We tried Stuka attacks and artillery shoots. We had assault troops attacking it; they achieved nothing, but suffered heavy losses. The Russians had dug themselves in too well. We thought that about four hundred men was a more or less correct estimate of the enemy's strength. In normal circumstances a force of that size should have surrendered after a fortnight. After all, the Russians were completely cut off from the outside world. Nor was there any chance of supply by air, as at that time we had undoubted air superiority. Now and then at night small single-seater open aircraft tried their luck and dropped an insignificant quantity of supplies to the encircled Russians. One must not forget that Russians are not like normal soldiers where supplies are concerned. On many occasions we found out how little they needed.

This Balka was a thorn in our side, but we could not count on reducing it by starving the garrison. Something had to be done.

Having exhausted all the wiles and arts which our training as staff officers had taught us, we thought it would be a good thing to allow the real fighting man a chance. Therefore we called in our lieutenants. Three of them were instructed to go into the matter and think up something useful. After three days they reported back and submitted their plan. They suggested subdividing the Balka into several sectors and putting tanks and anti-tank guns opposite the holes of the Russians on the slopes below. Then our assault troops were to work themselves down to these holes and smoke them out.

Everything went according to plan—the Russians didn't even wait to be fetched personally from their holes but followed the invitation of a few hand-grenades and other explosives. We were very surprised when we counted our prisoners and found that instead of four hundred men we had captured about *a thousand*. For nearly four weeks these thousand men had subsisted on grass leaves and on a minimum of water which they dug up by sinking a deep hole into the ground. What is more, they not only had lived on so little, but put up a stiff fight to the very end.

Colonel H. R. Dingler, 3 Motorized Division

XIV Panzer Corps was losing up to five hundred men a day and on one occasion, after adding up the totals, General von Wietersheim informed his Commander-in-Chief:

"Sir, I can work out the exact day on which I shall lose my last man, if the situation is allowed to continue like this." He received the reply:

"Are you commanding 6th Army, Wietersheim, or am I?"

Stalingrad Holds Out

Stalingrad is still holding out, and the impression is gaining ground that it may well hold. The Germans, it seems, are no longer even trying to capture it at one swoop, but simply slice it up like a sausage—and that will take some doing. A lot of people in Moscow think that if Stalingrad holds for another six weeks, the Germans may have to pull out of the Caucasus.

Alexander Werth

On 9 November, Adolf Hitler made his annual speech in the Bürgerbräu Beer Cellar before the Nazi "old-guard":

"I wanted to get to the Volga and to do so at a particular point where stands a certain town. By chance it bears the name of Stalin himself. I wanted to take the place, and do you know, we've pulled it off, we've got it really, except for a few enemy positions still holding out. Now people say: 'Why don't they finish the job more quickly?' Well, the reason is that I don't want another Verdun. I prefer to do the job with quite small assault groups. Time is of no consequence at all."

Many of the soldiers at Stalingrad listened to these

words. They cannot even have shaken their heads over
them, since they must have seemed so incomprehensible.
One soldier, however, seated in a dug-out on the northern
perimeter, buried his head in his hands and murmured:

"My God, quite small assault groups . . . if he had only
at least reached full corporal!"

ENCIRCLEMENT

On 20 November things began to happen around
Stalingrad. 16 Panzer Division, our neighbour on the
right, received orders to leave their present positions at
once and move to the western bank of the Don by way of
Kalatsch. Something very serious must have happened.

On 21 November we heard from our supply troops who
were stationed on the east bank of the Don and south of
Kalatsch, that Russian tanks were approaching the town
from the south. Other supply units stationed in the area
west of the Don informed us by wireless that Russians
were approaching Kalatsch from the north. It was clear
that the *encirclement* of Stalingrad would soon be a
reality. We realized how difficult it would be to break that
ring with the forces at our disposal—their weakness was
only too apparent.

If the Russians decided to advance with powerful forces
in the area west of the Don their line of encirclement
would be a very hard nut to crack.

Colonel Dingler

22 November, 18.00 hours
Army encircled. Despite heroic resistance whole of
Tsaritsa Valley, railway from Sovietski to Kalatsch, the
Don bridge at Kalatsch, high ground on west bank as far
as Golubinskaia, Olskinskii and Krainii inclusive now in
Russian hands.

Further enemy forces are advancing from the south-east

through Businovska northwards and also in great strength from the west.

Situation at Surovikino and Chir unknown.

. . . . The Don now frozen and can be crossed. Fuel supplies almost exhausted. Tanks and heavy weapons will then be immobilized, ammunition situation acute, food supplies available for a further six days.

Paulus

Paulus, his superior (the commander-in-chief of Army Group B), and General Zeitzler, Chief of Staff of the German Supreme Command, all saw the necessity of breaking out of the trap, but Hitler refused to allow this.

Despite the exceptional gravity of the decision to be taken, with the far-reaching consequences of which I am well aware, I must report that I regard it as necessary to accept General Paulus's proposal for the withdrawal of 6 Army. My reasons are as follows:

1. The supplying of the twenty divisions that constitute this army is not feasible by air.

2. Since the probable future developments do not offer any certainty of a rapid penetration of the encircling enemy forces from the outside, the attack to relieve 6 Army cannot, in view of the time required to assemble the relieving force, be mounted before 10 December.

. . . . However, I believe that a break-through by 6 Army in a south-westerly direction will result in favourable developments to the situation as a whole.

With the total dissolution of 3 Roumanian Army, 6 Army is now the only fighting formation capable of inflicting damage on the enemy. The proposed direction of attack, opening towards the south-west and then being followed by the northern wing advancing along the railway from Chir to Morosovskaia, will result in a relaxation of the existing tension in the Sventnoie-Kotelnikovo area.

. . . . I am well aware that this proposed operation will entail heavy losses, particularly in arms and equipment.

But these will be far less than those that must ensue if the situation is left to develop, as it must do, in existing conditions, with the inevitable starving-out of the encircled army as the certain result.

Colonel-General Freiherr von Weichs,
C.-in-C. Army Group B

It is a crime to leave 6 Army where it is. The entire army must inevitably be slaughtered and starved. We cannot fetch them out. The whole backbone of the Eastern front will be broken if 6 Army is left to perish at Stalingrad.

General Zeitzler

6 Army is temporarily encircled by Russian forces. It is my intention to concentrate 6 Army in the area [here followed a more precise definition of the area between Stalingrad-North-Point 137—Marinovka-Zybenko and Stalingrad-South]. 6 Army must be left in no doubt that I shall do everything to ensure that it receives its supplies and that it will be relieved in due course.

I know the brave 6 Army and its C.-in-C., and I also know that it will do its duty.

Adolf Hitler, 24 November

Supplies

6 Army can only hold fast if it is supplied with the necessities of life, fuel, ammunition and food and other clearly specified *matériel,* and if it can be assured of relief from outside the encirclement within a short period of time. What we need in the way of supplies has been stated in unambiguous terms. It is now up to the Supreme Command to calculate by means of a staff study whether these large quantities can be delivered, how, and then to issue the necessary orders. So far as 6 Army is concerned, all we can do is to report what exactly it is that the encircled troops need: it is not up to us to say how those needs can and will be met. . . . In view of the general

situation, a withdrawal by 6 Army would appear the more useful course to follow, but I cannot make such a decision from 6 Army Headquarters, since it presumes an inability on the part of the Supreme Command to meet 6 Army's requirements concerning the delivery of supplies and the breaking of the encirclement from without. . . .

General Paulus, 24 November

Night after night we sat in our holes listening to the droning of the aircraft engines and trying to guess how many German machines were coming over and what supplies they would bring us. The supply position was very poor from the beginning, but none of us thought that hunger would become a permanent thing.

We were short of all sorts of supplies. We were short of bread and, worse, of artillery ammunition, and worst of all, of petrol. Petrol meant everything to us. As long as we had petrol our supply—little as it was—was assured. As long as we had petrol we were able to keep *warm*. As there was no wood to be found anywhere in the steppe, firewood had to be fetched from the city of Stalingrad by lorry. As we had so little petrol, trips to the city to fetch firewood had to be limited to the bare minimum. For this reason we felt very cold in our holes.

Until Christmas 1942 the daily bread ration issued to every man was a hundred grammes. After Christmas the ration was reduced to fifty grammes per head. Later on only those in the forward line received fifty grammes per day. No bread was issued to men in regimental headquarters and upwards. The others were given watery soup which we tried to improve by making use of bones obtained from horses we dug up. As a Christmas treat the Army allowed the slaughtering of four thousand of the available horses. My division, being a motorized formation, had no horses and was therefore particularly hard hit, as the horseflesh we received was strictly rationed. The infantry units were better off as they were able to do some "illegal" slaughtering.

Colonel Dingler

It was my task to attempt to supply the 6 German
Army by air . . . but our resources were far too
inadequate. We lost over five hundred transport planes
trying to bring in ammunition and food for the quarter of
a million men encircled in the city. Food soon became so
short that the troops had to eat horses that had been
frozen in the snow for weeks. It was useless to attempt to
break out once we had been surrounded because there was
nothing behind us but hundreds of kilometres of open,
frozen steppes. In any case we had been ordered by the
Führer to hold Stalingrad. We always underestimated the
Russian strength in the winter of 1942.

                                        Lieutenant-General Pickert

*On 24 November von Manstein assumed command of
Army Group B, having been promoted to Field-Marshal.
He thus came directly under Hitler's command.*

Hitler as Supreme Commander

Now that I had come immediately under Hitler in my
capacity as an army group commander, however, I was to
get my first real experience of him in his exercise of the
supreme command.

When considering Hitler in the role of a military leader,
one should certainly not dismiss him with such clichés as
"the lance-corporal of World War I".

He undoubtedly had a certain eye for operational
openings, as had been shown by the way he opted for
Army Group A's plan in the west. Indeed, this is often to
be found in military amateurs—otherwise history would
not have recorded so many dukes and princes as
successful commanders. In addition, though, Hitler
possessed an astoundingly retentive memory and an
imagination that made him quick to grasp all technical
matters and problems of armaments. He was amazingly
familiar with the effect of the very latest enemy weapons
and could reel off whole columns of figures on both our

own and the enemy's war production. Indeed, this was his favourite way of sidetracking any topic that was not to his liking. There can be no question that his insight and unusual energy were responsible for many achievements in the sphere of armaments. Yet his belief in his own superiority in this respect ultimately had disastrous consequences. His interference prevented the smooth and timely development of the Luftwaffe, and it was undoubtedly he who hampered the development of rocket propulsion and atomic weapons.

Moreover, Hitler's interest in everything technical led him to over-estimate the importance of his technical resources. As a result, he would count on a mere handful of assault-gun detachments or the new Tiger tanks to restore situations where only large bodies of troops could have any prospect of success.

What he lacked, broadly speaking, was simply *military ability based on experience*—something for which his "intuition" was no substitute.

. . . . Hitler had a masterly knack of psychologically adapting himself to the individual whom he wished to bring round to his point of view. In addition, of course, he always knew anyone's motive for coming to see him, and could thus have all his counter-arguments ready beforehand. His faculty for inspiring others with his own confidence—whether feigned or genuine—was quite remarkable. This particularly applied when officers who did not know him well came to see him from the front. In such cases a man who had set out to "tell Hitler the truth about things out there" came back converted and bursting with confidence.

Field-Marshal von Manstein

Having closed the trap, the Russians began to grind down the Germans within it.

On 2 December the enemy made his first attack on 6 Army. Like those which followed on the 4th and 8th of the month, it was bloodily repulsed by the courageous troops in the pocket. Fortunately the supply position now appeared more favourable than we had originally dared to expect, for on 2 December the army reported that by existing on a reduced scale of rations and slaughtering a large proportion of the horses, it could—reckoning from 30 November—manage with its present stocks for twelve to sixteen days. At the same time the state of the weather encouraged us to hope for an improvement in the rate of air supplies, a record load of three hundred tons being flown into the pocket on 5 December. (Unfortunately this was to remain an all-time high.) Nonetheless it was clear that no time must be lost in making contact with 6 Army on the ground and fetching it out of the pocket.

Field-Marshal von Manstein

The Second Winter Comes

The weather conditions were bearable during the first days of December. Later on, heavy snowfalls occurred and it turned bitterly cold. Life became a misery. Digging was no longer possible as the ground was frozen hard and if we had to abandon our lines this meant that in the new lines we would have no dugouts or trenches. The heavy snow diminished our small petrol supplies still further. The lorries stuck in the snow and the heavy going meant a larger consumption of petrol. It grew colder and colder. The temperature remained at a steady twenty or thirty degrees below freezing-point and it became increasingly difficult for aircraft to fly in.

Colonel Dingler

Then one night the great freeze-up began, and winter was with us, the second grim winter in that accursed country. Like a black cloak the frost folded over the land. A supplies truck came round and brought us greatcoats, gloves and caps with ear-flaps. Despite this issue, we froze miserably in our funk-holes. In the morning we would be numb with cold, our rifles and guns completely coated with thick hoar-frost. As it left our mouths our breath was as dense as cigarette smoke and immediately solidified over the side-flaps of our caps its glittering crystals of ice. When shells came over, each detonation rang out with a new, hard resonance and the clods of earth which were thrown high were like lumps of granite.

Though apparently completely healed, last year's frost-bites on my heels began to be very painful again. I dared not let myself think of how long this cold would be with us, dared not remember everything would still be frozen up at the end of March.

We just lay in our holes and froze, knowing that twenty-four hours later and forty-eight hours later we should be shivering precisely as we were now, and vainly longing to be relieved. But there was now no hope whatsoever of relief, and that was the worst thing of all.

. . . . The day came when one realized that it was some time since a single truck had dared attempt the journey from our front to the rear base. Scattered Russian units had occupied every approach. At first they attacked any vehicle which came along only if it was night, then they attacked day and night continuously. When it came to that, all supplies columns were for a time linked up—trucks, sleighs, officers' cars—and moved off together in convoy, flanked by armoured stuff and motor-cycle units. In that way essential communications were kept going for a time. But now even this last link had been completely cut.

Frenzied counter-attacks, accompanied by huge losses, failed completely. Slowly but surely the Soviet wedges in the sides of our wedge grew broader, and the German divisions were thrown back, on the one side far beyond the Don, on the other eastwards, back on to that great mass of ruins, the city of Stalingrad.

. . . . The truth was slowly borne in on us, as, dragging all they had with them, the remnants of defeated division after division fell back from all sides before the on-pressing enemy, crowding and cramming into the heart of the cauldron. Gradually the columns of converging transport blocked all roads. On the road guns were blown up, and weapons of all kinds, tanks included, which had come to a standstill from want of fuel. Fully laden lorries, bogged in the snow, went up in flames. Munition dumps were sprung. Vast supplies of provisions and clothing had to become huge fireworks, not to fall into enemy hands. Installations erected at enormous effort were wiped out wholesale. The country for miles around was strewn with smaller equipment—tin hats, gas-masks in cases, ground-sheets, cooking utensils, ammo pouches, trenching tools, even rifles, machine-pistols and grenades. All of this stuff had been thrown away because it had become a mere hindrance, or because the men who carried it had become the wounded in their endless columns, with blood-soaked bandages and tattered uniforms, summoning the last vestiges of their strength merely to drag themselves on through the snow. Or else the equipment had belonged to the countless men now rigid and dead, of whom nobody took any more notice than we did of all that abandoned material.

Completely cut off, the men in field grey just slouched on, invariably filthy and invariably louse-ridden, their weary shoulders sagging, from one defence position to another. The icy winds of those great white wastes which stretched for ever beyond us to the east lashed a million crystals of razor-like snow into their unshaven faces, skin now loose-stretched over bone, so utter was the exhaustion, so utter the starvation. It burned the skin to crumpled leather, it lashed tears from the sunken eyes which from over-fatigue could scarce be kept open, it penetrated through all uniforms and rags to the very marrow of our bones. And whenever any individual could do no more, when even the onward-driving lash of fear of death ceased to have meaning, then like an engine which had used its last drop of fuel, the debilitated body ran down and came to a standstill. Soon a kindly shroud of snow covered the object and only the toe of a jackboot or an arm frozen to stone could remind you that what was

now an elongated white hummock had quite recently been
a human being.

Away two thousand kilometres to the west was another
world, a home country, a wonderful motherland. There
one imagined the glad laughter of little ones and men who
were happy too. There, people slept in soft warm beds;
there, at midday they sat down to eat as much as they
liked from clean white table-linen. And there, on Sunday,
when the church bells brought people out of doors, they
all dressed in their best and the whole family took its
stroll, with pet dog trundling after. Neighbours raised their
hats to each other, folk asked after each other's health,
forecast the weather and exchanged the latest talk of the
town. And if you were a bit out of sorts, the children
tiptoed and dared not speak above a whisper, and the
doctor came, with most serious mien, to say you really
ought not to take such things so lightly.

Bereft of initiative, we allowed ourselves to be driven,
crawling ever onward, obeying senseless orders to take up
ever new positions in hollow or dug-out and offer a
resistance which was already totally devoid of military
meaning. Mechanically we aimed our guns with frozen
fingers, banging away into the ocean of snow back whence
we had just come. Just as when tipsy men feel pain less, it
was only dully now that we sensed the biting cold, the
emptiness of our bellies, even that nagging fear of the final
end. It seemed to us a matter of real indifference when the
night sorties which the Luftwaffe flew to bring us in
supplies became smaller and rarer, when the only warm
food began to be a thin broth with rare cubes of sweetish
horsemeat, or that we often had to do with no more than a
couple of slices of bread all day.

We buried our head in the snow till our breath melted
the white stuff away, but still could not help hearing the
bubbling sound of the enemy mortars, by old habit
counting the seconds till they burst in destruction nearby.
We felt the earth shudder under the H.E.s, or we watched

the countless rocket volleys of the Stalin-organs as they came roaring down out of the overcast grey skies, spraying their fiery stuff over enormous areas till the very snow seemed red hot.

In spite of all this we still again and again experienced sheer astonishment when we saw that we were not the only ones whom for the time being death had spared, that there was still much tenacious life in this inferno of bellowing steel, and that that life was manifesting itself now even at that moment by sending red and violent flares into the heavens, warning of attack, warning of tanks, and urgent cries for help. And then we fired straight into the storming, yelling mass of Bolsheviks, and fired automatically as robots until at last the mammoth tanks, clattering down on us, compelled yet another withdrawal farther back still into the cauldron which with every day grew smaller.

Benno Zieser

Russian Tactics

Practically every Russian attack was preceded by large-scale infiltrations, by an "oozing through" of small units and individual men. In this kind of warfare the Russians have not yet found their masters. However much the outlying areas were kept under observation, the Russian was suddenly there, in the very midst of our own positions, and nobody had seen him come, nor did anybody know whence he had come. In the least likely places, where the going was incredibly difficult, there he was, dug in and all, and in considerable strength. True, it was not difficult for individual men to seep through, considering that our lines were but thinly manned and strong-points few and far between. An average divisional sector was usually more than twelve miles broad. But the amazing fact was that in spite of everybody being alert and wide awake during the whole night, the next morning entire Russian units were sure to be found far behind our front line, complete with equipment and ammunition, and

well dug in. These infiltrations were carried out with
incredible skill, almost noiselessly and without a shot
being fired.

General von Mellenthin

*Von Manstein's armies included Italians, Roumainians
and other more or less willing allies of Germany.*

Italians in the Snow

When it snowed we had to keep very careful look-out
for sudden raids. One night while I was going round with
my white shirt over my overcoat, like a ghost, I noticed a
Russian patrol trying to slip round under the strong-point.
I couldn't see the Russians but felt their presence a few
paces from me. I stood silent and still. And they were
silent and still. I felt they were looking round in the dark
as I was, their weapons at the ready. I was so frightened I
almost began trembling. What if they captured and took
me away? I tried to control myself but the veins in my
throat were throbbing hard. I really was frightened.
Finally I made up my mind; I shouted, threw the grenades
I had in my hand, and jumped down into the trench.
Luckily one of the grenades went off. I heard the Russians
running and by the flash saw them retreating into the
nearest bushes. From there they opened fire with a
machine-gun. Meanwhile some of Pintossi's men had
arrived. We began to fire too from the top of the trench.
One of us hurried off to get the machine-gun. We fired it
and then moved it a few yards. The Russian patrol replied
to our fire but slowly drew farther back. Then they stopped
some way off and began firing continuously with a heavy
machine-gun. But eventually it got too cold, they went
back to their dugouts and we to ours. If they'd been able to
capture one of us they might have been sent home on
leave. In the morning, in sunlight, I went out to look at the
tracks they'd left. They'd been farther away than I'd
supposed the night before, and I smoked a cigarette and
looked at their positions on the other side of the river.

Every now and again one of them got up to take snow
from the top of the trench. They'll be making tea, I
thought. I felt I'd like a little cup, too. And I looked at
them as one looks at a peasant scattering manure in the
fields.

Sergeant Mario Rigoni Stern

*In some respects, Russian tactics had changed little
since the disastrous Finnish campaign of 1939-1940.*

Russian tactics are a queer mixture; in spite of their
brilliance at infiltration and their exceptional mastery of
field fortification, yet the rigidity of Russian attacks was
almost proverbial. (Although in some cases Russian
armoured formations down to their lowest units were a
conspicuous exception.) The foolish repetition of attacks
on the same spot, the rigidity of Russian artillery fire, and
the selection of the terrain for the attack betrayed a total
lack of imagination and mental mobility. Our Wireless
Intercept Service heard many a time the frantic question:
"What are we to do now?" Only a few commanders of
lower formations showed independent judgment when
faced with unforeseen situations. On many occasions a
successful attack, a break-through, or an accomplished
encirclement was not exploited simply because nobody
saw it.

But there was an exception to this general clumsiness:
the rapid and frequent exchange of units in the front
line. Once a division was badly mauled, it disappeared
overnight and re-appeared fresh and strong at some other
place a few days afterwards.

That is why fighting with Russians resembles the classic
contest between Hercules and the Hydra.

General von Mellenthin

*On 12 December von Manstein attacked in an attempt
to relieve Paulus. On the 18th von Manstein, acting
directly against the Führer's instructions, ordered Paulus to
leave Stalingrad and break out to the west, where the*

*relieving troops were no more than forty miles away.
Paulus refused. By Christmas Eve the attempt at relief
had failed, and Manstein found the problem taken out of
his hands.*

6 Army was doomed; nothing could save Paulus now.
Even if by some miracle a break-out order had been
wrung from Hitler, even if the exhausted and starving
troops had cut through the Russian ring, the means did
not exist to get them back across the icy steppe to Rostov.
The army would have perished on the march, as surely as
Napoleon's veterans between Moscow and the Berezina.

Hitler took the Stalingrad area under his personal
command; it was designated as a "War Theatre under the
Supreme Command". He assumed direct responsibility for
everything regarding Stalingrad.

General von Mellenthin

Mass Grave

Every seven seconds a German soldier dies in Russia.
Stalingrad—mass grave.

Moscow Radio: constantly repeated
propaganda broadcast

"Unless a miracle happens, the game is up."
G.O.C., 23 Panzer Division

It was often asked, "Is there nobody prepared to tell
Paulus the truth?" To which the answer was, "Before 24
December there was no need, since there was still a hope
that 6 Army might break out. After 24 December there
was no point, for what is the purpose of telling a man
condemned to death that he must surely die?"

Christmas Eve

The company laughed long and loud at the reference to
"rickety old Father Christmases".

The man, who could only raise his right arm, then said:
"To-day is the evening men call Christmas Eve and to-
morrow is the day when, two thousand years ago,
salvation was to have been brought to the world. These
two days were to bring us peace. We are faced by an
enemy who does not recognize that day or its eve. We do
not know these men against whom we fight, nor would it
occur to us to shoot at them, had it not been for this war.
We are told where to go, and what to do. You are only a
handful, but this evening you should render unto God
what is God's, and when this hour has passed render once
more unto Caesar what belongs to Caesar. We wish peace
to our homeland, that same peace which is the promise of
Christmas Eve, we wish that the candles on their trees
may burn quietly, that the hands which are clasped
beneath the tree may be unhurried, that those at home
may think not of the winter but of the spring that is to
come, that if we should return we shall find warm hearts
to welcome us, and that our homeland may hold its head
high and never need look to the front for an example."

Five Letters from Stalingrad

My hands are done for, and have been ever since the
beginning of December. The little finger of my left hand
is missing and—what's even worse—the three middle
fingers of my right one are frozen. I can only hold my mug
with my thumb and little finger. I'm pretty helpless; only
when a man has lost any fingers does he see how much he
needs them for the very smallest jobs. The best thing I can
do with the little finger is to shoot with it. My hands are
finished. After all, even if I'm not fit for anything else, I
can't go on shooting for the rest of my life. Or would I still
make a gamekeeper, I wonder? That's a pretty grim kind
of humour, I know. The only reason I write such things is
to keep my nerves steady.

A week ago Kurt Hahnke—you may remember him
from the lectures we attended in '37—played the
Appassionata on a grand piano in a little side street by the

Red Square. Not a thing one sees every day of the week—a grand piano planted in the middle of a street. The house it came from had to be demolished, but I suppose they took pity on the piano and fetched it out beforehand. Every private soldier who passed that way had thumped around on it: where else, I ask you, would you find pianos standing out in the street?

Anon.

I was horrified when I saw the map. We're quite alone, without any help from outside. Hitler has left us in the lurch. Whether this letter gets away depends on whether we still hold the airfield. We are lying in the north of the city. The men in my battery already suspect the truth, but they aren't so exactly informed as I am. So this is what the end looks like. Hannes and I have no intention of going into captivity; yesterday I saw four men who'd been captured before our infantry re-occupied a strong-point. No, we're not going to be captured. When Stalingrad falls you will hear and read about it. Then you will know that I shall not return.

Anon.

For a long time to come, perhaps for ever, this is to be my last letter. A comrade who has to go to the airfield is taking it along with him, as the last machine to leave the pocket is taking off to-morrow morning. The situation has become quite untenable. The Russians are only two miles from the last spot from which aircraft can operate, and when that's gone not even a mouse will get out, to say nothing of me. Admittedly several hundred thousand others won't escape either, but it's precious little consolation to share one's own destruction with other men.

Anon.

To return to the present position. Of the division there are only sixty-nine men still fit for action. Bleyer is still alive, and Hartlieb as well. Little Degen has lost both

arms; I expect he will soon be in Germany. Life is finished
for him, too. Get him to tell you the details which you
people think worth knowing. D. has given up hope. I
should like to know what he thinks of the situation and its
consequences. All we have left are two machine-guns and
four hundred rounds. And then a mortar and ten bombs.
Except for that all we have are hunger and fatigue. B. has
broken out with twenty men on his own initiative. Better to
know in three days than in three weeks what the end looks
like. Can't say I blame him.

Anon.

We have no winter clothes. There are five pairs of
ersatz valenki per company—great big straw boots on
wooden soles. They do not warm the feet and are almost
impossible for walking. We have been swindled, and have
been condemned to death; we shall die of the war or of
frost.

Anon.

The Russian Ultimatum: 8 January 1943

To the Commander-in-Chief of the German 6 Army,
Colonel-General Paulus, or his representative, and to all
the officers and men of the German units now besieged in
Stalingrad.

6 German Army, formations of 4 Panzer Army, and
those units sent to reinforce them have been completely
encircled since 23 November 1942.

The soldiers of the Red Army have sealed this German
Army Group within an unbreakable ring. All hopes of the
rescue of your troops by a German offensive from the
south or south-west have proved vain. The German units
hastening to your assistance were defeated by the Red
Army, and the remnants of that force are now
withdrawing to Rostov.

The German air transport fleet, which brought you a
starvation ration of food, munitions and fuel, has been
compelled by the Red Army's successful and rapid

advance repeatedly to withdraw to airfields more distant from the encircled troops.

. . . . The situation of your troops is desperate. They are suffering from hunger, sickness and cold. The cruel Russian winter has scarcely yet begun. Hard frosts, cold winds and blizzards still lie ahead. Your soldiers are unprovided with winter clothing and are living in appalling sanitary conditions.

You, as Commander-in-Chief, and all the officers of the encircled forces know well that there is for you no real possibility of breaking out. Your situation is hopeless, and any further resistance senseless.

In view of the desperate situation in which you are placed, and in order to save unnecessary bloodshed, we propose that you accept the following terms of surrender:

1. All the encircled German troops, headed by yourself and your staff, shall cease to resist.

2. You will hand over to such persons as shall be authorized by us, all members of your armed forces, all war materials and all army equipment in an undamaged condition.

3. We guarantee the safety of all officers and men who cease to resist, and their return at the end of the war to Germany or to any other country to which these prisoners of war may wish to go.

4. All personnel of units which surrender may retain their military uniforms, badges of rank, decorations, personal belongings and valuables and, in the case of high-ranking officers, their swords.

5. All officers, non-commissioned officers and men who surrender will immediately receive normal rations.

6. All those who are wounded, sick or frost-bitten will be given medical treatment.

Your reply is to be given in writing by ten o'clock, Moscow time, 9 January 1943. It must be delivered by your personal representative, who is to travel in a car bearing a white flag along the road that leads to the Konny siding at Kotlubanj station. Your representative will be met by a fully-authorized Russian officer in District B, five hundred metres south-east of siding 564 at 10.00 hours on 9 January 1943.

Should you refuse our offer that you lay down your arms, we hereby give you notice that the forces of the Red Army and the Red Air Force will be compelled to proceed with the destruction of the encircled German troops. The responsibility for this will lie with you.

> Representing Headquarters Red Army
> Supreme Command,
> Colonel-General of the Artillery Voronov
> The Commander-in-Chief of the Forces of the Don front,
> Lieutenant-General Rokossovsky

On Hitler's orders, Paulus rejected the demand for surrender.

On 16 January the Russians resumed their attacks to the west and south, and pushed forward remorselessly towards Gumrak, the last airfield remaining to the beleaguered garrison. Whenever the Russians met determined resistance they stopped and attacked somewhere else. By 19 January the ring round 6 Army had grown very tight, and Paulus held a conference with his corps commanders. It was seriously proposed that on 22 January all troops in the "fortress" should rise as a man, and break out in small groups in an endeavour to reach the German lines on the Don. As Dingler comments, "This was a plan which despair alone could suggest", and it was quietly forgotten.

During this period various senior commanders and staff officers received orders to fly out of the Stalingrad ring. Among these was Colonel Dingler, whose shattered 3 Motorized Division was then holding a small sector near the water tower of Voroponovo. Together with General Hube, the commander of XIV Panzer Corps, he was to leave Stalingrad and try to improve the supply position of those in the ring. It was with a heavy heart that he left his men behind, and he did not do so before discussing the order with his Divisional Commander and other officers, who saw a ray of hope in this mission. The one and only transport vehicle left to the division—a motor-cycle combination—brought him to the Gumrak landing ground; the road was covered with dead soldiers, burnt-out tanks, abandoned guns, indeed, all the debris of an army in the last stages of dissolution. The airfield presented a similar picture of destruction—a snowy desert littered with aircraft and vehicles. Everywhere lay the corpses of German soldiers; too exhausted to move on, they had just died in the snow.

General von Mellenthin

THE END

6 Army to High Command: 24 January

. . . . Troops without ammunition or food. Contact maintained with elements only of six divisions. Evidence of disintegration on southern, northern and western fronts. Effective command no longer possible. Little change on eastern front: eighteen thousand wounded without any supplies of dressings or drugs; 44, 76, 100, 305 and 384 Infantry Divisions destroyed. Front torn open as a result of strong break-throughs on three sides. Strong-points and shelter only available in the town itself; further defence senseless. Collapse inevitable. Army requests immediate permission to surrender in order to save lives of remaining troops.

Paulus

Adolf Hitler to 6 Army: 24 January

Surrender is forbidden. 6 Army will hold their positions to the last man and the last round and by their heroic endurance will make an unforgettable contribution towards the establishment of a defensive front and the salvation of the Western world.

Adolf Hitler

31 January

12.18 hours. The dropping of supplies on the Red Square no longer possible, on the Engineer barracks unsafe and on the tractor factory doubtful.

12.30 hours. Enemy forces directly outside the door. The end of the struggle is no longer in doubt.

15.10 hours. From 6 Army Headquarters to VIII Flying Corps and Air Signals Battalion 129 through 9 Anti-Aircraft Division:

Remainder of Stalingrad Headquarters signing off today. Good luck and greetings to the homeland.

> Lieutenant Wachsland, 6 Army Headquarters

The Russians stand at the door of our bunker. We are destroying our equipment.

This station will no longer transmit.

> 6 Army Headquarters, 05.45 hours

On this day, General Paulus was promoted to the rank of Field-Marshal.

A Message to Stalin

Carrying out your order, the troops on the Don Front at 4 p.m. on 2 February 1943, completed the rout and destruction of the encircled group of enemy forces at Stalingrad. Twenty-two divisions have been destroyed or taken prisoner.

> Lieutenant-General Rokossovsky,
> Commander of the Don Front
> Lieutenant-General Malinin,
> Chief of Staff of the Don Front

The battle for Stalingrad has ended. Faithful to its oath to fight to the last breath, 6 Army under the exemplary leadership of Field-Marshal Paulus has been overcome by

the enemy's superior force and by adverse circumstances.
German High Command official communiqué,
3 February

Captured German Officers

The most unforgettable of them was Lieutenant-General von Arnim, a cousin of the other Arnim who was to be captured in Tunisia a few months later. He was enormously tall, with a long twisted nose, and a look of fury in his long horse-like face with its popping eyes. He had a stupendous display of crosses and orders and mantelpiece ornaments. He, no more than the others, had any desire to explain why they had allowed themselves to be trapped at Stalingrad, and why they had been licked. When somebody put the question, he snarled and said, "The question is badly put. You should ask how did we hold out so long against such overwhelming numerical superiority?" And one of the sulking ones in the background said something about hunger and cold.

But how they all hated any suggestion that the Red Army was a better army and a better-led army than theirs! When somebody suggested it, Von Arnim snorted and went almost purple with rage.

. . . . One thing astonished me about these generals: they had been captured only a couple of days ago—and they looked healthy, and not in the least undernourished. Clearly, throughout the agony of Stalingrad, when their soldiers were dying of hunger, they were continuing to have more or less regular meals. There could be no other explanation for their normal, or almost normal, weight and appearance.

The only man who looked in poor shape was Paulus himself. We weren't allowed to speak to him; he was only shown us. (We could then testify that he was alive and had not committed suicide.) He stepped out of a large cottage—it was more like a villa—gave us a look, then stared at the horizon, and stood on the steps for a minute or two, amid a rather awkward silence, together with two other officers; one was General Schmidt, his Chief of Staff, a sinister, Göring-like creature, wearing a strange fur cap made of imitation leopard skin. Paulus looked pale and sick, and has a nervous twitch in his left cheek. He had more natural dignity than any of the others, and wore only one or two decorations.

Alexander Werth

Post-Mortem

Hitler: "They have surrendered there formally and absolutely. Otherwise they would have closed ranks, formed a hedgehog, and shot themselves with their last bullet. When you consider that a woman has the pride to leave, to lock herself in, and to shoot herself right away just because she had heard a few insulting remarks,* then I can't have any respect for a soldier who is afraid of that and prefers to go into captivity. I can only say: I can understand a case like that of General Giraud; we come in, he gets out of his car, and is grabbed. But——"

Zeitzler: "I can't understand it, either. I'm still of the opinion that it might not be true; perhaps he is lying there badly wounded."

Hitler: "No, it is true. . . . They'll be brought to Moscow, to the G.P.U. right away, and they'll blurt out orders for the northern pocket to surrender too.** That Schmidt will sign anything. A man who doesn't have the courage, in such a time, to take the road that every man has to take some time, doesn't have the strength to withstand that sort of thing. He will suffer torture in his soul. In Germany there has been too much emphasis on training the intellect and not enough on strength of character. . . .

* Nothing is known of the incident Hitler refers to.
** A small part of the German forces, under the command of Lieutenant-General Streicher of XI Corps, was still holding out north of Stalingrad at this time. This unit surrendered on the day following this conference.

". . . . Here is a man who sees fifty or sixty thousand of his soldiers die defending themselves bravely to the end. How can he surrender himself to the Bolsheviks? Oh, that is——"

Zeitzler: "That is something one can't understand at all."

Hitler: "But I had my doubts before. That was the moment when I received the report that he was asking what he should do. How can he even ask about such a thing. From now on, every time a fortress is besieged and the commandant is called on to surrender, he is going to ask, 'What shall I do now?' . . . ."

Zeitzler: "There is no excuse. When his nerves threaten to break down, then he must kill himself."

Hitler: "When the nerves break down, there is nothing left but to admit that one can't handle the situation and to shoot oneself. One can also say the man should have shot himself just as the old commanders who threw themselves on their swords when they saw that the cause was lost. That goes without saying. Even Varrus gave his slave the order: 'Now kill me!' "

Zeitzler: "I still think they may have done that, and that the Russians are only claiming to have captured them all."

Hitler: "No."

After the Battle

The steep river bank covered with the black entrances to trenches and dugouts resembled a cave town.

Over one of the dug-outs I read a sign half washed-out by rain: *General Rodimtsev's Headquarters*.

This, then, was that narrow strip of land along the river to which our troops had clung tenaciously throughout the siege, which they had held although to hold it was obviously impossible—a fortress one or two hundred yards wide. A command—spoken, not shouted—from divisional headquarters was heard by the men in the forward positions. One had to crawl from dug-out to dug-out, for to raise one's head was asking for sudden death.

A Happy New Year, Comrades! said a sign over the entrance to one of the dug-outs and I pictured them standing face to face with death, drinking to victory on that New Year's Eve. Unfortunately, I was unable to reconstruct the story of the heroes of Chuikov's and Rodimtsev's divisions, for all those who had taken part in that great battle had moved on to the west before I arrived. But I did see the monument to the Defence of Stalingrad.

It is not a monument in the accepted sense. Just a plain wall with the soot-scrawled inscription: *Here Rodimtsev's Guards Stood to the Death.*

Boris Agapov

Doubt

We all had friends on the Russian Front and we tried not to talk too much about them to each other. But one day an old friend of mine—Edith Wieland—wrote, begging me to visit her, as she had just lost her husband in the battle. I found, as she opened the door, a thin, old woman in black, not the proud, confident Edith I had known. She began to cry as she asked me inside.

In the lounge she showed me her husband's last letter from Stalingrad. He asked her to forgive him for anything he might ever have done to hurt her. He had never at any time wanted to hurt her. It was for her alone that he was now living and he loved her more than his life. This was no empty phrase he wrote, because they were now facing death, and it would only be a matter of days or weeks. But as long as he felt his death served a purpose he would be willing to give his life for the Fatherland. He implored her never to give up, no matter what might come, and to bring up their children—the youngest only two months old—in the spirit they had agreed upon.

I was utterly shaken. I could see him standing before me in his officer's uniform, so proud and with the Iron Cross on his chest and the stars of a *Hauptmann*. He had been a strong and virile man, honest as the day.

"Was he wounded when he wrote this letter?" I asked Edith.

"No," she said quickly. "I have been told he was not wounded. He met his death with open eyes. He was perfectly well and strong."

I looked down at the carpet. What kind of death then had he met? As if Edith could guess my thoughts, she said, "They have written that death came instantaneously. He got a bullet through the head as he came round the corner of a house."

While I was searching desperately for the right words, Edith spoke again. "There is one thing that haunts me. I have heard a rumour that they could have escaped, but that Hitler forbade it!"

I was frightened. I had not heard that rumour myself at the time. "No! Impossible!" I said. "It would be plain murder. Hitler would never do such a thing. You know that, surely?"

Very slowly Edith lifted her head. "I am not so sure," she said in a low voice. "I keep re-reading that sentence in Albert's letter ('as long as I feel my death serves a purpose'), that doesn't sound a bit like Albert. It sounds as though his confidence was waning, and he was beginning to doubt."

                                        Else Wendel, housewife.

4

THE TIDE TURNS IN THE
PACIFIC: MIDWAY

By the spring of 1942 the Japanese had established a defensive perimeter which ran from Burma round Sumatra and Java and along the northern coast of New Guinea to the western Solomons, then turning north and embracing parts of the Gilbert and Marshall groups and Wake Island. The Kurile Islands off the coast of Siberia marked the northern extremity of the perimeter. In late March and April Japanese naval and air forces had raided far out into the Indian Ocean, attacking Ceylon and British naval forces with fair success and then returning to their defensive ring. With freedom of action within it and inexhaustible supplies of food and raw materials, the Japanese considered themselves in a position to fight on indefinitely. Within a few months they had achieved their aim and had reached the zenith of their success. General MacArthur, arrived in Australia from the Philippines, prepared to defend the Southern Continent and plan counter-strokes.

General MacArthur Arrives in Australia

THE President of the United States orders me to break through the Japanese lines and proceed from Corregidor to Australia for the purpose, as I understand it, of organizing the American offensive against Japan, a primary object of which is the relief of the Philippines. I came through and I shall return.

General MacArthur

Long before the Allied victories began; while, indeed, their forces were still being driven from Burma and the Philippines, the Japanese people in their homeland had received grim warning of what was to come two years later. On 18 April 1942 General Doolittle flew sixteen B-25 bombers off the U.S.S. Hornet *and bombed Tokyo. This totally unexpected stroke, though isolated, administered a salutary shock to Japanese morale, so far borne along on the flood-tide of victory. Rudimentary air-raid precautions were hurriedly instituted.*

Thirty Seconds over Tokyo

We were about two minutes out over the bay when we all of us seemed to look to the right at the same time, and there sat the biggest, fattest-looking aircraft carrier we had ever seen. It was a couple of miles away, anchored, and there did not seem to be a man in sight. It was an awful temptation not to change course and drop one on it. But we had been so drilled in what to do with our four bombs, and Tokyo was now so close that I decided to go on.

There were no enemy planes in sight. Ahead, I could see what must have been Davey Jones climbing fast and hard and running into innocent-looking black clouds that appeared round his plane.

It took about five minutes to get across our arm of the bay, and, while still over the water, I could see the barrage balloons strung between Tokyo and Yokohama, across the river from Tokyo.

There were no beaches where we came in. Every inch of shoreline was taken up with wharves. I could see some dredging operations filling in more shoreline, just as we were told we would see. We came in over some of the most beautiful yachts I've ever seen, then over the heavier ships at the wharves and low over the first of the rooftops. I gave the ship a little more throttle, for we seemed to be creeping along.

In days and nights of dreaming about Tokyo and thinking of the eight millions who live there, I got the impression that it would be crammed together, concentrated, like San Francisco. Instead it spreads all over creation, like Los Angeles. There is an aggressively modern sameness to much of it and now, as we came in very low over it, I had a bad feeling that we wouldn't find our targets. I had to stay low and thus could see only a short distance ahead and to the sides. I couldn't go up to take a good look without drawing anti-aircraft fire, which I figured would be very accurate by now because the planes that had come in ahead of me all had bombed from fifteen hundred feet. The buildings grew taller. I couldn't see people.

I was almost on the first of our objectives before I saw it. I gave the engines full throttle as Davenport adjusted the prop pitch to get a better grip on the air. We climbed as quickly as possible to fifteen hundred feet, in the manner which we had practised for a month and had discussed for three additional weeks.

There was just time to get up there, level off, attend to the routine of opening the bomb bay, make a short run and let fly with the first bomb. The red light blinked on my instrument board, and I knew the first 500-pounder had gone.

Our speed was picking up. The red light blinked again, and I knew Clever had let the second bomb go. Just as the light blinked, a black cloud appeared about a hundred yards or so in front of us and rushed past at great speed. Two more appeared ahead of us, on about the line of our wingtips, and they too swept past. They had our altitude perfectly, but they were leading us too much.

The third red light flickered, and, since we were now over a flimsy area in the southern part of the city, the fourth light blinked. That was an incendiary which I knew would separate as soon as it hit the wind and that dozens of small fire bombs would moult from it.

The moment the fourth red light showed I put the nose of the Ruptured Duck into a deep dive. I had changed the course somewhat for the short run leading up to the dropping of the incendiary. Now, as I dived, I looked back and out: I got a quick, indelible vision of one of our 500-pounders as it hit our steel-smelter target. The plant seemed to puff out its walls and then subside and dissolve in a black-and-red cloud.

Our diving speed picked up to 350 m.p.h. in less time that it takes to tell it, and up there in the front of the vibrating bomber I dimly wondered why the Japanese didn't throw up a wall of machine-gun fire. We would have to fly right through it.

I flattened out over a long row of low buildings and homes and got the hell out of there.

Captain Ted W. Lawson

Air-raid Precautions: Japan

The repeated air-raid drills took up a large part of the day when they were called. I took active part in only one of these drills and I think my neighbours were glad when I did not reappear. People looked at me instead of listening to the warden and that created too much confusion. Running uphill with pails of water, without spilling any water from the buckets, seemed to me a silly and tedious way to fight a war. We had to fill small bags with sand and stack them outside each dwelling, supposedly for use in putting out fires the air raids would start. We never knew and were never told whether that was the purpose of the sandbags or not, and I could only guess what the authorities had in mind. Additional fire protection was supplied by a large container of water outside each house and what looked like a huge fly swatter (to beat out the flames).

Sometimes a smudge pot would be placed in the lower branches of a tree, and the women would have to line up with pails of water to throw in an attempt to extinguish the smudge fire. Usually these exercises were at night when the women were exhausted from their household chores. The warden would shout "next", and I would hear the clap-clap of the wooden clogs and then the splash of the water.

. . . . The so-called shelter each household had to prepare in its garden was often only a deep hole, exposed and damp. These holes always depressed me; they looked so like open graves, gaping expectantly at us. Kikuya had to dig ours, and our new dog Kuri did his bit, too. Like a true war dog, he worked side-by-side with Kikuya, and I longed for a movie camera to record the scene.

Besides the shelter, every household had to have on hand one rucksack filled with supplies, bandages, a few first-aid articles, rice, a cooking-pan, and the padded hoods which we were required to wear. Many people were to be badly burned because of those hoods. The padding used was made of thick cotton, and when it caught fire the wearers were unaware of the blaze until it was too late to avoid serious burns. All women were requested to wear either *monpe* (the Japanese "pantaloons" I had learned to appreciate) or slacks, although slacks were frowned on as too Western. Permanents and nail polish were also considered in bad taste. But the Japanese woman, in spite of having been taught obedience from birth, rebelled at the prohibition of permanents. She continued to have her hair done, sometimes under great stress, and often incurring real danger during air raids. These governmental restrictions were shortsighted. The Japanese lady had always been a colourful, well-groomed person. She should not have been robbed of such attractiveness unnecessarily and forced to adopt drab, muddy colours in place of her gay, delightful kimono. A happy woman is a more efficient woman, even in war-time.

The men were requested to wear what was called "the national uniform", a dull khaki affair with puttees wrapped around the trousers. This uniform included a field cap identical with the army cap except it was without insignia.

On the eight of every month, to commemorate the beginning of the war, every man was required to wear the uniform and the women had to wear slacks or *monpe*. Anyone dressed otherwise was stopped at the exits of the stations and roundly scolded. Often some poor woman, harried and overworked, was forced to return home and dress again.

I noticed that many people cultivated flowers on top of their air-raid shelters. When the evening's work was done, they would sit in front of their shops and homes to admire the few blossoms they had been able to nurture.

Gwen Terasaki

Few nations can have enjoyed the full flush of unrelieved victory for so short a time as the Japanese. In fact, no sooner had they reached the limits of their advance within their original perimeter than the first of two battles which turned the tide of war took place.

In early May 1942 the Japanese launched the first stage of a three-fold operation to extend their perimeter. This stage was designed to begin the envelopment of northern and eastern Australia. They occupied the eastern Solomons and began to build an airfield on Guadalcanal, and then a strong naval force sailed to support a troop convoy heading for Port Moresby in eastern New Guinea. To meet them in the Coral Sea was an American force of approximately equal strength. On 4 May ensued the first naval action in history to be fought entirely in the air, in which the opposing fleets never came within sight or gunshot range of one another.

This battle of aircraft carriers ended with one sunk and one damaged on the American side and two damaged on the Japanese side, so the latter claimed the victory, but it was a hollow one, for the convoy destined for Port Moresby turned back.

THE BATTLE OF MIDWAY

Encouraged by an apparent victory in the Coral Sea, the Japanese pressed on towards the other objectives of their extending operation. One was the Aleutian islands of Attu and Kiska, cold lands in a world of fog, which they took without trouble and later abandoned. The other was the fortified atoll of Midway protecting Hawaii, towards which Admiral Yamamoto sailed with all the forces he could muster in the last week of May 1942. The decisive battle of the Far Eastern war was about to be fought.

The Battle of Midway took place on 4 June 1942. The Japanese Navy, excelling in carrier strength and flushed with victory after the Hawaiian attack, was unaware that operational secrets had leaked out. And so we fell into the trap laid by the enemy, who was forewarned of our movements. A severe defeat ensued for the Japanese. Midway was a crucial battle which reversed the whole position in the Pacific war.

Mochitsura Hashimoto

The Advance Guard sails from Japan

The fleet had formed a single column for the passage through the strait. Twenty-one ships in all, they cruised along at intervals of a thousand yards, resembling for all the world a peacetime naval review. Far out in front was Rear-Admiral Susumu Kimura's flagship, light cruiser *Nagara*, leading the twelve ships of Destroyer Squadron 10. Next came Rear-Admiral Hiroaki Abe's Cruiser Division 8—*Tone*, the flagship, and *Chikuma*—followed by the second section of Battleship Division 3, made up of fast battleships *Haruna* and *Kirishima*. (The first section of Battleship Division 3, *Hiei* and *Kongo*, had been assigned to Admiral Kondo's invasion force for this operation.) Behind *Kirishima* came large carriers *Akagi* and *Kaga,* comprising Carrier Division I, under Admiral Nagumo's direct command. Rear-Admiral Tamon Yamaguchi's Carrier Division 2—*Hiryu* and *Soryu*—brought up the rear, completing the Nagumo Force.

Presently a dozen or so fishing boats waiting for the tide hove into sight to starboard, and their crews waved and cheered as we passed. To port, the tiny island of Yurishima appeared to be floating on the surface of the sea, its thick covering of green foliage set off against the dim background of Aoshima. Beyond, the coast of Shikoku lay hidden in mist.

As the fleet steamed on, three seaplanes of the Kure Air Corps passed overhead, their pontoons looking like oversized shoes. The planes were on their way to neutralize any enemy submarines which might be lying in wait for us outside Bungo Strait.

Mitsuo Fuchida

The Interceptors

"In accordance with Commander-in-Chief Pacific Operation Plan 29-42, the *Hornet* got underway from Pearl Harbor, 28 May 1942, recovering the Air Group at sea, at 16.30, the same afternoon," begins the *Hornet's* Action Report for the Battle of Midway. As was usual, her aircraft had been stationed ashore when the ship was in port. They flew out to roost when she was a short time out of Pearl Harbor. Minutes after the planes were aboard, the speaker system blared throughout the ship:

"This is the captain. We are going to intercept a Jap attack on Midway."

That settled any doubts in the minds of the *Hornet* pilots.

Not all of Torpedo Eight was aboard. Six new Grumman Avengers, part of VT-8, were based on Midway. The *Hornet* pilots had been training for months, long before the ship got her final coat of paint, but not one was blooded. Their total average flying hours were somewhere around 285 each. Routine training was conducted en route, and most of the aircraft, in addition to combat air patrol, were scheduled for daily exercises. The force steamed on to a rendezvous with Rear-Admiral Frank Jack Fletcher's Task Force 17.

. . . . On 1 June, Mitscher wrote out a message for Commander Henderson to read over the bull horn: "The enemy are approaching for an attempt to seize Midway. This attack will probably be accompanied by a feint at western Alaska. We are going to prevent them from taking Midway, if possible. Be ready and keep on the alert. Let's get a few more yellowtails." Although some skippers, through oversight or intent, kept their crews in suspense, Mitscher tried to inform every man of what might be hanging beneath the next cloud.

The next day, at 14.00 the *Hornet* task force kept its rendezvous with the *Yorktown* northeast of Midway. Admiral Fletcher assumed tactical command of the entire American defensive force, but Nimitz, back in Pearl Harbor, still called the strategical signals. Halsey was ill, and Rear-Admiral Raymond Spruance had taken over Task Force 16, in which the *Hornet* rode.

Theodore Taylor

Contact

During the next hour there was a confusing succession of reported contacts on our force both by individual flying boats and by small numbers of enemy planes of unidentified type. There was also a further radio warning from *Tone*'s search plane at 05.55 that fifteen enemy planes were heading towards us. The formation raised its speed to twenty-eight knots, and *Tone,* after sighting three planes overhead at 06.43, began making smoke to provide concealment against attack. Since no attack took place during this entire period, however, some of the reported contacts must have been erroneous or on our own fighters patrolling overhead. But there was no question that enemy flying boats were shadowing us, skilfully manoeuvring in and out of the clouds to elude pursuit.

Each time one of the persistent PBYs was sighted, now to starboard, now to port, *Akagi*'s harassed fighter director would shout orders to our combat air patrol to go after it. The enemy pilots, however, were so adept at weaving through the clouds that the fighters merely exhausted themselves to no avail. While our own movements were thus observed and reported continuously, there was still no warning from our own search planes of any enemy task force.

Mitsuo Fuchida

Midway Attacked

. . . . The first Japanese air strike—thirty-six torpedo aircraft, thirty-six dive-bombers, and thirty-six fighters, under Lieutenant Tomonaga, was picked up by Midway radar forty-three miles north-west of the island. The alarm was sounded, every aircraft able to leave the ground took to the air, and at 6.16 a.m., when thirty miles out, the Marine Corps fighter squadron, twenty-six aircraft in all, encountered the Japanese van, but was out-numbered and almost annihilated. "The entire island," wrote an American officer, "was deadly silent after the buzz of the planes taking off. It was a beautiful sunny morning. The men all strained for a first glimpse, and I had to sharply remind the lookouts to keep the other sectors covered against surprise. Then we saw the Japs, and the tension snapped. A moment later we were in action." Although considerable damage was done to the installations on the island, few men were killed and none of the runways was rendered unusable. At 6.50 a.m. the attack was over.

Closing for the Kill

Shortly after 07.00, while Army B-17s were unsuccessfully attempting to damage the enemy from twenty thousand feet, the *Hornet*'s fighter pilots were called to deck; then the scout bombers were manned. Finally, Waldron's torpedo planes were ready. Hitting fast ships at sea is a job for planes that go in low. Then Mitscher spoke into the bridge microphone: "We intend to launch planes to attack the enemy while their planes are still returning from Midway. We will close to about a hundred miles from the enemy's position."

Theodore Taylor

Surprise

Already about an hour before Tomonaga's Midway strike planes got back to the carriers, however, there had been a development which completely altered the battle situation confronting Admiral Nagumo. *Tone*'s No. 4 search plane, which had been launched a full half-hour behind schedule, finally reached its three-hundred-mile search limit on course 100° at 07.20, and it then veered north to fly a sixty-mile dog-leg before heading back. Eight minutes later its observer suddenly discerned, far off to port, a formation of some ten ships heading south-east. Without waiting until it could get a closer look, the plane immediately flashed a message to the Nagumo Force: "Ten ships, apparently enemy, sighted. Bearing 010, distant two hundred and forty miles from Midway. Course 150°, speed more than twenty knots. Time, 07.28."

This vital message was received by the flagship only after several minutes' delay occasioned by the relaying of the message through *Tone*. When it reached Admiral Nagumo and his staff on *Akagi*'s bridge, it struck them like a bolt from the blue. Until this morning no one had anticipated that an enemy surface force could possibly appear so soon, much less suspected that enemy ships were already in the vicinity waiting to ambush us. Now the entire picture was changed.

Lieutenant-Commander Ono, the Staff Intelligence Officer, quickly plotted the enemy's reported position on the navigation chart and measured off the distance between it and our force. The enemy was just two hundred miles away! This meant that he was already within striking range of our planes, but if he had carriers, we were also within *his* reach. The big question now was what composed the enemy force. Above all, did it contain any carriers?

Mitsuo Fuchida

Strike

There was a cloud-flecked sky as Soucek gave orders to send the *Hornet*'s stingers off. The fighters, Grumman Wildcats, were first; Rhode's scouts in the Dauntlesses followed; then Johnson's dive-bombers, also in Dauntlesses; and lastly Waldron's heavy-bellied torpedo planes.

It took almost an hour for the launching and Mitscher bent over the railing, occasionally giving an order, and following each plane off with his eyes. Once the last torpedo plane was airborne, Mitscher was practically out of touch with the fight. Radio silence was maintained. Squadron commanders were in charge, with Stanhope Ring, a senior, over them. Mitscher could not contact, advise, or assist. He would have to wait until they got back to find out what happened.

Last-minute teletype instructions to the *Hornet*'s air group placed the enemy at a distance of 155 miles. The fighters and bombers climbed to nineteen thousand feet, flying at 125 m.p.h. Waldron stayed below a layer of cumulus clouds, nursing his planes along at 110 m.p.h. They breezed through the morning without knowledge that Admiral Nagumo had changed the course of his carriers and was retiring. When the bombers and fighters reached their supposed position, Nagumo and his carriers were not in sight. Stanhope Ring kept the air group travelling southwest.

But Jack Waldron, down below the blanket of clouds at fifteen hundred feet, unmindful that his fighter cover was not above, rolled the torpedo squadron northward on a strong hunch. He found Nagumo and the carriers *Hiryu, Akagi, Kaga* and *Soryu*. What Waldron then did has been called foolhardy, but it was also heroic. He rode his torpedo planes in against the carriers without fighter

protection; full into the ack-ack and whirling Zeros, hoping
to deliver his weenies and pickles. Waldron presented
fifteen solid targets to the Japanese gun gallery. Ensign
Gay was shot down and hid beneath a floating seat
cushion. He witnessed the Battle of Midway from that
bobbing seat and was picked up later.

The *Hornet*'s bombers and fighters were running low on
gas. But planes from the *Enterprise* and the *Yorktown*
arrived to convert three of Nagumo's carriers into flotsam.
The *Hiryu* sent her planes after the *Yorktown* in
retaliation. Meanwhile, back on the *Hornet,* Mitscher
stirred about the bridge uneasily. He knew little or nothing
of what was going on. Communications had been spotty
all morning. Action reports seeped in, but nothing to
indicate any decisive combat. Some of the planes had run
out of fuel and crash landed in Midway's lagoon; others
had refuelled at Midway. Survivors of the *Hornet*'s snipe
hunt banged down on deck to refuel. They didn't need to
rearm. They hadn't fought. Mitscher pushed on, holding
an easterly course at high speed to land his planes. The
first wheels hit the deck at 13.20. Rodee's scouts and part
of Bombing Eight fluttered in. Then they waited for the
fighters and for Torpedo Eight.

Ring and Rodee went to the bridge to tell Mitscher they
hadn't seen the enemy and knew nothing of Waldron.
Then Quillen, the rear gunner in Ensign White's dive-
bomber, reported that he thought he had heard Waldron's
voice on his radio: "What I heard was Johnny One to
Johnny Two. I am quite sure it was Lieutenant-
Commander Waldron's voice as I have heard him on the
air a number of times. I also heard him say, Watch those
fighters. Also, See that splash. Also, How'm I doing,
Dobbs? Also, Attack immediately. Also, I'd give a million
to know who did that. . . ."

And then there was silence. Thus they died, all except
one. Fifteen planes, each with pilot and crewman.

Japanese planes were attacking the *Yorktown*. Soon a
column of smoke reached into the north-west sky. Some
Hornet fighters were over there trying to ward off the

blows, and got three Zeros. The *Yorktown* was mortally wounded. One *Yorktown* pilot wobbled towards the *Hornet* and crashed down in a grind of ripping metal, his machine-guns peppering the island structure. Minutes later, the officer of the deck reported to Mitscher: five dead and twenty wounded. With Fletcher's Task Force 17 flag burning in the *Yorktown*, Rear-Admiral Raymond Spruance took local tactical command. A Japanese submarine finished the *Yorktown* later.

Spruance signalled Mitscher and the *Enterprise* to get the *Hiryu*. Her planes had destroyed the *Yorktown* and could do the same to the *Enterprise* and the *Hornet*. At 18.03, Mitscher launched sixteen bombers to join the *Enterprise* striking group. *Enterprise* pilots got there first and laid into the enemy carriers. The *Hornet* bombers circled at twenty thousand feet while nine B-17s attempted to bomb the *Hiryu*'s escorting battleships, missing by a wide margin. Then VB-8 pushed over into their dives, releasing bombs at low altitude for hits on a battleship and a heavy cruiser. The *Hornet* had finally drawn blood.

As more action reports drifted in, Mitscher informed the *Hornet* crew, "Four Japanese carriers are afire. Direct hits have been scored on their battleships and cruisers."

It was growing dark, and the *Hornet*, blacked out, soon blended into the night. How could her surviving bombers find the flight deck? Two planes angled towards the task force. Then others droned up. None of the *Hornet* pilots had qualified in night carrier landings.

"Turn on the truck lights," Mitscher ordered. The dim red beacons shone out from her masthead but the planes passed over. Mitscher knew the pilots could not possibly spot her deck. "Let's give them more light."

Two search beams climbed into the air over the *Hornet*: a string of lights outlined the flight deck to port.

Henderson said, "Captain, there must be subs here."

"The hell with the subs," Mitscher said, straining to glimpse the aircraft as they approached and finally landed.

He had thought Stan Ring was lost. Then Ring came up

to the bridge, sweaty and haggard. The surviving pilots gathered in the wardroom and pantry, happy to be alive, but the joy was tempered by concern about the still unreported torpedo-men.

Mitscher ordered Dr. Sam Osterlough to the bridge, and Sam came up with his pockets bulging and clinking. "How are they?" Mitscher asked.

"Some are a little shaky."

"Give them each a bottle and see to it personally that they go to bed."

Osterlough, on the way to deliver his "packages" to the pilots, stopped by Mitscher's cabin, pulled one of the two-ounce bottles of brandy out of his pocket, and placed it on the desk.

By now, it was obvious that Torpedo Eight was not returning. It appeared the *Hornet* had lost at least twenty-five aircraft and almost double that number of pilots and crewmen. The day's operations had not been good, but the bombers had partially recouped in the sunset attack. There were five bodies in readiness for burial from the gun accident. Luck had been very bad.

Theodore Taylor

The Slaughter of the Carriers

As our fighters ran out of ammunition during the fierce battle they returned to the carriers for replenishment, but few ran low on fuel. Service crews cheered the returning pilots, patted them on the shoulder, and shouted words of encouragement. As soon as a plane was ready again the pilot nodded, pushed forward the throttle, and roared back into the sky. This scene was repeated time and again as the desperate air struggle continued.

Preparations for a counter-strike against the enemy had continued on board our four carriers throughout the enemy torpedo attacks. One after another, planes were hoisted from the hangar and quickly arranged on the flight deck. There was no time to lose. At 10.20 Admiral Nagumo gave the order to launch when ready. On *Akagi*'s flight deck all planes were in position with engines warming up. The big ship began turning into the wind. Within five minutes all her planes would be launched.

Five minutes! Who would have dreamed that the tide of battle would shift completely in that brief interval of time?

Visibility was good. Clouds were gathering at about three thousand metres, however, and though there were occasional breaks, they afforded good concealment for approaching enemy planes. At 10.24 the order to start launching came from the bridge by voice-tube. The Air Officer flapped a white flag, and the first Zero fighter gathered speed and whizzed off the deck. At that instant a look-out screamed: "Hell-Divers!" I looked up to see three black enemy planes plummeting towards our ship. Some of our machine-guns managed to fire a few frantic bursts at them, but it was too late. The plump silhouettes of the American Dauntless dive-bombers quickly grew larger, and then a number of black objects suddenly floated eerily from their wings. Bombs! Down they came straight toward me! I fell intuitively to the deck and crawled behind a command post mantelet.

The terrifying scream of the dive-bombers reached me first, followed by the crashing explosion of a direct hit. There was a blinding flash and then a second explosion, much louder than the first. I was shaken by a weird blast of warm air. There was still another shock, but less severe, apparently a near-miss. Then followed a startling quiet as the barking of guns suddenly ceased. I got up and looked at the sky. The enemy planes were already gone from sight.

The attackers had got in unimpeded because our fighters, which had engaged the preceding wave of torpedo planes only a few moments earlier, had not yet had time to regain altitude. Consequently, it may be said that the American dive-bombers' success was made possible by the earlier martyrdom of their torpedo planes. Also, our carriers had no time to evade because clouds hid the enemy's approach until he dived down to the attack. We had been caught flat-footed in the most vulnerable condition possible—decks loaded with planes armed and fuelled for an attack.

Looking about, I was horrified at the destruction that had been wrought in a matter of seconds. There was a huge hole in the flight deck just behind the amidship elevator. The elevator itself, twisted like molten glass, was dropping into the hangar. Deck plates reeled upwards in grotesque configurations. Planes stood tail up, belching livid flame and jet-black smoke. Reluctant tears streamed down my cheeks as I watched the fires spread, and I was terrified at the prospect of induced explosions which would surely doom the ship. I heard Masuda yelling, "Inside! Get inside! Everbody who isn't working! Get inside!"

Unable to help, I staggered down a ladder and into the ready room. It was already jammed with badly burned victims from the hangar deck. A new explosion was followed quickly by several more, each causing the bridge structure to tremble. Smoke from the burning hangar gushed through passageways and into the bridge and ready room, forcing us to seek other refuge. Climbing back to the bridge, I could see that *Kaga* and *Soryu* had also been hit and were giving off heavy columns of black smoke. The scene was horrible to behold.

Akagi had taken two direct hits, one on the after rim of the amidship elevator, the other on the rear guard on the port side of the flight deck. Normally, neither would have been fatal to the giant carrier, but induced explosions of fuel and munitions devastated whole sections of the ship, shaking the bridge and filling the air with deadly splinters. As fire spread among the planes lined up wing to wing on the after flight deck, their torpedoes began to explode, making it impossible to bring the fires under control. The entire hangar area was a blazing inferno, and the flames moved swiftly towards the bridge.

Because of the spreading fire, our general loss of combat efficiency, and especially the severance of external communication facilities, Nagumo's Chief of Staff, Rear-Admiral Kusaka, urged that the flag be transferred at once to light cruiser *Nagara*. Admiral Nagumo gave only a half-hearted nod, but Kusaka patiently continued his entreaty: "Sir, most of our ships are still intact. You must command them."

The situation demanded immediate action, but Admiral Nagumo was reluctant to leave his beloved flagship. Most of all he was loath to leave behind the officers and men of *Akagi*, with whom he had shared every joy and sorrow of war. With tears in his eyes, Captain Aoki spoke up: "Admiral, I will take care of the ship. Please, we all implore you, shift your flag to *Nagara* and resume command of the Force."

At this moment Lieutenant-Commander Nishibayashi, the Flag Secretary, came up and reported to Kusaka: "All passages below are on fire, sir. The only means of escape is by rope from the forward window of the bridge down to the deck, then by the outboard passage to the anchor deck. *Nagara*'s boat will come alongside the anchor deck port, and you can reach it by rope ladder."

Kusaka made a final plea to Admiral Nagumo to leave the doomed ship. At last convinced that there was no possibility of maintaining command from *Akagi*, Nagumo bade the Captain good-bye and climbed from the bridge window with the aid of Nishibayashi. The Chief of Staff and other staff and headquarters officers followed. The time was 10.46.

On the bridge there remained only Captain Aoki, his Navigator, the Air Officer, a few ratings, and myself. Aoki was trying desperately to get in touch with the engine room. The Chief Navigator was struggling to see if anything could be done to regain rudder control. The others were gathered on the anchor deck fighting the raging fire as best they could. But the unchecked flames were already licking at the bridge. Hammock mantelets around the bridge structure were beginning to burn. The Air Officer looked back at me and said, "Fuchida, we won't be able to stay on the bridge much longer. You'd better get to the anchor deck before it is too late."

In my condition this was no easy task. Helped by some

sailors, I managed to get out of the bridge window and slid down the already smouldering rope to the gun deck. There I was still ten feet above the flight deck. The connecting monkey ladder was red hot, as was the iron plate on which I stood. There was nothing to do but jump, which I did. At the same moment another explosion occurred in the hangar, and the resultant blast sent me sprawling. Luckily the deck on which I landed was not yet afire, for the force of the fall knocked me out momentarily. Returning to consciousness, I struggled to rise to my feet, but both of my ankles were broken.

Crewmen finally came to my assistance and took me to the anchor deck, which was already jammed. There I was strapped into a bamboo stretcher and lowered to a boat which carried me, along with other wounded, to light cruiser *Nagara*. The transfer of Nagumo's staff and of the wounded was completed at 11.30. The cruiser got under way, flying Admiral Nagumo's flag at her mast.

Meanwhile, efforts to bring *Akagi*'s fires under control continued, but it became increasingly obvious that this was impossible. As the ship came to a halt, her bow was still pointed into the wind, and pilots and crew had retreated to the anchor deck to escape the flames, which were reaching down to the lower hangar deck. When the dynamos went out, the ship was deprived not only of illumination but of pumps for combating the conflagration as well. The fireproof hangar doors had been destroyed, and in this dire emergency even the chemical fire extinguishers failed to work.

The valiant crew located several hand pumps, brought them to the anchor deck and managed to force water through long hoses into the lower hangar and decks below. Firefighting parties, wearing gas masks, carried cumbersome pieces of equipment and fought the flames courageously. But every induced explosion overhead penetrated to the deck below, injuring men and interrupting their desperate efforts. Stepping over fallen comrades, another damage-control party would dash in to continue the struggle, only to be mowed down by the next explosion. Corpsmen and volunteers carried out dead and wounded from the lower first-aid station, which was jammed with injured men. Doctors and surgeons worked like machines.

The engine rooms were still undamaged, but fires in the middle deck sections had cut off all communication between the bridge and the lower levels of the ship. Despite this the explosions, shocks and crashes above, plus the telegraph indicator which had rung up "Stop", told the engine-room crews in the bowels of the ship that something must be wrong. Still, as long as the engines were undamaged and full propulsive power was available they had no choice but to stay at General Quarters. Repeated efforts were made to communicate with the bridge, but every channel of contact, including the numerous auxiliary ones, had been knocked out.

The intensity of the spreading fires increased until the heat-laden air invaded the ship's lowest sections through the intakes, and men working there began falling from suffocation. In a desperate effort to save his men, the Chief Engineer, Commander K. Tampo, made his way up through the flaming decks until he was able to get a message to the Captain reporting conditions below. An order was promptly given for all men in the engine spaces to come up on deck. But it was too late. The orderly who tried to carry the order down through the blazing hell never returned, and not a man escaped from the engine room.

As the number of dead and wounded increased and the fires got further out of control, Captain Aoki finally decided at 18.00 that the ship must be abandoned. The injured were lowered into boats and cutters sent alongside by the screening destroyers. Many uninjured men leapt into the sea and swam away from the stricken ship. Destroyers *Arashi* and *Nowaki* picked up all survivors. When the rescue work was completed, Captain Aoki radioed to Admiral Nagumo at 19.20 from one of the destroyers, asking permission to sink the crippled carrier. This enquiry was monitored by the Combined Fleet flagship, whence Admiral Yamamoto dispatched an order at 22.25 to delay the carrier's disposition. Upon receipt of this instruction, the Captain returned to his carrier alone. He reached the anchor deck, which was still free from fire, and there lashed himself to an anchor to await the end.

Meanwhile, uncontrollable fires continued to rage throughout *Kaga*'s length, and finally, at 16.40, Commander Amagai gave the order to abandon ship. Survivors were transferred to the two destroyers standing by. Two hours later the conflagration subsided enough to enable Commander Amagai to lead a damage-control party back on board in the hope of saving the ship. Their valiant efforts proved futile, however, and they again withdrew. The once crack carrier, now a burning hulk, was wrenched by two terrific explosions before sinking into the depths at 19.25 in position 30° 20' N., 179° 17' W. In this battle eight hundred men of *Kaga*'s crew, one-third of her complement, were lost.

Soryu, the third victim of the enemy dive-bombing attack, received one hit fewer than *Kaga,* but the devastation was just as great. When the attack broke, deck parties were busily preparing the carrier's planes for take-off, and their first awareness of the onslaught came when great flashes of fire were seen sprouting from *Kaga,* some distance off to port, followed by explosions and tremendous columns of black smoke. Eyes instinctively looked skyward just in time to see a spear of thirteen American planes plummeting down on *Soryu*. It was 10.25.

Three hits were scored in as many minutes. The first blasted the flight deck in front of the forward elevator, and the next two straddled the amidship elevator, completely wrecking the deck and spreading fire to petrol tanks and munition storage rooms. By 10.30 the ship was transformed into a hell of smoke and flames, and induced explosions followed shortly.

In the next ten minutes the main engines stopped, the steering system went out, and fire mains were destroyed. Crewmen, forced by the flames to leave their posts, had just arrived on deck when a mighty explosion blasted many of them into the water. Within twenty minutes of the first bomb hit the ship was such a mass of fire that Captain Ryusaku Yanagimoto ordered "Abandon ship!" Many men jumped into the water to escape the searing flames and were picked up by destroyers *Hamakaze* and *Isokaze*. Others made more orderly transfers to the destroyers.

It was soon discovered, however, that Captain Yanagimoto had remained on the bridge of the blazing carrier. No ship commander in the Japanese Navy was more beloved by his men. His popularity was such that whenever he was going to address the assembled crew, they would gather an hour or more in advance to ensure getting a place up front. Now, they were determined to rescue him at all costs.

Chief Petty Officer Abe, a Navy wrestling champion, was chosen to return and rescue the Captain, because it had been decided to bring him to safety by force if he refused to come willingly. When Abe climbed to *Soryu*'s bridge he found Captain Yanagimoto standing there motionless, sword in hand, gazing resolutely towards the ship's bow. Stepping forward, Abe said, "Captain, I have come on behalf of all your men to take you to safety. They are waiting for you. Please come with me to the destroyer, sir."

When this entreaty met with silence, Abe guessed the Captain's thoughts and started towards him with the intention of carrying him bodily to the waiting boat. But the sheer strength of will and determination of his grim-faced commander stopped him short. He turned tearfully away, and as he left the bridge he heard Captain Yanagimoto calmly singing *Kimigayo,* the national anthem.

Mitsuo Fuchida

On 5 June, Mitscher launched twenty-six bombers for a strike against the still burning carriers and battleships. The planes found only oil slicks to mark the major ships but attacked a destroyer leaving the scene. One again, they roared back over the task force in darkness, and once again, Mitscher lit up the *Hornet*. Out of gas, they sputtered in.

On 6 June, search planes fanned out to find the remnants. Running low on gas, Gee landed on the *Enterprise,* and unaware of his relative inexperience, the *Enterprise* sent him off on a long-range search mission. After a few hours he spied some ripples on the mirrored ocean and went down for a better look. Soon Gee relayed word that two groups of the Japanese fleet had been located. The pilot Mitscher had grounded in January thus vindicated himself completely.

Mitscher launched twenty-six bombers again, along with eight fighters. At 11.50, *Hornet* planes attacked two cruisers and a destroyer. The cruisers *Mogami* and *Mikuma* were sunk by dive bombing. A few weeks later, the pilots of *Hornet*'s VB-8 were nicknamed "The Bombing Fools" because of their low-altitude drops.

A little later that day, when the planes had returned and were being re-armed for a second strike, the *Hornet*'s radio intercepted a message from a Japanese admiral saying he was being attacked (by *Enterprise* planes). The *Hornet*'s planes made the second shuttle to the fleeing enemy, and then came home for a rest. The Battle of Midway was over.

                                                    Theodore Taylor

The End

On 7 June, with no enemy in sight and his ships in need of fuel, Yamamoto called off his vain pursuit and retired towards the homeland.

Mogami, in the meantime, had continued westward in her effort to lure the enemy. Through the untiring efforts of her crew, a speed of twenty knots was achieved by 15.15 despite the heavy bomb damage she had sustained and the loss of her bow. She was fortunate that no enemy planes had appeared since *Mikuma*'s sinking, and she was able to creep out of the very jaws of death, the last Japanese warship to come clear of enemy attacks in the Midway battle. Kondo's force finally rendezvoused with crippled *Mogami* and provided escort to Truk.

Further American attempts to hit the retreating Japanese Fleet this day were made by 26 B-17s from Midway, but the foul weather thwarted these efforts and no contacts were made. Alert to the possibility of attack by planes based on Wake Island, the enemy carriers also gave up the chase, and the action was over.

Thus fell the curtain on a spectacular and historic battle. Japan's sole consolation for the defeat lay in the minuscule success of having captured two Aleutian bases. The northern operations, resumed after their earlier cancellation, had progressed smoothly and led to the occupation of the islands of Attu and Kiska on 7 June. But these unimportant acquisitions were small compensation for the devastating fleet losses suffered to the south, and in the end they were to bog us down still deeper in the quicksands of defeat.

The catastrophe of Midway definitely marked the turning of the tide in the Pacific war, and thenceforward that tide bore Japan inexorably on towards final capitulation.

Mitsuo Fuchida

For Japan, Midway was to be what El Alamein and Stalingrad were to Germany later in the same year of 1942—the turning-point of their fortunes. Japanese expansion had been stopped.

5

THE PRISONERS

While the armies contended, another battle was being fought out less sensationally but just as bitterly behind barbed wire. The prisoners of war fought boredom and frustration in many ingenious ways, trying to raise their morale and make confinement less intolerable. The more enterprising and active among them planned constantly for the day of escape.

EUROPE

The Prison

THE Tower, which at various times had housed Saxon kings, fallen women, Communists, lunatics and dissident Czechs, was in the winter of 1941-1942 the seat of six hundred prisoners of war who had been sent to it from milder places, either on account of escaping or because they had otherwise by act or word incurred German displeasure. It was called *Sonderlager* ("Special Camp") and sometimes *Straflager* ("Punishment Camp"). A beetling spot, overlooking the small town of Colditz in the very middle of Germany, it was intended to be a firm and final immurement for these prisoners whose isolation was also, in the German view, a quarantine measure.

The mingling of nationalities was the brightest feature of the Tower. The Germans too seemed to feel a shy pride in this speciality which fluttered flaglike above the sterile landscape of the captor-captive situation.

English, French, Poles, Dutch and Belgians, though they had separate quarters and spent most of their time within their own groups, were all very much aware of each other. Membership of Colditz, however earned, seemed to vouch for a prisoner and thus enjoined a fellowship that slipped past national prejudice. Over and above that, the experience by which national groups different from your own in every obvious way were sharing an identical fate exerted a restraining, if not necessarily civilizing, influence. No nation, under those circumstances, ran amok in its specialized field of lunacy. Take sport. The British, instigators of a roughish game called "Stoolball", invited the slovenly, anaemic-looking French to play against them—and were beaten. The Poles, for whom all sport entailed a life-or-death defence of Polish honour, controlled, if they did not abandon, their most blatant grimness about defeat. The Dutch, though their rigid discipline and precision restrained them from playing much, cultivated an admiration for the English, associating themselves especially with their light sporty ways, and seemed in this to be making a deliberate effort, prompted by some new awareness, to lengthen the distance that separated them from their national neighbours, the humourless, wooden Germans.

The Belgians, who did not play at all, were the most intractably, individualistically unmilitary group. The French, worried about their own centrifugal tendencies, were genuinely scared when they contemplated the Belgians, seeing mirrored in them the extreme perils of civilianization. This fear was indirectly corroborated by Commandant Flébus the cat-eater, who said often that his

own soldierly character had never been properly
appreciated until he came to Colditz. The Belgian Army
had been very unpopular, he said, in pre-war Belgium.
Girls would not dance with men in uniform, on pavements
they were expected to give way to everybody, and
sometimes things were thrown at them. The Belgians of
Colditz, unshaven, shapeless, striking no attitude and just
as placid about large matters as about small, did look like
an unappreciated squad that had got captured by some
mistake. Yet they were perkily, serenely alive; and their
mere presence set quizzical limits to the exorbitances of
their neighbours.

There were hundreds of dreary days in Colditz. The
drive to escape and the campaign to harry the Germans
could never be wholly successful at the point where they
expressed, not their obvious purposes, but rather the
resolve of the prisoners to keep themselves active and to
resist succumbing to lethargy. From that point of view
there was always too much against them. There were
periods when the old looked old, the young did not look
fit, and the ardours of defiance, never an unforced growth,
failed to leap out. The Germans would find that they had
quiet parades and would patter secure along the files,
almost like nannies.

In such lethargic periods each nation slipped into its
special groove. Dutch, Poles and Belgians seemed to
hibernate, while the larger nations, the English and
French, fought the malaise in larger and dissimilar ways.

In that fight the French were the better equipped. They
had a knack of domesticating themselves. The British
prisoner's corner was his castle only if he could get out of
it. The *summum bonum* of the British cuisine was the
bread pudding, impatiently kneaded and left to bake as
best it might; a French prisoner could spend a happy day
contriving a *baba au rhum*. In the general field of manual
ingenuity there was not much to choose between them, but
the French often made things for their own sake whereas
the English always made them for a purpose—usually
escape. The French made mouse-tanks. The tanks were

toy-sized, built of small pieces of wood, and driven from inside by a mouse revolving on a ferris-wheel. The mouse visibly enjoyed this job. There was also a "Big Wheel" for the recreation of several families of mice. Mice lay about on a beach of sand while those who were feeling more active kept the wheel spinning by getting aboard the spokes. It was the particular sport of the bigger mice to leap suddenly from sand to spoke so that their weight set the wheel flying and tipped off all the little mice. Wondrous as these mouse-machines were, the spirit of Colditz was against them, and they were readily forgotten.

The French, who had no fear of convenience, considered that *les anglais* wittingly or unwittingly believed in subjecting themselves to inconvenience. Their own way of dealing with strain was to "exteriorize" and relax; whereas the British tended to produce more and more of it and press it down inside themselves harder and harder until they were at last exhausted and could fall virtuously asleep. British prisoners rejoiced, or said that they did, at being moved as often as possible from camp to camp, castle to castle, on the principle that moving was good for you—kept you fit and so on. It was looked at askance if anyone tried to make the corner in which he lived and slept more comfortable, personal, or home-like; such contrivances being dubbed disparagingly "life-boats", as constituting a mode of private self-salvage. Their search for inconvenience drove the British outside to the cobbles of the Colditz yard to spitting frenzies of shadow-boxing or to a hundred press-ups before breakfast. One, who on principle and on the coldest nights would never sleep under more than a single blanket, was not imitated; yet a wiry pride was taken in his unflinching austerity.

The French, in periods when escaping slackened off, fretted little. They never were so communally single-minded about escape as the English were. They rarely counted the world—even Colditz—well lost for it. There was a case where a French prisoner of war, offered a method which involved bribery of a German and some purchases through German channels, totted up the cost and decided that it was too high. French escapes were the outcome of individuality and daring rather than of collective patience and organization; a temperamental difference not obscured, though it *was* exaggerated, by obvious differences of situation, military and political, that made the rewards of escape less alluring for the French.

The interplay of national differences contributed a resilience and *élan* that often cushioned what otherwise was only noisy and hard. Anglo-French relations, more tortuously developed than others, provided a continual diversion due chiefly to the inevitable clashing impact of French curiosity on British sluggish phlegm. The French, passionately curious about changing events and "movements of opinion", found it incomprehensible even after months of enforced and intimate contact that their British opposites could get through the day without being bothered by events and without once changing their opinions on any subject.

There was a general pairing-off between the two groups, originally for exchanges of language-lessons, later widening into friendly acquaintances and friendships, and Anglo-French pairs would meet daily in the yard or in each others' quarters. *"Bonjour"* would lead straight to either *"Quoi de neuf?"* or *"Eh bien, qu'est-ce-que vous racontez?"* from the French side, whereupon the following dialogue (subject to variations) would develop:

"Bonjour! Quoi de neuf?"

"Oh, nothing particularly. Still here, I suppose."

"Yes I think so. Have you some interesting letters lately?"

"No—o, nothing very interesting. Rather dull really."

"But I think the situation is rather interesting at present?"

Pause. On English side, lighting and filling of pipe.

"The Germans admit to-day that they are retreating in Africa."

"About time they did admit it."

"Yes, I think so. It is better now than when you were at

El Alamein. I think you were very anxious then, yes?"

"Oh, not really."

"No?"

"Well, I mean we were a bit anxious, I suppose. But we never thought it would really come to anything."

"We were very anxious. Personally I thought the Germans should take Alexandria."

"Well, they didn't."

"No, of course not."

"Have a cigarette?"

"Thank you. And what about the danger from U-boats now? I think it is very serious. From the speech of your Mr. Alexander one has the impression that. . . ."

The British side would brace itself reluctantly; it certainly would not have read the speech. Yet all that was stimulating rather than irritating. The different groups in Colditz swallowed many a prejudice for the sake of this enlivening solidarity. Sometime they did more. Once, for instance, an English prisoner suffering from jaundice coughed up some blackish ersatz German jam which he mistook for blood. He was visited by a German doctor and also by a Polish prisoner-doctor. The German was sceptical about the blood. But the Pole was enthusiastic about it; urging a muscular injection to prevent internal bleeding; he marshalled phial, needle and syringe, and said, with a contemptuous gesture at the German:

"He doesn't think this necessary. I do. You can choose."

Seeing the sufferer inclined to refuse he became offended. The German *Arzt* smiled.

Refusal, it was plain, would precipitate Anglo-Polish discord. Poles were allies, German enemies. Polish nationalism was sensitive. The British officer endured the injection.

Giles Romilly and Michael Alexander

Tedium

It was lunch time. The biscuits had not been buttered.

No one had gone for the tea water. Five morose figures sat round a naked table. Presently Pomfret spoke. "It's a matter of principle. I've done it every day this week and now it's Friday. It's not that I mind doing it, but I've done more than my share. Clinton must do it to-day as a matter of principle." He advanced his chin obstinately. He was dressed in the full uniform of a flight-lieutenant. His collar, ironed with a tin of hot water, was frayed round the edges.

"That's all very well," said Bennett, "but it's lunch time and we're hungry. You and Clinton share the duty of cook and it's up to you to see that the meal is prepared." Bennett, apart from his odd assortment of clothes, might have been addressing a board meeting. He delivered his opinion as an ultimatum and glanced round the table for approval. His red, hairy arms were crossed upon the table. Having delivered his speech, he sucked his teeth with an air of finality.

"Well, I'm not doing it," said Pomfret. He appeared about to cry. "It's not fair! Just because he's digging a tunnel it doesn't mean that he can neglect all his duties in the mess. I'm fed up with doing two people's work. All they think about is their wretched tunnel. I'm sick to death of seeing them sitting in the corner whispering all evening. It was bad enough before they started the tunnel. Clinton was always missing at meal times. But for the last two months I've done all the work. It's not right, you know."

"That's for you and Clinton to settle between yourselves," said Bennett judicially. "What about our lunch? It's only a matter of buttering eight biscuits and walking over to the canteen for some hot water."

"That's not the point!" said Pomfret. "It's a matter of principle."

"So the whole mess suffers for the sake of your principles," put in Robbie, who was sitting at the head of the table disgustedly studying his finger-nails.

"It's not my principles at fault, it's Clinton's laziness."

"I don't call it laziness to dig a tunnel for several hours a day," said Robbie. "Surely you and he can come to some arrangement so that you both do equal amounts of work, but his share doesn't interfere with his tunnelling."

"You can't come to any arrangement with Clinton," said Pomfret. "He always forgets. He hasn't grown up yet. He's got no sense of responsibility."

"He's not the only one who hasn't grown up," said Robbie.

"This is all very well," put in Bennett, "but do we get our lunch?"

"I'm not doing it!" said Pomfret obstinately.

The five men looked at one another angrily. The food cupboard was sacred. No one but the cook was allowed to open it. It was a custom of the mess. In a life where hunger was ubiquitous, food had strict taboos. None but the high priest could approach the shrine.

"Supposing we split the mess in two," said Barton. "Let them mess together and we five will mess together. They can do what they like, then." Barton spoke with a genteel accent. His whole appearance was genteel, even to the crook of his little finger as he removed the cigarette from his mouth.

"They always do," said Pomfret fretfully.

"Well, what do you say?" asked Barton. "I think it would serve them right."

"Very likely buck them no end," said Robbie.

"I think we ought to do it," said Downes. "Howard and Wilde can't cook, anyway."

The party hesitated. It was a decision. Some of them had not made a decision for years. Some were reluctant to cast the three into the outer darkness of their disassociation.

"I think we should," said Pomfret.

"Let's take a vote," said Bennett, once more addressing the board of directors.

"I agree," said Downes.

"So do I," said Barton.

Bennett looked at Robbie, who thought of coping with the eccentricities of the other three. He decided not to risk it. Anyway, their tunnel would be finished soon.

"I think it's bloody childish," he said, "and it'll be damned inconvenient having two messes in one room."

"Would you rather go with them, then you can do all the cooking for them?" said Pomfret spitefully.

"No, I'll go with you," said Robbie, "but I don't like the idea of splitting up."

When the three came in from tunnelling they found the biscuits ready buttered and the tea water in the can. John had been working at the face, Peter half-way down, and Nigel at the tunnel entrance. John, who was yellow from head to foot with caked sweat and sand, threw himself on his bunk and closed his eyes.

"Lunch, John?" asked Peter.

"Not for the moment, thanks, old boy," said John.

"Feeling rotten?" asked Peter.

"I'm O.K. I'll be O.K. in a minute. I'll wash before I eat." He lay back with his eyes closed. His body was brown, but his face was colourless. His hair, matted with sand and sweat, was damp on his forehead. There were long streaks down his chest and arms where the sweat had washed away the sand. The sand was under his broken finger-nails and in his eyes. As he lay there, Peter could see that his nostrils too were filled with sand.

Pomfret cleared his throat. "I prepared the lunch to-day," he said.

"Thanks, old boy," said John. "Was it my turn?"

"It was your turn," replied Pomfret. "It has been your turn for the last three days. As a matter of principle I, at first, refused to do it to-day."

"Thanks for doing it all the same," said John. "I'll do the dinner."

"That will not be necessary," said Pomfret. "We five have decided to mess separately."

"After due consideration," said Bennett, addressing an audience of at least five hundred, "we have decided that we five shall mess on our own."

Pomfret looked at him angrily. After all, he was in the chair.

"We are tired of Clinton's impossible attitude,"

Bennett continued, "and we presumed that you three would want to be together. We have separated the food, and starting with dinner to-night, we shall cater for ourselves."

"O.K.," said Peter, "that suits us." In a way he was glad, as very soon they would begin to save their food for the escape. "What do you say, Nig?"

"*Blond genug,* old boy," replied Nigel.

So the mess was split into two and settled down to a new way of living.

Eric Williams

Escape

. . . . Escape is not only a technique but a philosophy. The real escaper is more than a man equipped with compass, maps, papers, disguise and plan. He has an inner confidence, a serenity of spirit which makes him a Pilgrim.

Airey Neave

The Way Out: Germany

Valenta had put Axel Zillessen on to the Keen Type. Axel wasn't his real name, but the one he'd chosen to use if he ever escaped from the compound so that he could travel as a Swede. He got everyone to call him Axel so he'd get used to it. Actually he was a wool buyer from Bradford, a tall young man with a slightly hooked nose and kinky hair; and with a charming and infectious enthusiasm Axel could talk the leg off an iron pot almost as fluently in German as in English.

The next time Keen Type came in the duty pilot's runner went and told Axel, and Axel strolled into the dusty compound where Keen Type was patrolling. He passed him a couple of times without speaking, and on the third time gave him a casual greeting and they exchanged a few words about the weather. The same thing happened next day. The third day they spoke for about five minutes.

Keen Type came in every day, and as soon as he did the runner warned Axel. By the end of the week Axel and the ferret were walking up and down together chatting for an hour. Gradually they got on to the war, Axel staying always on neutral ground, regretting the bombing and the suffering on both sides.

"It's ridiculous," he said. "Here are we, two ordinary people talking as civilized people, and if I put a foot over the warning wire you have to shoot me."

The Keen Type laughed.

"I have shot no one yet," he said mildly.

"But you would!"

"Only in the leg," said the Keen Type, "and with regret."

"That doesn't make it any more civilized."

"The bombing is not very civilized, either"—this rather resentfully.

"We didn't start it," said Axel, and veered off what could only be a bitter subject. "What are you going to do after the war?"

The ferret laughed without humour. "Why worry now? I don't think it's ever going to end, and if it does I probably won't see it."

"Look," said Axel, "when it's over we're going to need the co-operation of Germans who weren't mad Nazis. You won't be any enemy then."

The ferret considered the delicate implication but did not answer. Neither did he think to deny, as normally he automatically would, the clear inference that Germany was going to lose.

Axel took him to his room for the first time next day for a cup of coffee. "X" gave the room a little extra ration for this and whenever they wanted hot water for a brew they could claim time on the stove, no matter how many other pots were on it.

The others in the room—Dave, Laurie, Nellie and Keith—gave Keen Type casual welcome. He sat among them with a hot brew, a biscuit and a cigarette. It was more comfortable than padding round the dust of the compound, and it was interesting to hear the British and American point of view. It is a soldier's privilege—his only one—to grumble, but you couldn't grumble in the German Army unless you were tired of life and wanted to go to the Russian Front. Keen Type had a lot that he hadn't been able to get off his chest, and now he had a sympathetic and safe audience and he spoke with more and more freedom.

"What can we Germans do?" he said, after a week, sitting with his coffee and nibbling a piece of chocolate from a food parcel. "Against Hitler and the Gestapo—nothing."

"I'll tell you what you can do." Axel got up and sat down on the bunk beside him. "You can realize that the war is lost and nothing you do can help that. The sooner it's over the better. We're not going to be enemies for ever. Start regarding us as friends now." He added quietly, "We won't be forgetting our friend."

The duty pilot checked the Keen Type into the compound just after *appell* next morning and the runner slid off to warn Axel. He saw the Keen Type seemed to be following him, so he shied off. The ferret went straight into 105, knocked on Axel's door and put his head round the corner. "Keen Type here," he said with a friendly grin. "Can I come in?"

He stayed a couple of hours, and then he excused himself, saying he'd better put in an appearance in the compound or Glemnitz would be wondering what he was doing. He was much more leisurely this time in his patrolling. He reported to Axel's room every day after that for a brew, and when he reluctantly went out into the compound again he had a new benevolence. After a while, Roger took him off the danger list.

Valenta had detailed a German-speaking contact to every ferret and administrative German who came into the compound. The contact made friends with his man, fed him biscuits, brews and cigarettes and listened sympathetically to his grumbles and worries.

Funny people, the Germans. When you got them in a

bunch they were all Nazis (they had to be), but when you got the little people by themselves and worked on them for a while they didn't have any morale underneath. Inside they seemed naked and defenceless. You could bribe ninety per cent of them—including the officers—with a little coffee or chocolate.

In a way, I don't think you could blame them. Valenta's contacts were like white ants, nibbling away a little at a time at the German faith in victory. Hitler had said that if you tell a big enough lie people will believe it, but he rather overlooked the fact that once the lie is exposed everything else you've said is also disbelieved. It wasn't hard to get a German thinking that Hitler wasn't the angel of virtue, and then the rest of his edifice of wishful faith came tumbling down.

The contacts sympathized with their Germans that they had to fight Hitler's war, lamented with them about Gestapo persecution and poured out a stream of irresistible logic to show that Germany could never win. "Why, then," they said, "regard us as enemies? Soon you will want us as friends."

The talking wasn't only one-way. Delicate steering had the ferrets talking about the security measures they planned, about conditions in Germany, details of the area round the camp. Dozens of little snippets were picked up, and Valenta, who had done an intelligence course at Prague Staff College, put them all together with Roger.

Soon they knew all the paths around the camp, how far the woods stretched and the layout of Sagan town. They had timetables of all trains out of Sagan station and the prices of all tickets. They knew what foods were ration-free, where the Swedish ships lay in Stettin and Danzig, what guards were around them, what guards covered the Swiss frontier and the Danish frontier, and a thousand other handy hints on how to get out of the Third Reich.

"Why do you make such a bloody mess when you search the huts?" Axel asked the Keen Type.

"We have to be thorough," said the ferret. "Germans are always thorough. We have to take everything apart or we are in trouble with Glemnitz. And if we waste time putting everything together again we are in more trouble with Glemnitz."

"You never find anything."

"Orders," said Keen Type virtuously, "are orders."

"Orders don't say you have to make a bloody mess wherever you go," said Axel, who'd reached the stage where he could be a little stern with the Keen Type. "Last time you people went through my room you pinched half the wood-shavings out of my palliasse and it was spread all over the floor. It took me half an hour to clear up."

"It wasn't me," the Keen Type said apologetically. "I will do your room myself next time." He added reproachfully: "You must not forget that you are our prisoners. Do not expect too much."

"Don't forget you'll be our prisoners one day," Axel said, with flippant menace, though the Keen Type did not need much reminding. Axel had been wedging the thought into his mind for a couple of weeks.

"It'd help us all," Axel went on, "if we knew when we were going to be searched. We could have things a little more orderly and you wouldn't have to waste so much time going through all the mess. Be a help to you, too."

"You ask too much," said Keen Type, shaking his head in fright at the thought.

Axel carefully brought up the subject again next day, but it was a fortnight before he got Keen Type to tell him what huts were to be searched in the next few days, and after that it was easy. Roger nearly always got at least a day's notice of searches, and it was just a question of smuggling *verboten* stuff out of the hut next on the list, usually to the hut that was last searched. That was the safest spot of all. Once the ferrets had searched a hut it was usually immune till all the other huts had been searched and its turn came up again. It suited us.

"There's madness in their method," said Roger with satisfaction.

. . . . Roger went in search of Travis and found him in his room filing a broken knife into a screwdriver.

"Can you make me a rifle?" he asked, and Travis stared at him.

"It's for show, not for shooting," Bushell explained.

"What sort of rifle exactly?"

"German one. Imitation. We've got a new show on. D'you remember the time just before we moved they took a mob out from east camp to be deloused?"

"Yes," said Travis. "Someone on a new purge came in with wogs all over him."

"That's it," said Roger. "I think we can put on a couple of unofficial ones. We 've got to have some goons to go as escort. Guest is making the uniforms. You're going to make their guns."

"They'd have to be terribly good to pass the gate posterns, Roger," Travis said slowly. "I don't know that we can do it."

Roger swivelled his twisted eye on him. "I want them in a week," he said and walked out.

Travis, McIntosh and Muller tried to put on paper an accurate plan of a German military carbine and found they didn't have a clue about the detail and dimensions. Muller went and got Henri Picard out of the forgery factory. Picard, a young Belgian, was one of the best artists in the camp. Muller's idea appealed to him and he went away and cut a rough pair of calipers out of a piece of tin.

Coming off *appell* that afternoon, Muller started chatting to one of the guards and Picard stood just behind very carefully measuring with his calipers the width and depth of various parts of the carbine slung over the guard's shoulder. Then he stood beside him and calculated the length of the rifle, noting where the barrel came to about the height of his head and where the butt finished by his thighs. For the next day he cautiously trailed several guards, drawing rough detail parts of the gun.

Travis had noticed that about one in every three hundred bedboards was made of beech instead of pine and

Williams toured every hut and whipped every beech board he could find. They weren't thick enough to make a rifle, so they sawed and carved out each rifle in two halves, glued them together and clamped them to set in vices made of reinforced ping-pong net-posts. They carved out in wood the parts that were supposed to be metal, barrel, breech and bolt, and rubbed and polished them with a lump of graphite brought in by a tame German till they looked like blue gunmetal. The wooden parts that were really wood they stained with tan boot polish and rubbed till it looked perfect.

The clips round the barrels Muller made from strips cut off a metal jug; he used bent nails for the sling clips and belts for the slings. Muller didn't think the polished wooden barrel looked quite perfect enough, so he melted down silver paper from cigarette packets into lead and cast a proper barrel end in a soap mould. He polished it with graphite until it *was* perfect.

By happy chance, the grey of Luftwaffe uniforms was almost identical with R.A.F. grey-blue, and Tommy Guest used old R.A.F. uniforms to cut out several *unteroffiziers'* uniforms. Six of his amateur tailors hand-sewed them.

Muller made the little eagles that went on the lapels and the belt buckles by casting melted silver paper in soap moulds, carving the eagles in the mould himself. The belt buckle was perfect. One of the contacts got his goon to take off his tunic on a hot day while he drank his daily brew, and Muller stealthily pressed the buckle into the soap to make his mould. Guest cut a bit off the tail of a terrible old shirt of Kirby-Green's to make the colour patches on the uniforms.

Tim Walenn produced several beautifully forged gate passes (the originals had been brought in by a tame guard). The *unteroffiziers* would have to show the passes to get out of the camp with their party and Walenn's staff had hand-lettered them, working non-stop on the job for about a week. He took the passes to Roger.

"Which is the real one?" he asked.

Roger peered at them for a while.

"They're bloody good, Tim," he said. "I don't think I could pick them apart."

"As a matter of fact," Tim said, "they're all forgeries."

And the day it was all done and thirty-two men were getting their last briefing for the break, the German *unteroffiziers* came in without rifles. They all had pistols instead, in holsters on a belt. It was a new order. *Unteroffiziers* weren't going to carry rifles any more, and there had to be an *unteroffizier* on the fake delousing party. An ordinary *obergefreiter* (lance-corporal or private) wouldn't be allowed to escort a party out of the gate.

Roger really lost his temper this time and for two days he was quite unbearable. Travis and Muller weren't much better.

One of Tommy Guest's men had been a hand-bag maker in private life and Roger put him to work making imitation pistol holsters out of cardboard. He marked the cardboard to give it a leathery grain and rubbed it with boot polish and you couldn't tell the result from a real holster. McIntosh made a couple of dummy pistol butts out of wood and fixed them so they peeped coyly out of the holster flaps.

Roger planned the break in two phases. First, twenty-four men escorted by two *unteroffiziers* were to march out of the gate (they hoped) ostensibly bound for the delousing showers. Ten minutes after they were clear, Bob Van Der Stok, a Dutchman in the R.A.F. who spoke perfect German, was to march out a party of five senior officers for a "special conference" with the Kommandant.

Roger, Wings Day and the committee hand-picked the people to go, selecting men who'd been working hard for "X" and who'd been behind the wire for a couple of years or more. Roger himself toyed with the idea of going, but Wings and the others energetically talked him out of it. As Wings pointed out, there was a very fair chance of the alarm being given quite quickly, in which case many of them probably wouldn't get very far, and if Roger was caught again so soon after the last time he knew what to expect.

"Wait till you can get through 'Tom'," Day said. "You'll be out of the area by train then before they wake up to it."

Roger reluctantly agreed, partly because he was banking so much on "Tom". Floody wanted to go on the delousing party, too, but Roger vetoed the idea and they had a short, sharp argument. Arguments with Roger were often sharp and always short.

"We need you here for the tunnels," he told Floody flatly.

"God, I'm sick of tunnels!" Floody groaned. "I seem to send my life down a stinking hole in the ground. I want a change."

"Look, Wally," Roger said, "we're just getting somewhere now and everything's going like a bomb. Don't spoil it. We'll get 'Tom' out in a couple of months and then you can go for your life, but *not* now. You're needed here."

"But I'd be back," said Floody, spreading his hands appealingly. "They'd catch me. Nothing surer. I'll go on the delouser now and in two days I'll be back in the cooler. Then I can have a nice rest for a fortnight and come back fit. How 'bout that?"

"No," said Roger.

It was just after two o'clock on a warm afternoon that twenty-four men fell in outside 104, carrying bundles wrapped in towels, presumably to be dumped in the steam delousers. It would be too bad if the gate guards inspected them because they contained uniform jackets and pants converted to look like civilian clothes and little packets of concentrated food cakes made from oatmeal and breadcrumbs, milk powder, chocolate and sugar. In the pockets were maps, and a little German money. Two *unteroffiziers,* holsters at their waists, formed them into three ranks and they straggled off towards the gate laughing and joking with the fake heartiness people show as they climb into the dentist's chair. The atmosphere was a little electric. Roger and the envious Floody felt it one hundred yards away where they sat by a corner of a hut, unobtrusively watching.

The party stopped at the first gate and one of the *unteroffiziers* showed his pass. The guard hardly even looked at it and then the big barbed wire gates were swinging open. They marched to the next gate, the guard looked casually at the pass and in a few moments they were walking out into the road that curved into the pine wood. It was practically an anticlimax.

Three hundred yards down the road without a German in sight they turned sharply and vanished into the trees, then broke into a run for half a mile. Deep in the woods they changed into their travelling clothes and split up into ones, twos and threes.

At a quarter-past two Van Der Stok walked out of 110 with the second party and headed for the gate. Goodrich, the senior, was an American colonel of about forty, with a red, tough face and barrel chest. Beside him walked Bob Tuck, slim and elegant, a Battle of Britain ace with a D.S.O. and three D.F.C.s; then Bill Jennens, R.A.F. squadron-leader and compound adjutant with a voice like a drill sergeant and a face like a lump of uncarved granite. The other two were the lanky "Nellie" Ellan, who looked after the camp radio, and a Polish wing-commander.

Van Der Stok showed his pass at the first gate and they walked through. At the next, the guard was a little more conscientious and turned the pass over and looked at the back. (We found out later it was only a week before that the Germans had put a new mark on the back of the gate passes in case they were ever copied.) Van Der Stok's pass didn't have the mark and the guard looked suspiciously up at him. It was only then that his brain slowly grasped the fact that he had seen this man walking round the compound as a prisoner. He raised a shout and a dozen German soldiers came clumping out of the guardhouse.

Van Der Stok bowed disarmingly and raised his hands.

Broili came over from the *Kommandantur* in response to an urgent message. He was chief security officer, a plump little major with shiny black hair, given to monumental anger when prisoners escaped and patronizing politeness when they failed to. He greeted the little group jovially.

"Mr. Van Der Stok," he said roguishly, "you are improperly dressed. Ah, it is too bad, gentlemen"—with a happy grin—"the fortunes of war. Perhaps you will have better luck next time."

He congratulated the guard on recognizing Van Der Stok and the guard put his foot right in it.

"I thought it unusual, *Herr Major*, that two parties should leave the camp so close together," he said smugly, and Broili looked suddenly older.

"Two parties?" he asked in a voice of doom, and the guard told him.

"*Mein Gott, sechs und zwanzig*," shrieked Broili, and with a terrible look at Van Der Stok and Goodrich he ran for the guardhouse phone.

Paul Brickhill

The Tunnel

At this unhappy stage, when we were casting around to decide what to do with our tunnel, Peter Allan and Howard Gee (a newcomer), both excellent German speakers, reported the existence of a helpful Goon sentry. He was a sympathetic type, and he started smuggling for us on a small scale: a fresh egg here and there in return for English chocolate, or a pound of real coffee in exchange for a tin of cocoa, and so on. He ran a terrific risk, but seemed to do it with equanimity—perhaps too much equanimity—and we decided also to take a risk and plunge. At several clandestine meetings, in doorways and behind angles in the courtyard walls, Peter and Howard Gee primed the sentry and eventually suggested that he might earn some "big" money if he once "looked the other way" for ten minutes while on sentry duty.

The sentry fell for the idea. He was told that we would have to arrange matters so that he did a tour of sentry duty for a given two-hour period, on a given day, on a certain beat, and that in the ten-minute interval, between two predetermined signals, he was to stand (which was permitted) at one particular end of his beat. He was to receive an advance of one hundred *Reichsmarks* of his reward, which was settled at five hundred *Reichsmarks* (about £34), and the remainder would be dropped out of a convenient window one hour after the ten-minute interval. The sentry was told also that no traces would be left which could lead to suspicion or involve him in accusations of neglect of duty. To all this he listened and finally agreed. The escape was on!

The first escape party consisted of twelve officers, including four Poles. The French and Dutch were as yet newcomers, whereas the Poles were by now old and trusted comrades, which accounted for their inclusion. Further, the participation of officers of another nationality was decided upon for reasons of language facilities offered, and for camp morale. The Poles had been most helpful since our arrival; the majority of them spoke German fluently, some of them knew Germany well, and those of us who thought of aiming for the North Sea or Poland took Poles as travelling companions. A few decided to travel alone.

My mind was occupied with another problem—how to arrange for the entry of thirteen officers, twelve escaping and one sealing up the entry, into the canteen? During opening hours I examined the cruciform lock closely and came to the conclusion that, for the inside, I could dismount the lock almost completely, allowing the door to open.

The escape would have to be done after the evening roll-call and in darkness.

The fateful day was decided upon—29 May. I arranged to knock down the false wall the day before and extricate all our provisions and escape material. This was comparatively simple. During the two-hour lunch interval the canteen was locked. Before it was locked, however, I hid in a triangular recess which was used as a store cupboard and to which I had the key. When the canteen was locked up I had two clear hours to prepare everything. I removed the false wall, took out all our escape paraphernalia, hiding it in the cupboard, and prepared the tunnel exit so as to give the minimum amount of work for the final opening. After two o'clock, with a suitable screen of officers, I came out of the cupboard and all the stores were carried to our quarters.

The arrangements for the escape were as follows: Howard Gee, who was not in the first party, was to deal with the sentry. He would pass him the first signal on receipt of a sign from us in the tunnel. This was to be given by myself in the first instance at the opening end of the tunnel, passed to our thirteenth man on watch at the canteen window in the courtyard, who would then transmit it to our quarters by means of a shaded light. Gee could then signal to the sentry from an outside window. The "all clear" was to be given in the same way, except that our thirteenth man had to come to the tunnel exit and receive the word from me when I had properly sealed up the exit after all were out. A piece of string pulled out through the earth served the purpose. I would be over the wall at the far end of the lawn before the signal would be transferred to the sentry.

29 May loomed overcast and it soon began to rain. It rained all day in torrents, the heaviest rainfall we had ever had, but this would mean a dark night and it did not upset our plans. The sentry was told during the course of the afternoon what post he was to occupy. He was given his advance in cash and instructed to avoid the end of his beat nearest to the canteen on receipt of an agreed signal from a certain window, and to remain away from that end until another signal was given.

As the evening approached, the excitement grew. The lucky twelve dressed themselves in kit prepared during many months of patient work. From out of astonishing hiding-places came trousers and slouch caps made of grey

German blankets, multi-coloured knitted pullovers, transformed and dyed army overcoats, windjackets and mackintoshes, dyed khaki shirts and home-knitted ties. These were donned and covered with army apparel. Maps and home-made compasses appeared, and subdued last-minute discussions took place concerning routes and escape instructions. As the time passed, impatience for the "off" increased. I became alternately hot and cold, and my hands were clammy and my mouth was dry. We all felt the same, as I could tell by the forced laughs and the nervous jokes and banter which passed around.

I remained hidden in the canteen when it was locked up for the night, and dismounted the lock. When the evening *appell* sounded, I slipped out of the door behind a well-placed crowd of officers. If a goon pushed the door for any reason whatever we were finished. A wedge of paper alone held it. Sentries were posted for the *appell* at all vantage-points, and one stood very close to the canteen. Immediately after the *appell* we had to work fast, for all the prisoners then had to disperse to their rooms, the courtyard doors were locked, and every door tried by the German duty officer. All thirteen of us had to slip into the canteen behind the screen of assisting officers while German officers and N.C.O.s were in the courtyard, and the lock had then to be remounted on the canteen door in double-quick time. The twelve escapers had to appear on parade dressed ready in their escape attire suitably covered with army overcoats and trousers. Assembled rusksacks had been placed in order in the tunnel during the lunch-time closing hours in the same way as before.

The *appell* went off without a hitch. Colonel German, who had to stand alone in front, was looking remarkably fat, for he was escaping with us. He aroused no comment. Immediately after the "dismiss" was given, and almost in front of the eyes of the sentry nearby, the thirteen chosen ones slipped silently through the door until all were in.

"Where do we go from here?" asked one of the Polish officers who had not worked on the tunnel.

"Over the palisades!" I replied, pointing to the high wooden partition, over which sheets had already been thrown.

He grabbed them and started to climb, making a noise like a bass drum on the partition door. A loud "Sh! Sh!" as if a lavatory cistern was emptying greeted his effort.

"For God's sake!" I said, "you're not in Paderewski's orchestra now."

"No," replied the Pole dramatically from the top of the partition, "but his spirit is living within me this night!"

Luckily the din in the courtyard covered any noise we made at this juncture.

While the lock was remounted on the door, I removed my army uniform and handled it to our thirteenth man. He was to collect all discarded clothes, conceal them in the cupboard, and remove them with assistance next day. I went straight away to the end of the tunnel, closely followed by Rupert Barry, for we were going together, and started work on the last few inches of earth beneath the surface of the opening. It was dark by now outside, and the rain was still pelting down. It began pouring through the earth covering of the exit, and within five minutes I was drenched to the skin with muddy water. The lock-testing patrol tried the canteen door and passed. Soon all was quiet in the camp. Within an hour the sentry was reported by light flashes to be at his post. I gave the signal for him to keep away from the canteen window.

I worked frenziedly at the surface of grass, cutting out my square, and then slowly heaved the tray of the exit upwards. It came away, and as it did so a shaft of brilliant light shot down the tunnel. For a second I was bewildered and blinded. It was, of course, the light of the projector situated ten yards away from the opening, which lit up the whole of the wall-face on that particular side of the Castle, I lifted the tray clear. Streams of muddy water trickled into the tunnel around me. I pushed myself upwards, and, with Rupert's assistance from behind, scrambled out.

Once out, I looked around. I was like an actor upon a

stage. The floodlight made a huge grotesque image of my figure against the white wall. Row upon row of unfriendly windows, those of the German *Kommandantur*, frowned down upon me. The windows had no blackout curtains and a wandering inquisitive eye from within might easily turn my way. It was an unavoidable risk. Rupert began to climb out as I put the finishing touch to the tray for closing the hole. He was having some difficulty. He had handed up my rucksack and was levering himself upwards when I happened to look from my work at the wall in front of me, there to see a second giant shadow outlined beside my own crouching figure. The second shadow held a revolver in his hand.

"Get back! Get back!" I yelled to Rupert, as a guttural voice behind me shouted:

"*Hände hoch! Hände hoch!*"

I turned, to face a German officer levelling his pistol at my body, while another leaped for the hole. He was about to shoot down the opening.

"*Schiessen sie nicht!*" I screamed several times.

A bullet or two down that stone-and-brick-walled tunnel might have wrought considerable damage, filled as it was with human bodies. The officer at the hole did not shoot.

Gemans suddenly appeared from everywhere, and all the officers were giving orders at once. I was led off to the *Kommandantur* and conducted to a bathroom where I was stripped completely and allowed to wash, and then to an office where I was confronted by *Hauptmann* Priem.

He was evidently pleased with his night's work and in high spirits.

"*Ah hah! Es ist Herr Hauptmann Reid. Das ist schön!*" he said as I walked in, and continued:

"Nobody could recognize who the nigger was until he was washed! And now that we have the nigger out of the woodpile, what has he got to say for himself?"

"I think the nigger in the woodpile was a certain German sentry, was he not?" I questioned in reply.

"Yes, indeed, *Herr Hauptmann*. German sentries know

their duty. The whole matter has been reported to me
from the start."

"From before the start, maybe?"

"*Herr Hauptmann* Reid, that is not the point. Where
does your tunnel come from?"

"That is obvious," I replied.

"From the canteen, then?"

"Yes."

"But you have been locked into your quarters. You
have a tunnel from your rooms to the canteen?"

"No!"

"But yes! You have just been counted on *appell*. The
canteen has been locked many hours ago. You have a
tunnel?"

"No!"

"We shall see. How many of you are there?"

"So many I have never been able to count them
properly!"

"Come now, *Herr Hauptmann,* the whole camp or just
a few?"

"Just a few!"

"Good, then I hope our solitary confinement
accommodation will not be too overcrowded!" said Priem,
grinning broadly.

P. R. Reid

The Way Out: England

*During the whole of the war only one German prisoner
who had been confined in Britain eventually succeeded in
getting back to his own country. This man was Franz von
Werra, a Luftwaffe pilot who displayed unsurpassed
powers of tenacity and resource. His attempts to escape
from this country failed: shipped to Canada early in 1941,
he eventually crossed the border into the still-neutral
United States, returning by a devious route to Germany.
During one of his escapades in Britain, he posed as a
Dutch pilot and made his way to an airfield with the idea
of stealing an aircraft and flying it across the Channel.*

Realizing that the R.A.F. officer who was questioning him, known to him as "Mr. Boniface", was about to unmask him, von Werra acted.

Von Werra had got away from the office and "Mr. Boniface". But for how long? Time was now the supremely vital factor. Fractions of seconds mattered.

He sprinted back along the road he had travelled in the R.A.F. vehicle. There was not a soul in sight. When he reached the perimeter track he turned left, towards the group of camouflaged hangars and the gaggle of Hurricanes.

He slowed down to a walk near the first hangar, at the front of which construction work was being carried out. Builders looked down at him curiously from scaffolding. He dodged between a cement mixer and a heap of ballast, almost bumping into a labourer cutting open a cement bag.

He was out of sight of Headquarters. He did not start running again but walked briskly, purposefully. Past a wrecked aircraft and a row of twin-engined bombers. They were no good to him, but the wide sweep of the airfield made his nostrils twitch and his blood tingle. The orange red orb of the sun had risen above the rim of the airfield and frost sparkled on the grass.

The doors of the second hangar were wide open. It was full of aircraft in various stages of assembly.

Ahead was the group of Hurricanes. A mechanic wearing a black smock was dodging about near one of them. A trolley-acc. (accumulator trolley) was beside him. The Hurricane was about to be started up! There was only this one mechanic in sight and von Werra needed someone to explain the controls of the British fighter to him.

The mechanic looked up wonderingly as the little man in the unusual flying-suit approached.

"Good morning!" said von Werra. "I am Captain van Lott, a Dutch pilot. I have just been posted here. But Hurricanes I have not yet flown. Mr. Boniface, the

Adjutant, sent me down here so you should show me the controls and make a practice flight. Which one is ready for take-off? This one here?"

He looked the mechanic straight in the eyes and spoke with firmness and authority.

The mechanic looked puzzled. Then von Werra noticed that he was not in R.A.F. uniform, but wore civilian trousers and shirt and a striped tie.

"Haven't you come to the wrong place?" the man asked. "This is a private firm. We have nothing to do with the R.A.F. over there."

"I know. But Mr. Boniface said it was to you I should come. I don't have much time. . . ."

The mechanic pondered. Then the probable explanation dawned on him. The airman had said he was a "Captain", so he must be a ferry pilot from White Waltham, headquarters of Air Transport Command. Apparently he had come to take delivery of a Hurricane. It was a common occurrence for civilian ferry pilots, known by the courtesy rank of Captain, many of them foreigners speaking hardly a word of English, to collect aircraft which had been sent to the Rolls-Royce works for modification. Moreover, when they had to fly a type of aircraft new to them they often asked for a practical demonstration of controls and peculiarities, in addition to the printed pilot's notes which were issued to them. Of course, von Werra knew none of this.

"Ah!" said the mechanic, "then you must be a ferry pilot?"

Von Werra did not know the meaning of the word "ferry". But he thought it best to agree.

"Yes, of course," he replied.

"That's different," the mechanic said. "You'll have to see the A.I.D.* blokes."

Aieyedeeblokes? Von Werra couldn't cope with it.

"Look," he said. "I have no time . . . you shall show me the controls now, yes?"

* Aeronautical Inspection Directorate.

"I can't do anything until you've signed the Visitors' Book, and then you'll have to get your paper-work attended to. Hang on a minute, Captain. I'll go and fetch the manager."

The mechanic walked across the tarmac into the hangar. Von Werra stood leaning against the fuselage of the Hurricane. A brand-new beautiful Hurricane with not a scratch on it. A colossal beast, it seemed, twice as large as the Hurricanes he had encountered in air combat. He was tempted to climb into the cockpit and try to start the engine on his own. But it was no good. There were certain controls he must be sure about before he attempted to take off. If he got into the cockpit now it might wreck his chances altogether.

Familiar, nostalgic sounds issued from the hangar, as though from a cave: the beating of metal, the whirr of electric drills, somebody singing, somebody else whistling, the musical tinkle of a ring-spanner dropped on to concrete. At any minute "Mr. Boniface" would know the truth. The alarm would be sounded and every man on the aerodrome mobilized to hunt for him.

The mechanic came out of the hangar with a man wearing a khaki smock. They approached the Hurricane in a leisurely fashion, talking and looking at one another from time to time, apparently discussing something quite unconnected with the Dutch Captain. Von Werra remained leaning negligently against the fuselage, one arm stretched out along it, one flying boot crossed in front of the other, his body half covering the roundel painted on the side.

The man in the khaki smock, presumably the manager, smiled pleasantly and said:

"Good morning, Captain!" His manner was positive, as though his mind was already made up and he was dealing with an everyday occurrence.

"I hear you've come to collect a Hurricane," he continued. "If you'll come with me we'll get your paper-work fixed up."

"It shall take long? I have little time," von Werra

replied. "I just want to learn controls of the Hurricane."

"I'm afraid nothing can be done until you've signed the Visitors' Book. We'll soon fix you up, though."

Von Werra reluctantly followed the two men into the hangar. There was nothing else he could do. They walked with infuriating slowness. Fitters working on aircraft in the hangar stared down at him from staging, peered at him between undercarriages, craned their necks out of cockpits. He felt like a pickpocket at a police convention.

The mechanic remained in the works. Von Werra continued behind the manager. They reached the rear wall of the hangar and passed through a door into an asphalt yard. On the other side of it was a gate and a glass-sided lodge. A man in a blue uniform was sitting inside the lodge. Evidently a works policeman. The manager entered and spoke to him.

Through the window von Werra saw a large, solemn, white-faced clock on a wall. A couple of minutes to nine. His mouth opened and his brow furrowed as he watched the thin, central second hand sweeping round the dial. Then he bit his lip and looked away.

What was "Mr. Boniface" doing between the time the second hand moved from three to six? Perhaps that was the decisive quarter of a minute.

Though he looked away, the pointer continued to revolve in his mind's eye. He had to glance back. He expected to find the pointer at eight, but it was nearly at ten.

If only these idiots would hurry up!

The damned clock was making him lose his nerve. He fumbled for his cigarettes and matches with moist, quivering hands. Then he looked again at the pointer: twelve. The two men came out of the lodge.

As they emerged von Werra put away his packet of Player's and the box of Swan matches, making sure that they saw them. Then he idly flicked away the match with which he had lighted a cigarette.

" 'Morning, sir!" said the policeman brightly.

" 'Morning!" von Werra replied in the same tone.

"If you'll just sign along the next line, sir. . . ."

The entry had to be made across two pages, which were divided into columns. There were already half-filled with many different styles of handwriting. As he was afraid his German style might betray him, he decided to make his entry in printed characters. The first four columns were headed, Date, Name, Nationality and Address respectively, and presented little difficulty. He wrote:

21.12.40   van Lott   Dutch   Aberdeen

His anxiety not to betray himself by his entry did not prevent him from once again making the tell-take stroke over the "u" in "Dutch".

The fifth column was headed "Order". He had no idea what he should write under it, and the other entries in the column were indecipherable. He casually asked the policeman whether he wanted this item written out in full.

"No, it doesn't matter, sir. Just put 'see A.I.D.'."

Von Werra was none the wiser for his successful ruse. He asked the policeman to spell the words, but when he did so he was all the more confused. He had to write something. The manager was watching over his shoulder. The second hand was sweeping round the dial. Guards were probably searching every corner for him. Possibly Polish guards.

He made an entry of sorts, but the nearest he could get to "See A.I.D." was "Siocioed". The proper entry was later filled in by the policeman.

The next column was headed "Time of Arrival". The clock showed exactly nine o'clock, so von Werra wrote "09.00" (hours). (It must have been the policeman who subsequently filled in the time of departure—perhaps just to keep his books straight.)

"That's it, sir. Now everything's in order!" The policeman smiled happily, and von Werra's spirits soared. If "Mr. Boniface" would only give him another five minutes! He now felt so confident that when the manager asked him for his written orders covering the collection of the Hurricane, he replied firmly and without hesitation:

"My papers, parachute—all my kit—will come on a plane which shall land here soon—any minute. I will have instruction on controls to save time, yes?"

"Right ho," said the manager. "We can do that all right now you've signed the book. Come with me, Captain."

Meanwhile, the mechanic in the black smock had come out into the yard and was hanging about expectantly. The manager went over to him and told him to take the Captain back to the Hurricane and explain its instruments and controls in detail.

The manager went off in a different direction with a smile and a cheery wave of the hand.

"He'll fix you up all right," he said as he left.

Von Werra followed the mechanic back across the yard. There was a large notice on the outer wall of the hangar: "No smoking beyond this door." Von Werra dropped his cigarette and trod on it.

Back through the hangar. Every second counted. Would he see a group of airmen looking for him when he emerged on to the tarmac? The mechanic did not dawdle, but von Werra felt an urge to push him along still faster. Instead, he had to keep pace nonchalantly.

Out through the open front. A glance right and left. No R.A.F. uniforms in sight!

And there was the beautiful, brand-new Hurricane, with a coating of rime on its wings and——

Hell's teeth!—the accumulator trolley was no longer beside it. Nowhere in sight. Some other mechanic must have taken it away while he was signing that blasted book. Oh, well, he would just have to hope that he could start the engine using the battery in the aircraft.

The mechanic climbed up on one side of the cockpit and slid back the perspex hood.

A couple of seconds later von Werra was sitting at the controls, the strange-feeling stick in his hands, aghast at the completely unfamiliar lay-out and instrument panel. Leaning over him into the cockpit, the mechanic carefully explained the controls and instruments.

Von Werra hung on to his every word. But there was much he was unable to follow, too many words he did not understand. He could not absorb and retain all that information in so short a time. He almost panicked. Never mind all those details—what were the essentials?

The compass. Heavens! What kind of compass was that? Nothing like a Messerschmitt's. How did you set the damned thing? (He had determined before escaping from Swanwick that 120 degrees was the most direct course to fly from the Midlands to the Continent.)

"Set the compass to 120 degrees, for instance," he told the mechanic. The mechanic obliged. Von Werra looked from the reset compass to the sun shining through the perspex. Rubbish. It didn't make sense. He could not make heard or tail of the compass. To hell with it. Take off and keep the sun to port.

The stick. A monstrous contraption. As long as he didn't stand the aircraft on its nose when trying to take off. . . .

The hydraulic brake system. Incomprehensible. He had never seen anything like it. Ah, never mind. Hope for the best. As long as he didn't stand the aircraft on its nose.
. . .

The starter. Most important. Try it. The mechanic had already pointed out the starter button and the injection pump. What had he said was the proper drill? Von Werra could not remember.

It was a cold morning. Would the aircraft battery be strong enough to turn the engine through the stiff oil? If so, then in a minute he would be on the edge of the field. He would have to taxi along the perimeter road until the engine warmed up. In five minutes he would be airborne, setting course by the sun. In half an hour or so he would be approaching the familiar French coastline. Then— throw the kite flat on the deck on the cliff tops—never mind about the undercart—before the flak started flying about. He would have made it!

He glared at the starter button. He willed the battery to

be strong enough. God grant. . . It was almost a prayer.

Before the mechanic could anticipate his move, he jabbed the button.

Whirr—whirr. The propeller revolved twice, then stuck. Not a cylinder fired.

"Don't do that!" the mechanic cried in alarm. "Can't start without the trolley-acc.!"

"Fetch it, then!" von Werra ordered.

He must have it. He must make the mechanic get it. He must *hurry* him to get it.

"It's not available just now. Somebody else is using it." Just who did this little man think he was?

Von Werra bit his lip. He could not possibly have more than a few minutes left. He must have the trollery-acc. He must have it. He must have it at once. But if he tried to boss and hurry the mechanic, it would probably have the opposite effect; he would sulk and deliberately take his time. Or not fetch it at all.

He turned on the von Werra smile.

"Please get it, yes? I really am in a hurry."

The mechanic looked hard at the smiling Dutchman, then grinned himself.

"All right," he said. "I'll see if I can find it."

The aircraft swayed slightly as he stepped down off the wing. He moved off in the direction of the hangar.

Von Werra glanced back up the perimeter of the airfield. Surely any second men would come running round by the scaffolding on the end hangar. He must not think about it, but use these last few minutes to concentrate on the controls and the instrument panel. The air-speed indicator was graduated in miles per hour. He would have to convert that into kilometres. The altimeter showed height in feet. He would have to convert that into metres.

He heard a strange whining sound and looked out of the cockpit. The mechanic was coming across the tarmac standing on an electric truck, which was pulling the accumulator trolley.

Von Werra's heart thumped madly. His hands were clammy, his throat dry. Two more minutes! God grant nobody turned up.

The mechanic manipulated the truck with conscious expertness, swinging it round the starboard wing in a graceful sweep, halting it dead, with a clatter of couplings, so that the trolley-acc. was in exactly the right position. He jumped off the truck platform, went behind to the trolley-acc. and raised the armoured cable over his shoulder, preparatory to plugging it in.

The aircraft swayed. For a second von Werra did not grasp the significance of the movement. He operated the injection pump a couple of times, hoping it would be enough. A voice above him on the port side said quietly:

"Get out!"

He jerked his head back. At eye-level on the left-hand side of the cockpit, the sun was reflected on a highly-polished button of an Air Force officer's greatcoat. It gleamed too on the muzzle of an automatic pistol.

Von Werra's eye ran up the coat buttons, over a chin, a mouth twisted in a queer sort of grin and halted on a pair of cold, blue eyes.

It was "Mr. Boniface".

Prisoner's Return: Italy, December 1943

Descending the hill on the far side, I met three Italians on donkeys.

"Are there any Germans round here?" I asked them in Italian.

Suspiciously, they asked if I was German. Hearing I was English, their manner changed immediately. They embraced me and told me to keep going for half a mile when I would reach their village, Montenero, and find English soldiers everywhere.

"Niente tedeschi, niente tedeschi!" they laughed.

The sun broke through the morning mist as I came in sight of the village. Approaching it, I deliberately dawdled and finished the last mouthful of Italian bully.

"Well, here you are," I said aloud. "I suppose you'll remember the next minutes all your life."

And I was quite right.

From a hundred yards away the much-battered buildings appeared deserted. Then I noticed a Bren-carrier behind a wall, a few trucks under camouflage netting in a yard. As I limped slowly into the main street, a solitary shell whistled overhead, exploding somewhere at the farther end. A group of British soldiers, the first I had seen, in long leather waistcoats and khaki cap-comforters, chatted unconcernedly in a doorway across the cobbles from me. I glanced shyly at them, but they took no notice. Just another bedraggled peasant haunting the ruins of his home. . . .

The conventional inhibited Englishman is ill-equipped by temperament for such occasions. I would have liked to dance, to shout, to make some kind of demonstration. A Frenchman, an Australian, would have done it naturally, but somehow I could not. So I walked slowly on, holding off the pleasure of the long-awaited moment, the exclamation of surprise, the greeting from a compatriot.

English voices and laughter came from a house. I crossed the threshold and found, in what had been the peasants' kitchen but was now the usual military desolation of a billet, two half-dressed privates cooking breakfast. One of them saw me, standing there grinning at them.

"Christ, Nobby, look what the cat's brought in," he said.

I tried to be hearty but failed. "I've just come through. I'm soaked. Can I warm up by your fire?" I heard my bored voice say politely.

Neither of the soldiers was much surprised by this sudden entry of what was, to all appearances, a dank and bearded Italian, who spoke fluent English with a B.B.C. accent. Sensibly enough, they were more interested in breakfast.

"What are you? Escaped P.O.W. or something?"

"Yes."

It didn't cause much of a sensation and they asked no
more questions. They treated me, as they might have a
stray dog, with a sort of cheery kindness and without fuss.
In a few minutes I was sitting naked before their fire,
drinking a cup of char and feeling the warmth return to my
numbed body.

A corporal and others of the section came in for their
breakfast. My back view may have mildly surprised them.

"Bloke's an escaped P.O.W.," Nobby explained.

"Lucky sod. They'll send you home," the corporal said,
offering me a Player's.

Savouring every puff of the tobacco, every sip of the
tea, I wondered whether Amos was doing the same
somewhere nearby. We had so often pictured just this
situation in the past three months. Superstitiously, I put
off asking them if they had heard of him. If they had, they
would surely say so. And I didn't want to hear them say
they hadn't.

Long anticipated pleasures seldom come up to
expectation. Neither the tea, the tobacco nor even the
warmth were now quite as delicious as I had imagined
they would be. The scene was unreal, unbelievable.
Though the soldiers' gossip around me was vivid enough.

"Ginger, go and swipe some clothes for him off the
C.Q.M.S's truck," the corporal said to one of the men.

"Do you think the C.Q.M.S. can spare me something?"

"The C.Q.M.S. won't know," Ginger winked as he left
the room.

Certainly I was back with the British Army all right.

Later, in the miscellaneous garments swiped by Ginger
(the C.Q.M.S would, I am sure, have supplied them
voluntarily—but that, of course, would have been more
trouble) I visited R.H.Q. in another part of the village.
Nothing had been heard there of Amos and the C.O.
refused at first to credit my story that I had walked
through his outposts unobserved, until I traced my route
for him on the map. Evidently I had indeed walked slap
through C Company's position.

"Can't think why they didn't shoot you," the colonel

said irritably. "Remind me to have a word with the company commander about that," he added to his adjutant.

John Verney

THE FAR EAST

In Japanese eyes, a prisoner of war was not only defeated, he was also an object of contempt for having allowed himself to be captured. He had lost face; he was no longer entitled to be treated or considered as a human being. He was not.

Owing to the normal Oriental standards of treatment for the defeated, even civilians—men, women and children—who fell into Japanese hands fared little better. Starvation and brutality were their lot.

Out of three hundred thousand prisoners captured by the Japanese in the first months of the war in the Pacific one hundred thousand were already dead when the day of liberation dawned. The two hundred thousand survivors staggered emaciated and exhausted from unknown villages and prison camps scattered over the islands or in the interior of the Asiatic mainland from the rocky shores of the Banda Sea to the Burma jungle.

An almost unsurmountable barrier surrounded them. It was not only the physical prison which held them, or the enormous distances which separated them from their homes and their families and from those who were fighting to liberate them, but their complete isolation amongst a race whose language and customs were completely foreign to them. And, in addition, there was the wall of silence which their Japanese guards deliberately erected around them.

A letter took a year to reach the place of their imprisonment—and then the Japanese would often leave the post sacks lying unopened for some time.

Marcel Junod, International Red Cross

Capture

From the south the leading groups of Japanese came
swiftly through the grey light towards the town. The
advance scouts marched as quickly as the troops behind,
scarcely bothering to watch the sides of the roads for
ambushes, knowing that a properly laid ambush would be
impossible to detect however hard they strained their eyes.
It was easy for them to go forward so quickly and
impassively, for them the issue was simple. They could
either go forward and perhaps die gloriously, with the
absolute certainty of eternal bliss, or not go forward and
be even more certain of a swift death and utter disgrace.
There were a few to whom the gift of faith in heaven had
not been granted and there were some who feared the pain
of dying, but they would be ground on the millstone of
their own comrades if they allowed those sentiments to
show, and with a certainty that made the life of a leading
scout seem full of promise.

. . . . When it was light enough to see a few yards the
Japanese officer got to his feet. He felt numbed with cold
and his body ached with tiredness; it was so usual a
condition that he no longer thought about it. Soon the vile
fishy taste in his mouth would go and he would feel
hungry, perhaps they would come across some water once
they moved.

He told his senior N.C.O. to bring the men up to the
track immediately; in the meantime he walked towards the
dark patch on the dusty track that he knew was the
English soldier; perhaps there were some more lying dead
in the jungle. He drew his revolver from force of habit; he
was convinced that there was no one hiding in the jungle,
he had listened contemptuously to the cries for help and
the noise they had made as they crashed down the slope; if
his own men behaved like that he thought he would
commit suicide.

With his foot he rolled Clifton's stiff body over and
searched it, transferring everything of possible interest to

his haversack. Then he went on. He found more
bloodstains and left the track and pushed his way into the
jungle.

When he came back the men had fallen in on the track
and bowed as he reached them. He gave his instructions in
a low voice and they listened stolidly. When he finished he
walked to the head of the line of men and began to pick
his way through the jungle towards the ridge.

The group that he led were not picked men nor did they
receive any special pay, although their tasks were much
more dangerous than those that usually fell to the ordinary
Japanese infantry. But even so these groups were envied
by the others, it was not only more honourable, but also
part of their role was to spread fear by committing
atrocities and letting their handiwork be found by the other
side. It was exciting and amusing to watch your enemies
die bizarrely, and at the same time shocking and
horrifying to listen to them begging for mercy on their
knees, begging for the incomparable disaster of being
taken prisoners.

As far as the Japanese were concerned such men
deserved to die.

. . . . In the course of half an hour the back of the work
was broken. The cooks had made tea for themselves and
taken some to the two diggers; now they stood watching
them as they shovelled out the hard lumps of earth, sweat
running down their faces. The driver had managed to
unscrew the padlock on the front door and wandered
about the gloomy rooms lit by chinks of mote-flecked sun
that slipped through the shutters. The place was bare
except for a few rickety pieces of furniture, but he found a
tattered copy of *Blackwood*'s dated July 1926; he dragged
an armchair to the veranda and sat drinking his tea and
reading odd paragraphs that caught his eyes, his lips
forming the words.

He heard a slight noise and casually looked across to
his lorry, thinking that one of the wounded men might
have dropped something, but the lorry was broadside on
and he could see nothing. He went on reading and then

something moved into his line of vision. He looked up quickly . . . a few yards away were three men in uniform coming towards him, a young man in front carrying a thin revolver. He knew at once that they were Japanese, and he got up slowly, glad that he had left his rifle in the front of the lorry because he thought that as he was unarmed they would not shoot him. He was dazed by the shock, and all he could feel was bitterness, not against the Japanese but against his own people for allowing this to happen, allowing a lorry-load of dead and wounded to go unescorted and be captured.

The officer stood on the bottom step of the veranda and said something to him. The driver shook his head: "No speak Jap," he said very quietly as though they were in a conspiracy together. They stood for a few seconds looking at each other, and then the officer beckoned him to walk forward. He came down the steps and they prodded him gently in the back and made signs that he should go in front of them. They walked round the bungalow and past the cookhouse towards the group of men at the grave, the two soldiers on either side and the officer a few paces behind. Dobson stared at them uncomprehendingly, wondering for a moment if he was doing wrong by digging in the rest-house garden, thinking that maybe they were civil police.

"What's up?" he called out.

"I . . . I don't know," the driver answered, "they're Japs." There was a moment of frozen silence and then some dry earth pattered into the grave and one of the cooks turned quickly and started to run towards the trees that hid the river. He ran clumsily in a straight line and everyone watched him. It seemed to take a very long time to reach the edge of the trees and then there was a shot and he pitched forward and rolled against the slender trunk of one of the palms. The officer spoke harshly and waved his revolver in the directon of the lorry. They were too dazed to resist, their rifles which lay close at hand were as useless to them as twigs, movement towards them meant death and to die was unthinkable. Burns had died because he had run, they would not run and would live.

They started towards the lorry. While it was still hidden behind the bungalow they heard screams, and when they turned the corner they could see a little group of men prodding at a body on the ground. They came nearer and saw that Rasby's bandages had been torn off and his smashed jaw was being whipped at and prodded with little sticks; one man had pushed a long piece of bamboo into his mouth and was gouging at the back of his throat with the broken end while Rasby moved his head from side to side carefully, screaming when he could. The officer shouted to them and they stopped at once, shuffling back a few paces and watching the body move on the ground. The officer spoke again and one of the soldiers caught hold of the driver's shirt, ripping it down the front and dragging it off him. He rolled the shirt lengthways, and while someone held Rasby's arms he twisted it twice round the gaping mouth and jerked the knot as tightly as he could.

Some of the Japanese climbed into the lorry and threw everything out, others started tearing blankets into strips and gagged and bound the uninjured prisoners. Myler's and Rasby's clothes were torn off, and they were tied to the flamboyant tree under which the lorry stood. No one resisted, they were outnumbered and unarmed and they did not believe they would be killed. When all the baggage was thrown out of the lorry Dobson was sure that his party of Japanese knew nothing of the company marching towards them and intended driving them back to the town as prisoners. He thought it was much more likely that they would be shot by their own side than killed by the Japanese, who would have no time to waste on prisoners once they met the company. He couldn't understand why the two men should be stripped and tied to the tree so securely; it was dreadful but it wasn't happening to him.

Everything had now been thrown out and quickly examined, the tins of bully beef seemed to attract them more than anything else and their haversacks were bulging with them. He was seized roughly by two men and made to hop over to the lorry and then pushed in with the others. They lay on the floor waiting for the tail-board to be put up, but instead all the baggage started to be thrown in again, blankets first and then the heavier articles. They tried to escape from the soft suffocation of the blankets but they were only partially successful; the four of them managed to roll together to one side of the lorry, but they were smothered in blankets and heavy cases lay across them in confusion. They could hear the Japanese laughing and whispering outside and unscrewing the spare two-gallon tins of petrol. The driver was the first to interpret the sounds, but he did not understand that they were going to be burnt alive until one of the Japanese climbed into the lorry and poured petrol on the pile of luggage until it soaked into the blankets. The sudden knowledge seemed to separate his mind from his body, and he started jerking and heaving to escape from the stifling horror of the blankets, and the sounds that came from his throat and filtered through the gag infected the others and they too began to writhe in terror, strange sounds pouring from their blanket-stuffed mouths. There was a muffled explosion and they heaved their bodies this way and that, the flames reached down quickly, but to them the interval was timeless. The blankets blazed on their bodies and as the fire scorched them they made a last effort to burst loose and the driver stood upright in an oven of fire, blinded by the flames, his arms and body blazing like a torch. He managed to turn towards the open back and tried to step forward, he toppled across the burning cases and fell to the ground. His head lay in a puddle of fire. It was the last thing Myler saw before the petrol tank exploded and enveloped the whole flamboyant tree in flame.

Walter Baxter

Borneo: Civilians

Some days later in the prison compound, behind a thirty-foot wooden boarding, we listened to the first of many addresses by Japanese commanding officers,

ands openly, and sometimes they beat us for smiling
hem secretly.

he first guard we had in Berhala made a speech to us
r one week, on the eve of their departure. Before
ing it, they dictated their sentiments to me in broken
lish and told me to write them out in "literary" style.
result of our effort was this:

ENTLEMEN, LADIES AND WOMEN: Nipponese
ldiers are very kindly. We will pray for your health
ntil we meet again. To-morrow we go back to
andakan. We are very sorry for you. However, if you
et conceited we will knock you down, beat you, kick
ou, and kill you.

suggested that the last sentence was a trifle harsh, but
were particularly attached to it.

. . . In Kuching we learned to bow seriously. We had
ted instructions, demonstrations and practice. The
ponese orders for bowing were: Incline the body from
waist to a fifteen-degree angle, with head uncovered,
ds at the side, and feet together: remain thus to the
nt of five (silent); then recover. (If not knocked
n.)

he first time we were instructed in bowing in the
hing camp, we were being trained to present a good
arance for the visiting lieutenant-general for whom we
planted potatoes.

e day came, we were all assembled in ranks, the
s in front, the women and children behind, where it
oped we could do the least harm by our frivolous

The order was given to bow. The Sisters had
erful behinds, the bow made the behinds spring into
prominence; by standing too close and bowing too
we managed to meet the behinds with our heads.
sion and concussion reigned, and order was not
d. The lieutenant-general was hastened away to
the pigs, who had more respect for lieutenant-
s than we did, or else did not understand the

expressing the following sentiment: "You are a fourth-
class nation now. Therefore your treatment will be fourth-
class, and you will live and eat as coolies. In the past you
have had proudery and arrogance! You will get over it
now!"

Throughout three and a half years they did their best to
cure us of proudery and arrogance.

. . . . For a while we kept small bowls of oil with wicks
floating, which we burned at night to give us light. The oil
was coconut oil given as a ration. But soon the Japanese
stopped giving us oil, and we got so hungry we ate what
we had, and by that time we had burned up all the cloth
for wicks. So then we lived in the dark.

The barrack had no glass in the windows, just solid
wooden shutters. Although it wasn't the rainy season
when we arrived, it rained much of the time on Berhala,
the rain and wind driving furiously upon us from the sea
side of the island. At such times we had to have the
shutters closed tight, leaving no ventilation or light, either
by day or by night.

The building itself was made of loose shakes, with
cracks between, and the rain drove through. I lived on the
side exposed to the ocean wind. It rained almost every
night, and for six months I rolled up George's and my
sleeping things nightly and moved them to a dry spot, and
sat on them until the rain abated. I never could unroll
them in a dry spot, because there wasn't room enough.
The dry places were full of somebody else. Those nights
George slept with Edith and Eddie and Mrs. Cho, the
Chinese Consul's family, the four of them lying on her
feather mattress which her *amah* had rescued for her.

There were two cement latrine holes in camp. These
had no containers or outlets, and no manner of being
emptied, so after a few experiments we stopped using
them. Then the Japanese gave us two corrugated tin
buckets to use, and these we stood outdoors behind a
shelter.

We took turns disposing of their contents. At first we
dug holes in the compound and buried the refuse, but we

had no good digging tools, and there was a rock layer just under the topsoil; when it rained we couldn't get the refuse to stay below water level, and excrement floated about the compound. The compound became crowded with refuse holes, and the whole place stank. It was like nothing else I ever smelled. We didn't pass through that smell holding our noses. We simply ate, slept and lived in it.

In time the Japanese decided to permit us to empty the latrine buckets in the sea, five minutes' walk away, twice a day. The men's camp asked permission to do this work for us, but the Japanese refused, as they believed in equal rights for the sexes when it came to excrement. When it was my turn to empty the bucket, I used to carry George on one side and the bucket on the other. We carried the buckets out to the end of the wharf, experimented with the wind, dumped in the refuse. From thence it was carried back to the shore by the current, to the beach where we bathed.

It was a rule in camp that the bucket should be used for faeces only, as otherwise they filled up too fast, so one corner of the compound was used as a urinal. It did not offer the seclusion of those in Paris.

A hooded cobra was said to sleep in the latrine shelter at night, by one of the buckets. Some said they saw it, and all of us heard it. I never saw it there, but I know that there were cobras in the grass outside the compound. Whether the cobra was in the latrine or not, the idea of his being there was sufficient.

The change of diet for all of us, and a dysentery epidemic among the children, made it necessary to keep one latrine bucket in our sleeping quarters on rainy nights. The sounds of that bucket in use, the odour of it, the thought of it, make war more deadly and unendurable to me now than does the memory of all the bombs dropped over us in 1945.

. . . . On the island there were no officers in charge, and the eight guards were changed once a week. During the week they had complete power over us. To them island duty was a vacation; the lads relaxed in loin-cloths most

of the time, bathing, doing acrobatics, throwing prisoners, picking their noses, beating up distributing largesse, or lolling in the women playing footsy-footsy.

Our barrack was one big room with a loft ab no partitions. Each person occupied about fi feet. If the guard wanted to occupy it with y wasn't much you could do except roll over. No guards spent all their time lying down near us; a time they were drunk in the guardhouse.

Some of it was good clean fun, and boys will But sometimes boys are dirty boys, and one d being frisked, frolicked, bullied, chased, back-sl face-slapped by a young man with a gun. The gu the element of light-hearted gaiety from the game

Because there were buns, rice, and privileges from tolerating and encouraging the guards, and with which to discourage them, the fact that the us like tarts was sometimes justified. One good against collaborating was the fact that the g bedbugs.

They were not sadistic, or masochistic; the Oriental, or Occidental; they were just a gang young hoodlums who had complete power ove people who could not strike back.

Once a week a worn-out officer arrived i motorboat, and both made a loud noise searched the guards, and us, with equal susp by the motor, the guards could just get their time to reach the wharf's end and stand a could just get our forbidden diaries, b hidden in the grass and the latrines. W departed, everybody relaxed.

Life on Berhala was according to th guards—and they were whimsical. The kind. One guard gave his own buns to another distributed loaves of bread frequently fed us their own surplus, co food was terrible. Sometimes they

meaning of the phrase "dumb insolence", as we did. We were never again assembled together in one group to bow to a visiting general.

. . . . Every change was for the worse. Rules increased, food decreased, work increased, and strength decreased. Disappointments multiplied, and optimism was never verified. Hope itself seemed only a refuge for those who would not face facts.

Our food ration, then, as supplied by the Japanese per person per day, was as follows: one cupful of thin rice gruel, five tablespoons of cooked rice, sometimes a few greens, a little sugar, sometimes a little salt and tea. This was what the Japanese expected us to live on. Or did they expect us to live on it?

Additions to this diet were sweet-potato tops, which we grew ourselves. We used the tops because we were too hungry to wait for the potatoes to mature. Every square foot of the camp was in use for gardens, but the soil was exhausted, and we were exhausted. The last eight months of imprisonment it was almost impossible for us to do heavy work, but we did it. We arose before sunrise to finish the work inside camp, and then went outside the camp to work for the Japanese. By nine o'clock in the morning we were worn out.

By now soldiers were trading for and buying skinned cats and rats, people were eating snails and worms, all of us were eating weeds and grass, and plenty of us would have liked to eat each other.

I had meals of banana skins stolen from Japanese refuse barrels and boiled into soup.

. . . . Throughout their imprisonment a home-made radio was concealed—and functioned—in the British soldiers' camp.

The radio was never referred to in camp by name, but spoken of as Granny, Mrs. Harrison, the Ice Cream, the Old Lady, and several less polite terms. Knowing that the lives of its inventors and protectors were forfeit to its discovery, as well as the welfare of the whole camp, a security service of men was formed to guard the Old

Lady. These kept guard on the Japanese guards with more efficiency that the guards kept guard on them. Night and day a signal system of songs, whistles, and bird noises kept the Old Lady vigilant to the approach of danger in the shape of guards, officers and *Kempi-Tai*.

At first the soldiers' camp had electric light, and while this lasted the radio was run by electricity. Later when the electricity was discontinued, the radio ceased to function for a four-months' period, during which time the men were busy at work making a hand-power generator. It took them only one month to make the generator itself, but it had taken them three to make the tools with which to make the generator.

This hand-power generator was run by a flywheel, which was disguised as a barrel top. The wheel was turned by one man, and had to revolve at the rate of three thousand revolutions per minute in order to generate sufficient power for the radio. The man who turned the flywheel was given extra food and care in camp, and developed huge muscles in one arm and side from turning it. After sixty seconds of turning, the sweat poured from him like water, and he could turn for only a few minutes at a time.

. . . So humble were her beginnings, and so simple and inanimate the articles which finally in her being gained life and functions, that the Old Lady seems to have been truly created rather than built. The origins of her component parts were as follows:

The receiver was made from the stolen steering damper knob of a Norton motor-cycle.

The coil was made from a Gibbs' bakelite shaving-soap container.

The variable condenser was made from biscuit tins, stripped and remodelled.

The resistors and valves were made over from old hearing-aid amplifiers belonging to a deaf civilian. Without these, there could have been no Old Lady.

The resistor condenser panel was made from bakelite linen from an old map container.

The high-frequency choke was made from a Colgate's shaving-soap container.

The humdinger or small rheostat was made from stolen old brass, bakelite and wire.

Insulation was supplied by pieces of aeroplane glass stolen by soldiers working at the airfield.

The ignition coils were stolen from an old gun battery.

The rectifier was stolen by a soldier when on a working party in Kuching.

A fixed condenser was stolen from a motor-cycle in Kuching by a soldier on a working party.

And the generator was made of scrap iron, soft Swedish iron, and copper, these materials being stolen from the Nipponese stores, or salvaged from old machines, by men on working parties.

The Old Lady in the altogether was hidden in a soldier's mess tin, an unrewarding place for the only lady in the soldiers' camp to sleep.

. . . . Colonel Suga's picture of himself was as the cultured and beneficent administrator of the ideal internment camp of Kuching. He was always kind to the children, often brought them biscuits and sweets, supplied means for their teaching, gave them what liberty he could. They all liked him.

He had good and kindly impulses, and a real desire for inter-racial understanding. He was kind to me personally. I believe that he saved my husband from death.

Against this, I place the fact that all the prisoners in Borneo were inexorably moving towards starvation. Prisoners of war and civilians were beaten, abused and tortured. Daily living conditions of prison camps were almost unbearable.

At Sandakan and Ranau and Brunei, North Borneo, batches of prisoners in fifties and sixties were marched out to dig their own graves, then shot or bayoneted and pushed into the graves, many before they were dead. All over Borneo hundreds and thousands of sick, weak, weary prisoners were marched on roads and paths until they fell from exhaustion, when their heads were beaten in with rifle butts and shovels, and split open with swords, and they were left to rot unburied. On one march, 2,970 P.O.W.s started and three survived.

The Kuching prison camps were scheduled to march on 15 September 1945 had peace not intervened. It was this abandoned order which Colonel Suga had read to me on the day peace pamphlets were dropped.

I have since heard reports of other Japanese prison camps outside of Borneo: in most of them conditions were better than ours, in few were they worse.

For these black chapters in captivity Colonel Suga, commander in Borneo, must be held responsible.

What his orders were I do not know. No doubt he must obey them, or risk himself. Whether he attempted to save us I do not know, but I do know that it takes more even than physical courage to stand up for human values against patriotic zeal in wartime. Until the gun is held at your own head, until the whisper comes of "Traitor", you cannot know what you will do.

Agnes Newton Keith

25 March 1945

First Allied planes seen to-day. Three years ago I would have been delirious with joy. To-day I have neither energy nor heart for excitement. Too little food.

Diary entry

.... The British soldiers' camp stretched along the side of our road. I was walking up that road on the way to Colonel Suga's office one day when something caught my attention. All over the soldiers' camp I saw small camp-fires glowing, with little pots of various sorts smoking over them. And I thought I smelled ... chicken! I stopped and stared and sniffed. The Jap sentry near by me said nothing. All this was unusual—fires, food and silent sentries.

A miserably thin-looking soldier in a loin-cloth, so close to the barbed wire that I could see him wink at me, sang out recklessly, "Happy days are here again!" A boy near him shouted, "It won't be long now, lady!" Two others bellowed out the familiar camp phrase, "They'll be coming up the river when they come!" Somebody else chanted the soldiers' favourite:

Let the Chinese and Dyaks and the Dutchmen fight about it,
They can have their Borneo. We can do without it. . . .

and all over the camp I could hear snatches of *Yankee Doodle Dandy*. I saw then that every British soldier within sight was smiling at me, and waggling thumbs up, and the Jap sentry nearby, instead of shouting and shaking his gun, just glared with gummy eyes and did nothing.

I remembered what Harry had told me. I walked on, thinking. None of the scraggy Indonesian chickens that usually fluttered about on the road between camps were visible to-day. Slowly I began to see the connection between the road without chickens, and the soldiers' camp-fires with. It had been chicken that I smelled all right!

The soldiers would not have been killing the chickens from which they occasionally got stray eggs if they did not have good reason to believe that peace had come, nor would the Nipponese sentries have been allowing them to build camp-fires. That smell of chicken cooking will always in my mind be the first harbinger of peace.

The next day the Nipponese sent us a double ration of rice and sago flour. We had already received our August rations, complained at their scarcity, and been answered, "There is no more rice in Kuching." When the double ration arrived we knew something had happened.

Meanwhile the Japanese officers denied the rapidly spreading rumours of peace, and the Japanese guards believed their officers, so convinced had they always been of their own invincibility.

. . . . A Douglas C-47 flew very low over camp. A door opened in the centre, and two blond airmen leaned far out,

waving and shouting and laughing at us. We had crowded
to the entrance of the camp when we heard the plane
flying low, and now we waved back, jumping and
cheering, not knowing what was happening, but sure that it
was good.

The C-47 circled camp and returned, swooping even
lower as she neared us. The centre door opened again, the
men were leaning out waving, and suddenly, to our
delight, out of the door came a long torpedo-shaped
object. It shot downward; then, just before reaching the
ground, a parachute unfurled above it, and the torpedo
settled softly to the ground, between the entrance gates of
our camp. The thirty-four kids fell upon it. On the six-foot
torpedo was printed the word BREAD.

People have asked me since if we raced for this first
bundle of food, and tore it open and fought over it. Such
an action would have horrified us. We might have felt like
it, but we could not have done it. Mean tricks we had
learned in captivity, but an equal division of rations had
become sacred.

In any case, half-starved though we were, that first
parachute meant so much more to us than food that we
were not even tempted. Even more than our bodies, our
hearts had starved—for contact with our own people, for
a touch of the friendly hand. The word on that parachute
spelled *Bread,* but it meant, *You Are Not Forgotten.* The
greatest satisfaction we could get from its contents was
ours already.

Twenty-five parachutes descended that day. At first the
Japanese held us back; but by the time the planes had left
we had raced forward and started salvaging the parachutes
themselves, which we saw would be priceless for shirts
and pants. Some of those first parachutes—made speedily
into pants—were walking around on children and mothers
within twenty-four hours.

In addition to bread we received that day boxes
containing tinned tongue, ham, rabbit, milk, butter,
chocolate, biscuits, sugar, custard powder, soap, toilet
paper, Red Cross medical supplies and a little clothing.

During all this people continued to go mad. George leaped into the air like a puppy, women jumped and waved and screamed, tears flowed, noses were blown, hearts pounded, laughter and cheers poured out. All but myself; I went very silent, in a cold sweat, with an asinine smile, and no words for my feelings. I could only nod my head, yes, yes, in agreement with everyone that this was the greatest moment of *our* war.

. . . While awaiting liberation I was requested by Colonel King, the English medical officer who had been in charge of the British soldiers' camp during captivity, to visit their camp. If I was going to write, he said, I must know the truth. So Harry, two other civilians, and I accompanied Colonel King into camp the next day.

When I entered the soldiers' compound I was instantly struck by its utter barrenness compared to our own. It was an eroded brown wasteland crossed by washed-out gullies with row after row of withered palm-leaf huts with ragged, limping men coming from them.

. . . . Before Colonel King took me through the sick huts he asked me if I had a strong stomach for shocking sights. I said that I hoped I had. When I saw the conditions I was not concerned about my stomach, which had stood up to everything for years, but I was disturbed at the distress which I feared I might cause the patients. They were almost naked, covered with ulcers, and in such a state that I felt they would resent my intrusion, if they had strength for resentment. If they had any active wish now, it must be to crawl away from all eyes and die.

But I found I was wrong. Great as their physical misery was, their boredom was even greater, and this I could relieve. For they, like the stronger men in camp, were avid for sight, sound or smell of a woman. Soon we all talked together, and examined ailments together; soon we could scarcely move through the huts for patients describing their symptoms and showing their wounds. Finding that they liked seeing me helped me to move naturally amongst sights which Colonel King had properly described as shocking.

The bodies of all the men were shrunken from starvation, with the bones showing like skeletons, the skin dried and shrivelled, while the skulls with their deep-set eyes seemed unnaturally large.

All patients had ulcers caused by malnutrition and lack of circulation, many covering an entire leg, chest, arm or thigh. Many had a gangrenous condition of feet, hands, testicles. Some had a condition of the fingers and toes which can only be described as dissolving away; the tips of the digits were open and bloody and they seemed to be bleeding off.

I was told that of two thousand British soldiers who had been brought to Kuching from Singapore as prisoners, seven hundred and fifty now survived. Of this number six hundred and fifty were ill, and not thirty men in the whole camp remained strong enough to form a working party.

Four years before, these soldiers had been fittest of the fit. This was what a war fought in captivity had done for them. I was glad I had seen them. I would never forget them. I wished that anyone who spoke philosophically of "the next war" could see them.

Agnes Newton Keith

Manchuria

The first thing we saw was a big yard around which were sheds made of concrete.

The yard was empty and there was nothing in the sheds. Where were the prisoners?

"They're at work," Matsuda replied with a great display of nonchalance.

"Well, will you please take us to where they are working?"

"Oh, that's quite impossible. It's too far."

"Perhaps we can at least see their representatives?"

"Na. Na. An unforeseen hindrance."

Not for the first time in my career as a delegate of the International Committee of the Red Cross I felt anger rising hot in my breast. But I had to keep calm. An unpleasant incident on this very first "visit" might create difficulties better avoided. And incidentally the colonel was taking us towards a building which appeared occupied.

"And here is our magnificent hospital," he announced with one foot on its first step.

At the top of the steps stood four men in shirts and shorts at attention. They were the first prisoners of war I had seen in Manchuria.

As our procession mounted the steps after him the four men bowed low, their arms kept tightly to their sides, until their heads were almost on a level with their knees.

In a low voice, and making an effort not to show the indignation which was boiling up in me, I said:

"That's not the manner in which soldiers of an Occidental army salute."

"No, it's the Japanese manner," replied Colonel Matsuda with his eternal and impenetrable smile.

We were taken along a corridor with sick-rooms on either side. Standing by the wall near each door were three or four sick prisoners, all of whom bowed low as we approached. Those prisoners who were unable to rise were seated tailor-fashion on their beds, their arms crossed on their chests, and they too bowed as low as their bandages, wounds or mutilations would permit. When the last Japanese officer had passed they resumed the upright position, their eyes raised fixedly to the ceiling. Never once did their eyes meet ours.

The palms of my hands were wet and Margherita was as white as a sheet. This was indescribably horrible. Matsuda tried to lead us on but I stopped before a group of four prisoners, three British and an American.

"Is there a doctor amongst you?" I asked, trying to keep my voice firm and not betray the emotion I felt.

No one answered, and the Japanese behind me kept silent.

I stood directly in front of a big fellow who towered above me. I could see only his chin and his stretched neck as he looked up at the ceiling. Not a muscle stirred and I repeated my question. There was still no reply and I turned grimly to Matsuda.

"Why doesn't he reply?" I asked. "Isn't he allowed to?"

The Japanese were stupefied at my audacity, but Matsuda was evidently unwilling to risk an unpleasant incident and he indicated one of the men standing against the wall with the others.

"This Australian is a doctor," he said.

I went towards my Australian colleague with outstretched hand. I had to overcome a lump in my throat to get out the banal words:

"How do you do?"

The man lowered his eyes, but not to me. It was at Matsuda he looked. It was the colonel's permission he sought. After several seconds which seemed incredibly long his hand slowly rose to mine. I took it and shook it warmly, trying to convey to him all the emotion and sympathy I felt and hoping he would afterwards communicate them to his comrades.

I told him as briefly as possible who I was and why I had come and I tried to get into conversation with him. He replied slowly and in monosyllables and each time before he spoke I could see that he silently sought the approval of Matsuda over my head.

"Will you accompany me on a tour of the wards?" I asked finally.

This time Matsuda intervened.

"No," he said. "A Japanese doctor will accompany you."

I felt it was impossible to insist further, and I let go the man's trembling hand which stiffened back to the attention against his side whilst his eyes rose again to the ceiling.

. . . . We walked towards the grey house, which was less like a prison than a miner's block in the Borinage. A long corridor went from end to end of it with doors on either side, seven on the left and eight on the right.

In surroundings which were so like the familiar surroundings we knew at home I had difficulty in realizing

that I was about to come face to face with the hero of
Corregidor, the defender of Singapore, the Governor of
the Dutch East Indies and twelve other soldiers of high
rank whose armies were still fighting everywhere in the
Pacific.

And suddenly a disturbing sight presented itself.

There they stood upright and motionless in the middle
of the room. I should not have been able to distinguish
their faces even if I had not involuntarily turned my head
away because they bowed low, their arms close to their
bodies, as soon as the sabre of Matsuda rapped on the
floor.

It seemed to me that the last man in the row refused to
submit to the humiliation and remained upright.

"General Wainright."

My emotion was so great that I could hardly utter the
words I had to speak. He maintained an icy reserve
towards the Japanese around me. Nothing, it seemed, had
broken his spirit. His voice was still vibrant as he replied
to the pitiful and absurdly abrupt questions which were all
I was allowed to ask him.

"How are you?"

"Not bad. My right hip is giving me rather less trouble
now."

"I am happy to tell you that your family is well and that
they received your last message safely."

"Thank you."

His face lit up at my last question.

"Have you any request to make?"

"Certainly. Can I make it now?"

"No," put in Matsuda at once. "It will have to be made
in writing to Tokyo."

The ghost of a sceptical smile passed over General
Wainright's lips.

The door was closed behind us. The interview was at an
end. It had not lasted two minutes.

I left the house almost hustled out by the Japanese, who
seemed to fear that I would shout the "goodbye" that
struggled for expression. I had been able to see them and

let them see me; that was all. But at least they now knew that we were aware of their place of detention.

Only prisoners who had been cut off from their world for three years and had seen nothing around them but yellow faces could appreciate the full significance of that pitiful result: two months' journey from Europe to China, via Egypt, Persia, Moscow and Siberia, for two minutes restricted conversation with one prisoner of war in Manchuria.

Marcel Junod

EXTERMINATION

There was another kind of prisoner whose one object was simply to survive. These were the men, women and children of every nationality whose crimes were political or racial: they had spoken or written or acted against the Nazis, or they happened to belong to one of the races marked down for organized extermination. They went to concentration camps, where they were kept just alive while their bodies or their labour served some useful purpose, and then, if they were not dead already, they were killed.

The Jews

As far as the Jews are concerned, I want to tell you quite frankly that they must be done away with in one way or another. The Führer said once, "Should united Jewry again succeed in provoking a world war, not only will the blood of the nations which have been forced into the war by them be shed, but the Jew will have found his end in Europe." I know that many measures carried out against the Jews in the Reich at present are being criticized. It is being done intentionally, as is obvious from the reports on the morale, to talk about cruelty, harshness, etc. Before I continue, I want to beg you to agree with me on the following formula: We will on principle have pity on the German people only and nobody else in the whole world. The others, too, had no pity on us. As an old National Socialist I must say this: This war would be only a partial success if the whole of Jewry should survive it, while we had shed our best blood in order to save Europe. My attitude towards the Jews will, therefore, be based only on the expectation that they must disappear. They must be done away with. I have entered into negotiations to have them deported to the East. A great discussion concerning that question will take place in Berlin in January, a discussion to which I am going to delegate the State Secretary, Dr. Bechler. It is to take place in the Reich Security Main Office with S.S. Lieutenant-General Heydrich. A great Jewish migration will begin, in any case.

But what should be done with the Jews? Do you think they will be settled down in the *Ostland* in villages? This is what we were told in Berlin: why all this bother? We can do nothing with them either in the *Ostland* or in the *Reichskommissariat*. So liquidate them yourselves.

Gentlemen, I must ask you to rid yourselves of all feeling of pity. We must annihilate the Jews, wherever we find them and wherever it is possible, in order to maintain the structure of the Reich as a whole.

> Hans Frank, Governor-General of Poland, Cracow,
> 16 December 1941

Auschwitz

I am twenty-nine years of age, from Lublin, Poland, where I was arrested on 19 May 1940 because I was a Jewess. I received no form of trial, was first kept at Lublin for a year and then was sent to Auschwitz, where I arrived in the autumn of 1941. My husband, who was not a Jew, was a lieutenant in the Polish Army and was also arrested. At the camp all our personal belongings were taken away. We had to leave our clothes behind and we were taken into a shower-bath. As my hair was cut very short I asked for a cloth to put round my head as I was freezing, and a

Kapo who was in charge of the shower-bath started to hit us very severely. The clothes we were given consisted of a long sort of coat and a silk blouse without any sleeves. We had already had a number tattooed on our arms. For a whole day we were left naked in that sort of shower-bath, and then at last we were led into Block No. 25. There were sort of cages in three parts in this block and very often we slept seven or eight in one part of this cage, getting one blanket issued amongst eight persons. There were no mattresses or palliasses. 3.30 a.m. was the normal time to get up in the morning.

What happened when you got up in the morning?—Everybody had to leave the block for a roll-call which lasted until eight or nine o'clock in the morning. We had to stand to attention in lines of five, and if we moved we were hit in the face or had to kneel down holding a heavy stone in our arms. For the first six weeks we did not work at all as we were in a sort of quarantine. Whilst I was fetching food one day I fell down and broke my leg, and was taken to the camp reception station, and was in hospital at Christmas 1941.

What happened on the day before Christmas Day?—There was a big selection in Block No. 4, the hospital block. Over three thousand Jewish women had to parade in this selection, which was under the charge of Hoessler. We had to leave our beds very quickly and stand quite naked to attention in front of him and the doctors, Enna and Koenig. All those who could not leave their beds had their numbers taken, and it was clear to us that they were condemned to death. Those whose bodies were not very nice looking or were too thin, or whom those gentlemen disliked for some reason or other, had their numbers taken, and it was clear what that meant. My number also was taken. We stayed in Block No. 4 for a night and the next day were taken to Block No. 18. About half-past five in the evening trucks arrived and we were loaded into them, quite naked like animals, and were driven to the crematorium.

When you reached the crematorium, what happened

there?—The whole truck was tipped over in the way they do it sometimes with potatoes or coal loads, and we were led into a room which gave me the impression of a shower-bath. There were towels hanging round, and sprays, and even mirrors. I cannot say how many were in the room altogether, because I was so terrified, nor do I know if the doors were closed. People were in tears; people were shouting at each other; people were hitting each other. There were healthy people, strong people, weak people and sick people, and suddenly I saw fumes coming in through a very small window at the top. I had to cough very violently, tears were streaming from my eyes, and I had a sort of feeling in my throat as if I would be asphyxiated. I could not even look at the others because each of us concentrated on what happened to herself.

What was the next thing you remember?—At that moment I heard my name called. I had not the strength to answer it, but I raised my arm. Then I felt someone take me and throw me out from that room. Hoessler put a blanket round me and took me on a motor-cycle to the hospital, where I stayed six weeks. As the result of the gas I had still, quite frequently, headaches and heart trouble, and whenever I went into the fresh air my eyes were filled with tears. I was subsequently taken to the political department and apparently I had been taken out of the gas chamber because I had come from a prison in Lublin, which seemed to make a difference, and, apart from that, my husband was a Polish officer.

After you came out of hospital, how were you employed?—In the beginning I was employed in cleaning the room of the *Blockälteste* and in washing in the laundry. Later on I was employed on latrine fatigues. With my own hands I had to clean whatever was in the latrines and there were no brooms or brushes or any sort of cleaning material given to me. It was considered a good job because sometimes we would warm ourselves near the stove, or even wash a shirt. Our food consisted of coffee in the morning, half a litre of vegetable soup for lunch,

sometimes only a quarter, and in the evening a ration of
bread, sometimes something with it, other times without,
and sometimes coffee. For a few days I worked in the
kitchen, but as the work was too hard for me I was put on
a working party called "Kanda", which consisted of
sorting out the belongings which came from other people
who went to the crematorium. I got this through the
influence of the *Blockälteste* with whom I was working
previously.

Dachau

I, Franz Blaha, being duly sworn, depose and state as
follows:

I was sent as a prisoner to the Dachau Concentration
Camp in April 1941, and remained there until the
liberation of the camp in April 1945. Until July 1941 I
worked in a Punishment Company. After that I was sent
to the hospital and subjected to the experiments in typhoid
being conducted by Dr. Mürmelstadt. After that I was to
be made the subject of an experimental operation, and
only succeeded in avoiding this by admitting that I was a
physician. If this had been known before I would have
suffered, because intellectuals were treated very harshly in
the Punishment Company. In October 1941 I was sent to
work in the herb plantation, and later in the laboratory for
processing herbs. In June 1942 I was taken into the
hospital as a surgeon. Shortly afterwards I was directed to
conduct a stomach operation on twenty healthy prisoners.
Because I would not do this I was put in the autopsy
room, where I stayed until April 1945. While there I
performed approximately seven thousand autopsies. In all,
twelve thousand autopsies were performed under my
direction.

From mid-1941 to the end of 1942 some five hundred
operations on healthy prisoners were performed. These
were for the instruction of the S.S. medical students and
doctors and included operations on the stomach, gall
bladder, spleen and throat. These were performed by

students and doctors of only two years' training, although they were very dangerous and difficult. Ordinarily they would not have been done except by surgeons with at least four years' surgical practice. Many prisoners died on the operating table and many others from later complications. I performed autopsies on all these bodies. The doctors who supervised these operations were Lang, Mürmelstadt, Wolter, Ramsauer and Kahr. *Standartenführer* Dr. Lolling frequently witnessed these operations.

During my time at Dachau I was familiar with many kinds of medical experiments carried on there with human victims. These persons were never volunteers but were forced to submit to such acts. Malaria experiments on about twelve hundred people were conducted by Dr. Klaus Schilling between 1941 and 1945. Schilling was personally asked by Himmler to conduct these experiments. The victims were either bitten by mosquitoes or given injections of malaria sporozoites taken from mosquitoes. Different kinds of treatment were applied, including quinine, pyrifer, neosalvarsan, antipyrin, pyramidon and a drug called 2516 Behring. I performed autopsies on bodies of people who died from these malaria experiments. Thirty to forty died from the malaria itself. Three to four hundred died later from diseases which proved fatal because of the physical condition resulting from the malaria attacks. In addition there were deaths resulting from poisoning due to overdoses of neosalvarsan and pyramidon. Dr. Schilling was present at the time of my autopsies on the bodies of his patients.

In 1942 and 1943 experiments on human beings were conducted by Dr. Sigismund Rascher to determine the effects of changing air pressure. As many as twenty-five persons were put at one time into a specially-constructed van in which pressure could be increased or decreased as required. The purpose was to find out the effects of high altitude and of rapid parachute descents on human beings. Through a window in the van I have seen the people lying on the floor of the van. Most of the prisoners who were made use of died as a result of these experiments, from internal haemorrhages of the lungs or brain. The rest coughed blood when taken out. It was my job to take the bodies out and to send the internal organs to Munich for study as soon as they were found to be dead. About four hundred to five hundred prisoners were experimented on. Those not dead were sent to invalid blocks and liquidated shortly afterwards. Only a few escaped.

Rascher also conducted experiments on the effect of cold water on human beings. This was done to find a way for reviving aviators who had fallen into the ocean. The subject was placed in ice-cold water and kept there until he was unconscious. Blood was taken from his neck and tested each time his body temperature dropped one degree. This drop was determined by a rectal thermometer. Urine was also periodically tested. Some men lasted as long as twenty-four to thirty-six hours. The lowest body temperature reached was nineteen degrees C., but most men died at twenty-five degrees C., or twenty-six degrees C. When the men were removed from the ice water attempts were made to revive them by artificial warmth from the sun, from hot water, from electrotherapy or by animal warmth. For this last experiment prostitutes were used and the body of the unconscious man was placed between the bodies of two women. Himmler was present at one such experiment. I could see him from one of the windows in the street between the blocks. I have personally been present at some of the cold-water experiments when Rascher was absent, and I have seen notes and diagrams on them in Rascher's laboratory. About three hundred persons were used in these experiments. The majority died. Of those who lived many became mentally deranged. Those not killed were sent to invalid blocks and were killed, just as were the victims of the air-pressure experiments. I only know two who survived—a Jugoslav and a Pole, both of whom have become mental cases.

Liver-puncture experiments were performed by Dr. Brachtl on healthy people, and on people who had diseases of the stomach and gall bladder. For this purpose a needle was jabbed into the liver of a person and a small piece of liver was extracted. No anaesthetic was used. The experiment is very painful and often had serious results, as the stomach or large blood vessels were often punctured and haemorrhage resulted. Many persons died of these tests, for which Polish, Russian, Czech and German prisoners were employed. Altogether these experiments were conducted on about 175 people.

Phlegmone experiments were conducted by Dr. Schütz, Dr. Babor, Dr. Kieselwetter and Professor Lauer. Forty healthy men were used at a time, of whom twenty were given intra-muscular, and twenty intravenous, injections of pus from diseased persons. All treatment was forbidden for three days, by which time serious inflammation and in many cases general blood poisoning had occurred. Then each group was divided again into groups of ten. Half were given chemical treatment with liquid and special pills every ten minutes for twenty-four hours. The rest were treated with sulphanamide and surgery. In some cases all of the limbs were amputated. My autopsy also showed that the chemical treatment had been harmful and had even caused perforations of the stomach wall. For these experiments Polish, Czech and Dutch priests were ordinarily used. Pain was intense in such experiments. Most of the six hundred to eight hundred persons who were used finally died. Most of the others became permanent invalids and were later killed.

In the autumn of 1944 there were sixty to eighty persons who were subjected to salt-water experiments. They were locked in a room and for five days were given nothing to swallow but salt water. During this time their urine, blood and excrement were tested. None of these prisoners died, possibly because they received smuggled food from other prisoners. Hungarians and gypsies were used for these experiments.

It was common practice to remove the skin from dead prisoners. I was commanded to do this on many occasions. Dr. Rascher and Dr. Wolter in particular asked for this human skin from human backs and chests. It was

chemically treated and placed in the sun to dry. After that
it was cut into various sizes for use as saddles, riding
breeches, gloves, house slippers and ladies' handbags.
Tattooed skin was especially valued by S.S. men.
Russians, Poles and other inmates were used in this way,
but it was forbidden to cut out the skin of a German. This
skin had to be from healthy prisoners and free from
defects. Sometimes we did not have enough bodies with
good skin and Rascher would say, "All right, you will get
the bodies." The next day we would receive twenty or
thirty bodies of young people. They would have been shot
in the neck or struck on the head so that the skin would be
uninjured. Also we frequently got requests for the skulls
or skeletons of prisoners. In those cases we boiled the
skull or the body. Then the soft parts were removed and
the bones were bleached and dried and reassembled. In
the case of skulls it was important to have a good set of
teeth. When we got an order for skulls from Oranienburg
the S.S. men would say, "We will try to get you some
with good teeth." So it was dangerous to have a good skin
or good teeth.

Transports arrived frequently in Dachau from Studthof,
Belsen, Auschwitz, Mauthausen and other camps. Many
of these were ten to fourteen days on the way without
water or food. On one transport, which arrived in
November 1942, I found evidence of cannibalism. The
living persons had eaten the flesh from the dead bodies.
Another transport arrived from Compiègne in France.
Professor Limousin of Clermont-Ferrand, who was later
my assistant, told me that there had been two thousand
persons on this transport when it started. There was food
available but no water. Eight hundred died on the way and
were thrown out. When it arrived after twelve days more
than five hundred persons were dead on the train. Of the
remainder, most died shortly after arrival. I investigated
this transport because the International Red Cross
complained, and the S.S. men wanted a report that the
deaths had been caused by fighting and rioting on the way.
I dissected a number of bodies and found that they had

died from suffocation and lack of water; it was mid-summer and a hundred and twenty people had been packed into each car.

In 1941 and 1942 we had in the camp what we called invalid transports. These were made up of people who were sick or for some reason incapable of working. We called them *Himmelfahrt* Commandos. About a hundred or a hundred and twenty were ordered each week to go to the shower baths. There, four people gave injections of phenol evipan, or benzine, which soon caused death. After 1943 these invalids were sent to other camps for liquidation. I known that they were killed because I saw the records, and they were marked with a cross and the date that they left, which was the way that deaths were ordinarily recorded. This was shown both on the card index of the Camp Dachau and the records in the town of Dachau. One thousand to two thousand went away every three months, so there were about five thousand sent to death in 1943, and the same in 1944. In April 1945, a Jewish transport was loaded at Dachau and was left standing on the railroad siding. The station was destroyed by bombing, and they could not leave. So they were just left there to die of starvation. They were not allowed to get off. When the camp was liberated they were all dead.

Many executions by gas or shooting or injections took place in the camp itself. The gas chamber was completed in 1944, and I was called by Dr. Rascher to examine the first victims. Of the eight or nine persons in the chamber there were three still alive, and the remainder appeared to be dead. Their eyes were red and their faces were swollen. Many prisoners were later killed in this way. Afterwards they were removed to the crematorium, where I had to examine their teeth for gold. Teeth containing gold were extracted. Many prisoners who were sick were killed by injections while in hospital. Some prisoners killed in the hospital came through to the autopsy room with no name or number on the tag which was usually tied to their big toe. Instead the tag said, "Do not dissect."

I performed autopsies on some of these and found that

they were perfectly healthy, but had died from injections. Sometimes prisoners were killed only because they had dysentery or vomited, and gave the nurses too much trouble. Mental patients were liquidated by being led to the gas chamber and injected there or shot. Shooting was a common method of execution. Prisoners would be shot just outside the crematorium and carried in. I have seen people pushed into the ovens while they were still breathing and making sounds, although if they were too much alive they were usually hit on the head first.

The principal executions about which I know from having examined the victims, or supervised such examinations, are as follows: In 1942 there were five thousand to six thousand Russians held in a separate camp inside Dachau. They were taken on foot to the Military Rifle Range near the camp in groups of five hundred or six hundred and shot. These groups left the camp about three times a week. At night we used to go out to bring the bodies back in carts and then examine them. In February 1944, about forty Russian students arrived from Moosburg. I knew a few of the boys in the hospital. I examined them after they were shot outside the crematorium. In September 1944 a group of ninety-four high-ranking Russians were shot, including two military doctors who had been working with me in the hospital. I examined their bodies. In April 1945, a number of prominent people who had been kept in the bunker were shot. They included two French generals, whose names I cannot remember, but I recognized them from their uniform. I examined them, after they were shot. In 1944 and 1945 a number of women were killed by hanging, shooting and injections. I examined them and found that in many cases they were pregnant. In 1945, just before the camp was liberated, all *Nacht und Nebel* prisoners were executed. These were prisoners who were forbidden to have any contact with the outside world. They were kept in a special enclosure and were not allowed to send or receive any mail. There were thirty or forty, many of whom were sick. These were carried to the crematorium on stretchers. I examined them and found they had all been shot in the neck.

From 1941 on, the camp became more and more overcrowded. In 1943 the hospital for prisoners was already overcrowded. In 1944 and in 1945 it was impossible to maintain any sort of sanitary condition. Rooms, which held three hundred or four hundred persons in 1942, were filled with a thousand in 1943, and in the first quarter of 1945 with two thousand or more. The rooms could not be cleaned because they were too crowded, and there was no cleaning material. Baths were available only once a month. Latrine facilities were completely inadequate. Medicine was almost non-existent. But I found, after the camp was liberated, that there was plenty of medicine in the S.S. hospital for all the camps, if it had been given to us for use.

New arrivals at the camp were lined up out of doors for hours at a time. Sometimes they stood there from morning until night. It did not matter whether this was in the winter or in the summer. This occurred all through 1943, 1944 and the first quarter of 1945. I could see these formations from the window of the autopsy room. Many of the people who had to stand in the cold in this way became ill from pneumonia and died. I had several acquaintances who were killed in this manner during 1944 and 1945. In October 1944 a transport of Hungarians brought spotted fever into the camp, and an epidemic began. I examined many of the corpses from this transport and reported the situation to Dr. Hintermayer, but was forbidden, on penalty of being shot, to mention that there was an epidemic in the camp. He said that it was sabotage, and that I was trying to have the camp quarantined so that the prisoners would not have to work in the armaments industry. No preventive measure were taken at all. New healthy arrivals were put into blocks where an epidemic was already present. Infected persons were also put into these blocks. So the thirteenth block, for instance, died out completely three times. Only at Christmas, when the epidemic spread into the S.S. camp, was a quarantine established. Nevertheless, transports continued to arrive.

We had two to three hundred new typhus cases and a hundred deaths caused by typhus each day. In all, we had twenty-eight thousand cases and fifteen thousand deaths. In addition to those that died from the disease, my autopsies showed that many deaths were caused solely by malnutrition. Such deaths occurred in all the years from 1941 to 1945. They were mostly Italians, Russians and Frenchmen. These people were just starved to death. At the time of death they weighed fifty to sixty pounds. Autopsies showed their internal organs had often shrunk to one-third of their actual size.

The facts stated above are true: This declaration is made by me voluntarily and without compulsion. After reading over the statement I have signed and executed it at Nuremberg, Germany, this 9th day of January 1946.

Dr. Franz Blaha

The Perfectionist

The overhauling of vans by groups D and C is finished. While the vans in the first series can also be put into action if the weather is not too bad, the vans of the second series (Saurer) stop completely in rainy weather. If it has rained, for instance, for only one half-hour, the van cannot be used, because it simply skids away. It can only be used in absolutely dry weather. It is now merely a question of whether the van can be used only when it stands at the place of execution. First, the van has to be brought to that place, which is possible only in good weather. The place of execution is usually ten to fifteen kilometres away from the highway and is difficult of access because of its location; in damp or wet weather it is not accessible at all. If the persons to be executed are driven or led to that place, then they realize immediately what is going on and get restless, which is to be avoided as far as possible. There is only one way left; to load them at the collecting point and to drive them to the spot.

I ordered the vans of group D to be camouflaged as

house-trailers by putting one set of window shutters on each side of the small van and two on each side of the larger vans, such as one often sees on farmhouses in the country. The vans became so well-known that not only the authorities but also the civilian population called the van "death van" as soon as one of the vehicles appeared. It is my opinion the van cannot be kept secret for any length of time, not even camouflaged.

Because of the rough terrain and the indescribable road and highway conditions, the caulkings and rivets loosen in the course of time. I was asked if in such cases the vans should not be brought to Berlin for repairs. Transportation to Berlin would be much too expensive and would demand too much fuel. In order to save these expenses I ordered them to have the smaller leaks soldered. . . . Besides that I ordered that during application of gas all the men were to be kept as far away from the vans as possible, so that they should not suffer damage to their health by the gas which eventually would escape. I should like to take this opportunity to bring the following to your attention: After the application of gas several commands have had the unloading done by their own men. I brought to the attention of the commander of these S.K. concerned the immense psychological injuries, and damage to their health which that work can have for those men, even if not immediately, at least later on. The men complained to me about headaches which appeared after each unloading. Nevertheless they do not want to change the orders, because they are afraid prisoners called for that work could use an opportune moment to flee. To protect the men from those risks, I request orders be issued accordingly.

The application of gas is not usually undertaken correctly. In order to come to an end as fast as possible, the driver presses the accelerator to the fullest extent. By doing that the persons to be executed suffer death from suffocation, and not death by dozing off as was planned. My directions now have proved that by correct adjustment of the levers death comes faster, and the prisoners fall asleep peacefully. Distorted faces and excretions, such as could be seen before, are no longer noticed.

To-day I shall continue my journey to group B, where I can be reached with further news.

Dr. Becker, S.S. *Untersturmführer*

Sachsenhausen

These hangings take place on the parade ground, and everyone has to look on. Our Norwegian comrades have seen any number of them. Nor are these executions lacking in their "heroic episodes". A German was hanged for attempting to escape. He talked of freedom on the scaffold, freedom for the German people which would soon come. He turned to the Commandant, who attends the executions, and calmly said, Well, it was his turn now, before long it would be the Commandant's. When the rope was put round his neck, he raised his hand and waved and smiled to his comrades for the last time. It must be a good deal worse to look on when the unhappy man or men scream, weep and struggle, Once there were seven hanged at the same time.

Odd Nansen

Solitary Confinement

Sunday, 20 February 1944

It is Bella's birthday to-day, I have never been so heavy-hearted as in this morning hour. The whole weight of my many failures towards Bella crushes me. I have been mean, indifferent and unkind towards her—she who is the pearl of my life. What is the good of regretting it now? It is deeds which count. To-day I feel a great need to pray. I can't manage all this alone. I will pray when the bells of Holy Trinity ring. I will pray to be allowed to live and fulfil the law of life and love at Bella's side. Oh Bella! I long for you. My heart is more tender towards you than my back is from the whipping at Victoria Terrasse.

Believe me, Bella, I write this in an hour which is full of pain and terrors.

The sun is shining upon a beautiful Norwegian winter day. Here at 19 M* are over three hundred good Norwegians imprisoned because they did their duty towards their country. Well—Nazism will never take root in Norway. That is worth great sacrifice. Seen in this light the fate of the individual is not worth mentioning. But this is not *London News.*** It is my diary which comforts and strengthens me. . . . One summer day when Norway is once again a free country Bella and I will walk in the woods and sing: "What is the country where you live called?" Happiness!! Oh God, I beg for this. Bella! A new bond goes between us from 19 Mollergaten to Grini. We suffer for our cause and are comrades in what is for us a new sense of the word.

Comrade Bella.

We will live and love.

                                                    Peter Moen

* The Gestapo prison in Oslo where Moen, chief of the whole Norwegian underground press, was put in solitary confinement. On his deportation to Germany in September 1944 he lost his life when the ship struck a mine. His diary, written on toilet paper with a tack, was discovered after the war (Ed.)

** The best-known of the clandestine newspapers of the Norwegian resistance movement (Ed.)

6

THE ORDEAL OF THE CITIES:
BOMBS ON GERMANY —
V-WEAPONS ON ENGLAND

While German bombs were falling on England in 1940, the Royal Air Force had already begun to attack Germany's war industries and domestic morale. Until the spring of 1942 these raids achieved little, but during the same year the introduction of radar position-finding devices allowed really accurate night bombing for the first time, mainly on the Ruhr.

Woe to the One who Loses

THE worst part of the raids for me, however, was being separated from my children. Were they all right; and if I were killed what would happen to them? I did not tell Heiner of these anxieties. Perhaps I should have done but I felt it was a personal matter. We often talked about the war and the bombing of England and how long they would last out.

"Do you think they can stand much more?" I asked him

one night. It was just after the bombing of Coventry. "The whole town has gone . . . a town with two hundred thousand people in it! I should die if I thought that Wolfgang and Klaus would ever have to go through the things those English children must have suffered."

"If you start thinking that way in a war you will end up by committing suicide," he told me. "You've got to be hard, and think: 'It's the enemy or me and the sooner they give in the better!' "

"That's a frightful creed," I protested.

"War is a frightful thing, and it's no use thinking about it too much when you are in the midst of one. I'm glad for that reason that I shall never be called up. I might start thinking when I was in a plane and be too paralyzed to drop the bombs."

"But surely we needn't bomb civilians as we did at Coventry."

"It's easier said than done. Targets are close together sometimes. Bombs fall where they are not meant to."

I was silent.

"Coventry was a reprisal raid, anyway. For the bombing of our towns," he added.

"I wonder who started first?" I wanted to know.

"I'll tell you after the war. No one knows the truth while it is going on," he told me.

"But will you know the truth even after the war?"

"Oh, yes," laughed Heiner. "We'll know then. The man who starts a war is the one who loses it!"

"Which means England will be blamed for starting the air-raids on civilians?" I asked.

"Don't forget Hitler's speech in September when he threatened: 'If they attack our cities we will destroy theirs.' I'm afraid these air-raids are now such a mix-up of attack and counter-attack that one can never fix the blame fairly and squarely. This is now a total war, and woe to the one who loses it. It will be total destruction."

                                        Else Wendel, housewife

Security

Empty your pockets, Tom, Dick and Harry,
Strip your identity; leave it behind.
Lawyer, garage-hand, grocer, don't tarry
With your own country, your own kind.

Leave all your letters. Suburb and township,
Green fen and grocery, slip-way and bay,
Hot-spring and prairie, smoke stack and coal tip,
Leave in our keeping while you're away.

Tom, Dick and Harry, plain names and numbers,
Pilot, observer, and gunner depart.
Their personal litter only encumbers
Somebody's head, somebody's heart.

John Pudney

Bombers from Britain

If you live in Sussex or Kent nowadays (or I suppose in a good many other counties besides), you know before getting out of bed and pulling aside the blackout if it's a nice day. A clear dawn has a new clarion—the deep and throbbing roar of hundreds of planes, outward bound. They may be sailing high towards the coast, flashing or shining in the light of the sun that's not yet up over the horizon. Sometimes they look white and as graceful as gulls against the blue; at others they look black and sinister as they come and go between the clouds. But the impressive thing—the thing that makes land-girls pause in their stringing of the hopfields and makes conductors of country buses lean out and look up from their platforms—the impressive thing is the numbers. Never in the Battle of Britain, in the days when the Luftwaffe was beaten over these fields and woods, did the Germans send over such vast fleets. Never were their bombers four-engined monsters, such as these of the Americans which go out in their scores and hundreds. Sometimes you will see one big formation coming, say from the north, others from the north-east, others from the west, all heading for a common rendezvous. Their courses often converge, and a stranger to the scene might hold his breath seeing the approach of disaster as the formations close in. At the moment when it looks as if they must collide, he sees with relief that they're at different heights; and they make a brief, fascinating cross-over pattern and sail on as easily as an express train flies over complicated points. As their roar fades with them, another rises until things on the kitchen mantelshelf tinkle and rattle as they catch the vibration. Up over the beechwoods on the hill, the leading formation of a second wave of heavies appears, followed by others and still others. Some days it will go on like this pretty well all day—not all heavies, of course, but twin-engined bombers of various kinds, fighter-bombers and fighters. There are always lots of Marauders, packed together, flying very fast—reminding one of those sudden clouds of migrating birds which appear from nowhere and as quickly vanish. They have an appointment abroad, and they're keeping it,

Pat Smithers

The Last Trip

The sense of apprehension, normally dissolved as soon as they were airborne, was still with him. The last trip was always the worst. When you began a tour, risks were part of it, inevitable, natural. In retrospect, the risks seemed suicidal. His determination was worn and thinned like an old chisel. At the beginning, you did not care: you were full of expectation. Now expectation had hardened into experience. So many of your friends were dead. Sometimes their faces laughed at you from the bottom of a tankard at a mess party, momentarily. They were dead and you were alive: and, on this last trip, there was so much to lose.

. . . ."PORT GO!"

His heart stopped.

At once he rolled into a steep dive to port, conscious only of a great surge of fear.

Out of the corner of his eye he saw tracer going over their starboard wing and, ahead of them, the splutter and wink of the self-exploding cannon shells.

He heard Taffy's voice exultant, hysterical. "Got you, you bastard, got you!"

Then the voice was cut off.

Flames were coming in puffs from the cowling of the starboard outer engine. Every moment they became thicker, feeding on the slipstream.

"Feather the starboard outer," he shouted to the second dickey.

. . . . Jesperson turned towards him. He put his hands to his ears and shook his head.

"Feather it, you bloody fool!"

He stabbed his finger towards the feathering button. Was the man deaf, crazy? The fire was licking and leaping round the outboard motor. He cut back on the throttle and switched off the master fuel cock.

The engineer leaned over Jesperson and pressed the feathering button. With immense relief he watched the propeller steadily stopping. As it slowed the flames subsided. Looking at his instruments, he saw the aircraft was commencing to spiral and the speed was building up. Quickly he corrected, taking the load off his foot with the rudder trim. When he looked up again, the flames were out.

Jesperson was pointing to his ears.

"What is it?" Peter said. He flicked the microphone switch. "What is it?"

He could not hear himself speak. His plug must be out. No wonder Jesperson could not hear him. He felt for the plug. It was firmly home. Again he flicked the mike switch. Silence. The intercom was dead. He was isolated, walled in by the engine noise.

He signalled "W-W-W" on the call light.

He was alone in a nightmare world of possible emergencies.

He pressed the emergency switch on his R/T set. Still the roaring, lonely silence, swirling round him like a sea. He pressed each switch in turn on the 1196. Nothing.

He began to sweat.

Finding himself thirty degrees off course, he swung the aircraft fiercely round. Jesperson leaned towards him, took off his oxygen mask and shouted. Peter shook his head. He could not hear a thing. Then, faintly above the noise of the motors, came the words: "My helmet is u/s."

Rage swept over him. He felt he could take Jesperson by the throat. The dim, stupid fool, sprawled over half the cockpit, unable to feather an engine, telling me his blasted helmet is u/s when nobody in the kite can hear a thing. As if his helmet mattered; or his head.

Suddenly, like a miracle, came the wireless operator's voice, crackling at first, then clear as a bell.

"Hallo, skipper; hallo, skipper; can you hear me?"

"Loud and clear."

Thank God. Good old Nobby.

"Bloody good show, Nobby," he said.

Then, after a moment's pause: "Everybody all right—rear-gunner?"

"O.K., skipper. I got him. He came so close I could have hit him with a stick."

"Good boy, Taff."

. . . . "I think we'll press on," said Peter. "What do you feel, nav?"

"Och, we might as well. We're past Denmark. We might as well get on with it."

"How about that turret, mid-upper?"

"It'll be O.K., skip. It works all right manually."

Thank God that was over.

Well, we shall not be in time to do any supporting. That's one consolation, anyway. And the bombing height's only fifteen thousand. We should just about maintain that height on three motors.

"Did you use the graviner, engineer?"

"No, skip. When we feathered the engine, the fire went out by itself."

"Was it a petrol fire?"

"Don't know."

I would not fancy being three thousand feet below everybody else. He remembered a daylight sortie when things went wrong and bombs began falling round them and an aircraft ahead had been sliced in half. Down spun the two halves; grotesque, down, down, twisting like a leaf, while everyone waited for the white flowering of the parachutes. But there was no flowering—only of flame as the aircraft hit the ground.

Searching port, searching starboard.

Having trimmed the aircraft to fly comfortably on three engines, Peter felt master of the situation once more, though the silhouette of the feathered propeller was a stark symbol of insecurity. Jesperson no longer aroused his irritation. The aircraft was obviously a good one. Already he had an affection for it. They had a fighter to their credit—first blood on his last trip—and no serious damage: and, surely, it was unlikely that on this one operation they would run into all the bad luck in the world. He looked at the silhouette of Jesperson's helmeted head and, behind him, Dicky Wagstaffe crouched by his instrument panel. What were they thinking, he wondered, two faceless enigmas.

Always he was searching for fighters.

They were well over the Baltic now—what about a trip to the Baltic for your summer holidays?—eating up time and distance. I shall be glad, he thought, when we're coming back. I could almost wish time suspended. I could wish to freeze this stream that carries us remorselessly towards the target glare.

Searching port, searching starboard.

It must have been an isolated fighter that attacked us. We have seen no flares, no sign of other aircraft being jumped on. How stupid it would have been if we had been flicked out of the sky as if by the idle movement of some divine finger. It has happened to so many. There would be no baling out over the sea if we really started burning.

. . . . On the approach to the target—long and straight from the west—Peter trimmed the aircraft as carefully as he could. This is the last time, he thought, and we will make a good job of it. We must drive the last nail home as sweetly and truly as the rest.

In the clear September night the target seemed to be much nearer than it really was. He settled down in his seat, bracing himself against the fear which began to rise in him, fear like a dark pool, deepening with every operation and threatening always to burst the barriers of his control. The firm contact of arm-rest and seat and throttle enabled him more easily to master it.

Ahead the attack, a fiery parasite upon the body of a city, began to writhe terribly into life, following the cycle he had seen so often. He saw the first flares, the target markers going down, the incendiaries budding, flowering, the short bright blossoming of the bombs. He watched the searchlights swinging and swaying, and the gradual growth of the flak-cloud.

Out of the corner of his eye he saw Jesperson gazing motionless, and the feathered propeller stark beyond him.

Nearer they flew, nearer.

Slowly the glare from the ground began to fill the cockpit with that strange sinister light. To and fro went the long knives. The turbulence of the air was growing. Every so often the aircraft shook itself like a small ship struck by a wave.

He felt the tension in his stomach. He braced himself in the seat, determined, at the same time, to keep his hands and feet relaxed.

"Bomb-doors open."

Carefully he held the heading.

Carefully he narrowed the focus of his mind down to his instruments, excluding everything that waited, on the edge, to shiver his concentration into fragments.

They were shocked and jolted by the air.

Now, like the beak of a giant bird, the flak rapped at

their egg-shell of metal and perspex. Imperiously the raven-fear came knocking, knocking. With all his strength he must guard the little crystal core of his will. Yet he kept hands and feet gentle. Relax, yet don't relax.

"An S turn to starboard, skipper," came Bron's voice, eager.

Then, in an agony of haste—"Enough, enough. On heading."

"On heading," said Peter, his voice coming calm from the turmoil of his mind.

"Steady"—lovingly—"steady."

The sky above was sown with fighter flares. The piercing searchlights were pale upon them. He saw a Lancaster blow up into a great slow balloon of fire.

Coax her through the turbulence. Ride her lightly through the rocking air. Keep that little pointing needle central, quite central.

"Steady, steady."

How much longer.

It can't be much longer.

This is the last time, the last time.

He felt his control slipping little by little, as a handful of dry sand diminishes the more quickly the tighter it is grasped.

"Bombs gone."

Henry Archer and Edward Pine

Bombs Gone

Mr. Wolter was becoming nervous. "Have you heard?" he asked one morning, "they are dropping bombs on West Berlin now on a bigger scale. It's serious. I had a real taste of it last night," he added. "They dropped bombs on the block of flats in the Bayerischer Platz. It smashed all our windows and shook the whole house. We were in the cellar, of course. The women and children didn't take it too well. The noise and screaming, it was frightful." He looked up for sympathy.

"Yes," I agreed. "It's bad for the women and children."

"It was bad enough for me," added Mr. Wolter with a wry smile. "I had enough, I can tell you. I couldn't sit down there scared to death with people screaming all round me. I had to go out and do something. I went along to the Bayerischer Platz. It was the most frightful sight."

He had got up now and was pacing about on his blue carpet. I had never seen him moved in this way before. Enthusiastic, optimistic, bitter and confident. I had seen all that in my boss, but not this pity and horror.

"It's easy to say, it was just a rubble heap, and leave it at that. But to me, and I passed the place every day, you know, it was the end of the most sumptuous and beautiful block of flats in Berlin. When I went there in the middle of last night it was still burning."

"And the tenants?" I interrupted.

"Dead! Practically all of them, I should say. They can't have lived through that heat. We worked like niggers for the rest of the night trying to dig an entrance to the cellars, but when I left to come to the office this morning they still hadn't got through. They now have tractors and cranes on the job. When they do reach the cellars they will only find burned bodies, I think."

He was still walking nervously up and down. It took him some time to get down to work that morning. This was the first time he had seen bombing in his part of the town. It changed him in a night.

At lunch-time I went along to the Bayerischer Platz to see for myself. There were hundreds of sightseers, all people, who like me, had come to make sure that the British had really got to the heart of luxury Berlin with their bombs.

"Now we can call him 'Meyer'," said a man's voice beside me. He referred, of course, to Goering's boasts in 1939 that Berlin should never be bombed while he was in charge; if it was we could call him Meyer. A woman next to the man plucked at his sleeve and pulled him away. It was an unwise thing to say aloud in a crowd.

Suddenly the cranes stopped working. A murmur went through the crowd. "They've cleared the entrance . . . they are going in now. . . ." We stood on tiptoe, staring in horror and fascination. There was something moving, I could see at the entrance of the luxury block, something being brought out. A woman screamed sharply three times. It was the same awful scream that I heard from women later on when the Russians came.

"What's happening? What has she seen?" the people round kept asking. We surged forward to look. Police appeared and pressed us back. "Move on, now," they said. "This is no sight to stare at. You'll read about it soon enough in the papers."

Actually we didn't read the truth in the papers. What had happened in the flats was too terrible to be printed. The tenants had not burned but scalded to death. The water pipes of the central heating system had burst, and boiling water had poured into the air-raid cellar. They found women with their arms stretched out holding their children above their heads as they died. They found people crouched on the top of piles of chairs and tables as they clambered to escape the rising, boiling water. No wonder they didn't print these facts at the time. There were hundreds of other flats similarly constructed in Berlin. Few people would have sought shelter in those cellars had they known what might happen.

Else Wendel, housewife

The Shelters

This time it was in the Berlin streets. I stood in the centre of Berlin, in the Friedrichstrasse, looking in a shop window for some things I had come up from Kladow to buy. The sirens suddenly screamed out over the city. Immediately there was a dead silence all round. Shops closed, business people and gossiping women stopped talking. Then they began to run through the street. Women with children in their arms, or pushing prams; young children quite alone; old people appeared from the houses with blankets and bags. All of them ran, and no one spoke at all. All had a look of blank fear on their faces. In a few moments the trams and buses were empty, and cars were left abandoned by the side of the street. In two or three minutes the whole life of a city seemed to have disappeared. I stood completely alone except for an air-raid warden I noticed in the porch of a house opposite. Like a scene in a film, it seemed. Then, very frightened myself, I went over to the warden.

"Where is the nearest shelter?' I asked quickly.

He replied by roaring with laughter. "Where do you come from?" I told him, from my house outside Berlin.

He nodded. "Don't you know the shelters are packed like sardines? Why, people queue up long before an alarm for they have a sort of instinct for trouble on the way. Mind you, it's well worth it. The shelters are quite bomb-proof—which is more than these cellars are." He jerked his head to indicate the mass of rubble on each side of him. "Not one soul was rescued from those cellars," he said morbidly. "Not one," the warden repeated. "So now you know why the public shelters will be full."

I began to get more and more frightened. "But where shall I go, then? Can I go into the cellar of this house behind you?"

"No," he said brusquely. "We are full too. The only thing you can do is to go back to the S-Bahn (Metropolitan railway) and find shelter there in one of the underground tunnels."

"Isn't that about the most dangerous place in Berlin? Surely they always aim at the main railways?"

He shrugged his shoulders. "It's the only advice I can give you. Now, hurry and get off the streets. The Tommies will be here in no time. *Heil Hitler!*" He turned away.

I ran myself now, this time to the S-Bahn, and into one of the underground tunnels. I shrank back as I tried to descend the stairs, the tunnel was packed completely full. People were standing on the long, wide platforms, tightly pressed against each other, *in silence*. A man in a brown Party uniform told me that there was no room left here, I must go to tunnel C. I pushed my way on—still that awful silence as I moved.

"Try and move forward as much as you can," the warden of tunnel C told me. "In a minute all the passengers of the last train will be diverted here, then it will be really crowded."

So I walked forward on to the platform as far as I could. The passengers of the last train came down the stairs, again in silence. Soon we were tightly jammed against each other. I suppose if I had looked in a mirror I would have seen the same expression of intense fear and seriousness on my face as I had noticed in the running crowds a few minutes ago. The bombing began. We heard the bombs falling. Some were very near. We could distinctly hear the crash of the explosions and a rumbling noise of falling stones, then splintering glass—something like a gigantic cocktail-shaker.

I looked along the tunnel. The crowd stood motionless, listening. Nobody spoke. This silence! Like a vast crowd watching a funeral, it flashed through my mind. Or were we watching our own funeral? Until the air-raid ended nobody knew. Even the children amongst us did not stir. I was glad no child was near me. I could not bear the look on those tiny, pale faces, so unnaturally quiet. Suddenly there was a thundering bang right over our heads, or so it seemed to us. I felt as though the ground under my feet wavered for a second, then the lights went out and big clouds of smoke blew into our tunnel.

For the first time the crowd moved. They all surged forward towards the staircase to escape the smoke. None of us wished to be toasted alive by heat and smoke. If it was burning above our heads it was high time we got out. The lights came on again and a man in brown Party uniform stood at the top of the stairs and shouted, "Don't move. No one is permitted to leave the tunnel!"

The crowd obeyed automatically. We stood quite still in the thick smoke and waited. Children began to cry. The grown-ups near them took it in turns to pick them up and comfort them. Only one man spoke. He bent down and whispered in my ear: "If they manage to get a bomb in there," he indicated with his finger the wall opposite us, "where the Spree is flowing along, then it's good-night!"

I said nothing. I was too frightened to speak. To be drowned in that tunnel like a mouse in a bucket of water!

I went on standing motionless in silence like the hundreds round me, waiting . . . waiting . . . till at long last the all-clear sounded. Immediately Berlin became alive again. As if a spell had been lifted we all began to talk and laugh and joke again.

"That was a pretty near thing," said the man next to me . . . in quite a different tone of voice now.

Else Wendel

Attack and Counter-attack

Our night fighters tried to adjust themselves to the new British methods, and profited by them to a certain extent because the British markers not only showed the way to their bombers but also to our pursuing night fighters. In a certain way the disadvantages of the radio and radar interference were annulled by the effect of the markers. Another means of finding the bomber stream was the burning enemy bombers which had been hit and which could be seen from a great distance. As a result of this, our night fighters found the whereabouts, course and altitude of the bombers, visible in the glow of the fires that attracted our fighters from a distance of sixty miles as a candle attracts a moth. The British bombers were pursued until they were over the target and also on their return journey. The solid system of the limited defence areas were out of date. Now the fighters "travelled".

Colonel Adolf Galland, Luftwaffe

In 1943 the United States Air Force operating from Britain joined in on a large scale, but their daylight raids, unescorted for lack of long-range fighters, suffered terribly.

In the course of the year 1943 the emphasis shifted more and more to action against daylight raiders. Even though numerically the British raids against Germany were still stronger than the American and were undoubtedly a great trial for the civilian population, the American precision raids were of greater consequence to the war industry. They received priority attention over the British raids on our towns.

. . . . The first air-raid on Schweinfurt was a shock to the German High Command. If the German ball-bearing industry, their Achilles' heel, were to be destroyed or paralyzed, then the armament production of the whole Reich would suffer heavily. Speer, in a post-war report, pointed out that with a continuation of the raids the German armament industry would have been essentially weakened within two months, and in four months would have come to a complete standstill. But luckily the first raid on Schweinfurt and Messerschmitt-Regensburg proved a disaster for the enemy: 315 Flying Fortresses reached the target area, sixty were shot down, and over a hundred damaged. For the first time the losses were sixteen per cent of the airborne force and nineteen per cent of the actual raiding force. The most important air battle of the war so far ended with a success for the German air defence. About three hundred fighter aircraft took part. They assembled in the sector of Frankfurt, outside the range of the fighter escort, and were directed against the bulk of the bombers in close formation. The success cost us twenty-five and not 228 fighters, as the American communiqué claimed. . . . These first high losses, shown by films, descriptions and many reports which were published later, caused deep depression amongst the American crews and a sort of crisis in the Command. Raids of this nature were not repeated before the fighter escort brought the solution.

Colonel Adolf Galland

In the nights of the spring and summer of 1943 the Ruhr, Hamburg and Berlin were effectively damaged for the first time by an ever-increasing weight of bombs, Hamburg being almost obliterated in a succession of raids

*of a violence and duration never before experienced by
any city.*

Die Katastrophe

On the night of 25-25 July, after midnight, about
eight hundred heavy British bombers assembled over
England. This mass formation, passing over Lübeck,
approached from the north-east of Hamburg, the city with
a million population on the Elbe, the German sea-gate to
the world. A narrow, restricted area, comprising the
harbour and part of the inner city, was attacked mainly
with incendiaries and phosphorus canisters. The raid was
carried out in close formation with the greatest precision,
and was almost unmolested by the German defence. What
had happened?

Not one radar instrument of our defence had worked.
The British employed for the first time the so-called
"Laminetta" method. It was as primitive as it was
effective. The bomber units and all accompanying aircraft
dropped bundles of tinfoil in large quantities, of a length
and width attuned to our radar wavelength. Drifting in the
wind, they dropped slowly to the ground, forming a wall
which could not be penetrated by the radar rays. Instead
of being reflected by the enemy's aircraft they were now
reflected by this sort of fog bank, and the radar screen was
simply blocked by their quantity. The air situation was
veiled as in a fog. The system of fighter direction based on
radar was out of action; even the radar sets of our fighters
were blinded, the flak could obtain no picture of the air
situation, and the radar target-finders would not work. At
one blow the night was again as impregnable as it had
been before the radar eye was invented. Furthermore,
during this dark night—dark also for the Reich's
defence—the British used for the first time a new method
of approach—the "Bomber Stream". This is a compromise between the loose, stretched-out formation
on a broad front, as was usual for the night approach, and
the tightly packed formation in which daylight raids were

flown. The bombers flew in several waves on small fronts, each wave behind the other, as the single aircraft used to fly, with a synchronized course, altitude, speed and time—the E.T.A. They formed no definite formation; only occasionally two or more planes flew in visual contact. Out of many small raindrops which used to unite over the target area into a cloud-bursting bombing effect, a stream had already formed during the approach that broke through our defences in a bed five miles wide. Our already insufficient peripheral defences were powerless against this new method.

Colonel Adolf Galland

For several weeks the R.A.F. had dropped leaflets over Hamburg calling on the citizens to leave the city. No one left; everyone was too used to official exaggeration to believe anything very seriously. I still remember every detail of the hot, sultry July night when the first large-scale raid began. At first there was nothing unusual about it; people sat cowering in their damp cellars, children wept, the whistle of falling bombs, dull thudding hits, blasts of air which tore out windows and doors.

In none of this was there anything new. But what was new was the way in which it went on; while red flames still stood above the houses and the air was black with dust and dirt and the fire engines were clanging through the streets, the sirens went again. With a deep zooming sound the squadrons returned to the city. Again the sharp and clear bark of the 88 mm. guns alternated with the deep powerful hits of the heavy bombs.

At first I was not caught in the general mood of panic. "The British don't mean me," I thought. I had nothing to fear. Those men up there in the sky were fighting against the Nazis, too; we had the same enemy. However stupid it may sound, I felt instinctively that no British bomb could harm me. I was firmly resolved to stay in Hamburg and see what would happen. I wanted to witness the death of the city.

Claus Fuhrmann, half-Jewish, unemployed

Suddenly the sirens sounded again. Everybody jumped up. What did the enemy want now? Hadn't they done enough?

This time the harbour was attacked, the dockyards and factories in Wilhelmsburg. This raid lasted well over an hour. When it was over Mama decided to go in search of other friends on the far side of the city, friends she had not seen for some time. Anything was better than lying here homeless on the grass. She walked and walked, carrying her suitcase and the coat. It was still very hot, and the fires behind her were still burning. But this time she found her friends safe and their home intact. She was given food, allowed to wash in a minute basin of water, and then put to bed. That night there was no air-raid, nor on the Monday.

On the Tuesday night, 28 July, the bombers came back. In that one raid over thirty thousand people in Hamburg died. Mama and her friends went down into their cellar. The air warden stored sand and water and piled up tools ready for any digging that might be necessary.

It was the worst raid Mama had ever known. For hours they huddled there, with bombs crashing nearer, and the ceaseless rumblings of falling masonry. Then there was the loudest crash of all. The air warden ran out. He came back, his face grey. "Leave the cellar at once!" he called. "A phosphorus bomb has fallen at the entrance door. Quick, all of you. . . ."

An indescribable panic started. Mothers grabbed children and rushed madly away. People fell over each other and Mama was separated from her friends. She didn't see them again. Out in the street people just rushed blindly away from the bomb, thinking of nothing else. An old man came near Mama, who was now standing dazed and alone. "Come with me," he said. She picked up her suitcase and followed him. It was unbearably hot in the street.

"I can't go through this. There's a cellar there not burning, I shall go down there," she told him.

"Don't be a fool," he said. "All the houses here will catch fire soon; it's only a matter of time."

A woman with two children joined them. "Come on," said the old man. "This looks the clearest way."

There were walls of flame round them now. Suddenly into the square came a fire engine drawn by two startled horses. They swerved aside, and one of the terrified children rushed down a side street. The mother followed, leaving her boy behind. As the first child reached a burning house some blazing wood fell near her, setting her clothes alight. The mother threw herself on top of the child to try and smother the flames, but as she did so the whole top floor of the house opposite crashed down on the two of them.

The old man grabbed the boy's hand firmly. "You come with us," he ordered.

"I'll wait for my Mummy," said the boy.

"No," said the old man, trying to make his voice sound harsh. "It's getting too hot here. We will wait for your Mummy farther away from the fire."

Mama intervened quickly. "We will find the best way out, and then come back and fetch your Mummy."

"All right," said the little boy.

They went the same way as the horses, thinking the animals' instinct might have led them to safety. The boy fell down but got up, then fell down again.

"We can't go on like this," said the man, pulling them towards a cellar. "There's some water left here, pour it over your coats, and we'll put them over our heads and try that way."

Up in the square again, the man took a hasty glance round and then grabbed the boy's hand. "Now—come this way," he told them. Mama grabbed her suitcase. "Put it down," shouted the old man. "Save yourself, you can't bring that as well."

But Mama would not let go. She took the boy's hand in her left hand and the case in her right. Out in the square it was like a furnace. Sweat poured down her body as they began to run. The smoke seeped through the wet coats and began to choke them. Only for a few yards could she carry the suitcase, then she dropped it in the road and left it without another thought. The little boy ran between them, taking steps twice as fast as their own. He fell again, but was hauled to his feet. Were they still on the track of the horses? They didn't know, for every moment or two they had to turn to avoid burning wood and pylons which hurtled down from the houses around. Bodies were still burning in the road. Sometimes they stumbled against them. But on they went, with the little boy's feet running tap, tap, tap between them. A dog was howling madly somewhere. It sounded more pathetic and lost than they themselves. At last they came to a small green place, and ran to the centre of it and fell on their faces, the little boy between them. They fell asleep like exhausted animals, but only for a few minutes. The old man woke first.

"Wake up," he said, shaking them both. "The fire is catching up with us."

Mama opened her eyes. They were lying in a small field, and the houses on one side were now alight; worse than alight; some kind of explosive material was there as well, it seemed. A great flame was shooting straight out towards them. A flame as high as the houses and nearly as wide as the whole street. As she stared in fascination, the giant flame jerked back and then shot forward towards them again.

"My God, what is it?" she said.

"It's a fire-storm," the old man answered.

"The beginning of one. Quick, come along, there's no time to lose. In a minute there will be dozens of flames like that and they'll reach us; quick, come on, we must run. I think there's a small stream farther over this field."

Mama got up and bent over the boy. "Poor little thing, what a shame to wake him." She shook him gently. "Get up! We must run again."

The child did not stir. The man bent down and pulled him to his feet. "Come on, boy," he said. The child swayed and fell again. The man sank to his knees beside the child and took his hands.

"Oh, no!" he said in a shocked voice. "No, it can't be. My God, he's dead!" The tears began to pour down his blackened face. He bent down lower over the little figure and began to whisper to it.

"You were a good little boy, a very brave little boy," he said, stroking the child's face with a woman's tenderness. "As long as Hamburg has boys as brave as you she won't die." He kissed the child's face very gently. "Sleep well, little boy," he whispered. "Sleep well; you got a kinder death than your mummy and sister. They were burnt alive like rats."

Mama became nervous; another tongue of flame shot out from the side street. The roaring of the flames became stronger. The old man seemed quite oblivious now of their danger.

"Come on," she called out. "The boy is dead. We can't help him any more. Come on, we must go on."

The old man did not look up. "No," he said. "You go on by yourself. I shall die with this little boy."

Mama yelled through the roaring wind. "You're crazy! Come on!" The old man did not answer. He kissed the child's forehead again.

In despair, Mama grabbed the man in her arms and tried to pull him away. Sparks were now beginning to reach their coats. Suddenly a hot gust of wind blew their coats off their backs, sending them blazing through the air. This brought the man to life again. He jumped up and started to run. As they raced across the field, the flames crept behind them. Once they fell and then got up and ran on. The field seemed wider and wider as they raced towards the stream, but at last they reached it. Unable to say another word, they both fell on the banks and slept, or perhaps they fainted first and slept afterwards.

When they regained consciousness it was daylight, and they stumbled down into the stream and splashed their faces and hands. The water stung their scorched skin, but they did not mind. The old man told her he had lost two grandsons and his daughter-in-law in the fires last night.

"My son is in Russia. I don't know how I shall tell him when he returns," he said.

After a rest they decided to walk back into Hamburg. It seemed suicidal, but they both felt they must go and see what remained of the city. It was a terrible walk. They passed through one big square where corpses were piled up, corpses burned beyond recognition. Soldiers and police were sorting them out and loading them on to trucks.

"All of them were standing in the middle of the square when a fire-storm caught them. No one escaped," a woman said.

"Didn't I tell you?" said the old man to Mama. "A fire-storm finished everything and everybody."

The woman standing near them shivered. "I heard scream after scream. I shall never forget those screams. If there were a God, he would have shown some mercy to them. He would have helped us."

"Leave God out of this," said the old man sharply. "Men make war, not God."

Else Wendel

Trees three feet thick were broken off or uprooted, human beings were thrown to the ground or flung alive into the flames by winds which exceeded a hundred and fifty miles an hour. The panic-stricken citizens knew not where to turn. Flames drove them from the shelters, but high-explosive bombs sent them scurrying back again. Once inside, they were suffocated by carbon-monoxide poisoning and their bodies reduced to ashes as though they had been placed in a crematorium, which was indeed what each shelter proved to be. The fortunate were those who jumped into the canals and waterways and remained swimming or standing up to their necks in water for hours until the heat should die down.

A German secret report

After the last bombs of this series of raids had dropped

on Hamburg in the night of 2-3 August, we began to take stock: the amount of bombs dropped was approximately eighty thousand H.E. bombs, eighty thousand incendiary bombs and five thousand phosphorus canisters; a quarter of a million houses were destroyed, i.e. nearly half of the city; a million people were bombed out or fled. Shipping, industry and supply suffered great damage. The death-roll, only completed in 1951, six years after the war, numbered forty thousand, of whom five thousand were children.

A wave of terror radiated from the suffering city and spread throughout Germany. Appalling details of the great fires were recounted, and their glow could be seen for days from a distance of a hundred and twenty miles. A stream of haggard, terrified refugees flowed into the neighbouring provinces. In every large town people said, "What happened to Hamburg yesterday can happen to us to-morrow." Berlin was evacuated with signs of panic. In spite of the strictest reticence in the official communiqués, the Terror of Hamburg spread rapidly to the remotest villages of the Reich.

Psychologically the war at that moment had perhaps reached its most critical point. Stalingrad had been worse, but Hamburg was not hundreds of miles away on the Volga, but on the Elbe, right in the heart of Germany.

After Hamburg in the wide circle of the political and the military command could be heard the words: "The war is lost."

Colonel Adolf Galland

Morale

Reports from the Rhineland indicate that in some cities people are gradually getting rather weak in the knees. That is understandable. For months the working population has had to go into air-raid shelters night after night, and when they come out again they see part of their city going up in flames and smoke. The enervating thing about it is that we are not in a position to reply in kind to the English. Our war in the East has lost us air supremacy in essential sections of Europe and we are completely at the mercy of the English.

Dr. Goebbels

By 1943 both sides were developing jet-propelled aircraft.

In May 1943, Messerschmitt informed me that the test flights of his Me.262 prototypes had now progressed so far that he begged me to fly and judge one for myself. He was convinced of the future of the developed type. . . . With the Me.262 we had a hope of being able to give the fighter arm a superior aircraft at the very moment when Allied air superiority was opening up catastrophic prospects for Germany in the war in the air because of the increased range and overwhelming number of the American fighter escort.

I shall never forget 22 May 1943, the day I flew a jet aircraft for the first time in my life. In the early morning I met Messerschmitt on his testing airfield, Lechfeld, near the main works at Augsburg.

. . . . We drove out to the runway. There stood the two Me.262 jet-fighters, the reason for our meeting and for all our great hopes. An unusual sight, these planes without airscrews. Covered by a streamlined cowling, two nacelles under the wings housed the jet engines. None of the engineers could tell us how many horse-power they developed.

. . . . The flying speed of 520 m.p.h. in horizontal flight, which was fantastic at that time, meant an advance of at least 120 m.p.h. over the fastest propeller-driven aircraft. Inferior fuel similar to diesel oil could be used instead of octane, which was more and more difficult to get.

The chief pilot of the works made a trial demonstration with one of the "birds", and after refuelling I climbed in. . . . I took off along a runway fifty yards wide at a steadily increasing speed, but without being able to see ahead—this was on account of the conventional tail wheel with which these first planes were still fitted instead of the front wheel of the mass-produced Me.262. Also I could not use the rudder for keeping my direction: that had to be done for the time being with the brakes. A runway is never long enough! I was doing 80 m.p.h. when at last the tail rose, I could see, and the feeling of running your head against a wall in the dark was over. Now, with reduced air resistance, the speed increased quickly, soon passing the 120 m.p.h. mark and long before the end of the runway the plane rose gently off the ground.

For the first time I was flying by jet propulsion! No engine vibration, no torque, and no lashing noise from the air-screw. Accompanied by a whistling sound, my jet shot through the air. Later, when asked what it felt like, I said, "It was as though angels were pushing."

Colonel Adolf Galland

By spring of 1944 long-range fighters came into service which allowed the Americans to attack escorted. Thus, in spite of improved German aircraft, radar and night flying techniques, "round-the-clock" bombing was now possible for the first time. Even when the main Allied air effort was switched farther west to prepare the way for D-Day, Germany's respite was short and incomplete, and German war production, though never entirely crippled by the bombing, thanks to its excellent organization and plentiful labour resources, was decisively reduced. The Allied air forces had succeeded where the Luftwaffe and U-boats had failed; but at a terrible cost. Many hundreds of aircrew might be lost in a single raid; if, as sometimes happened, one in ten of perhaps a thousand attacking planes failed to return. Below them they would leave a shattered city and tens of thousands dead.

German Difficulties

The weather has to be mentioned as a last factor that destroyed, again to our disadvantage, the balance between attacker and defender which had somehow been re-established by a tremendous effort during the summer of 1943. While the attacking units flew in at an altitude of twenty-one to twenty-four thousand feet above the bad weather, in radiant sunshine high above rain, snow, or the icing-up danger zone, completing their effective raids with excellent navigational aids and bomb-sights, and while they took-off, assembled and landed again in tolerable weather conditions in England or Italy, our defending units, by force of circumstance, often had to be sent up in the very worst of weather. Neither crews nor aircraft were prepared for such demands.

. . . . The defensive fire of the bombers and the escorting fighters took great toll of our force. Numerous German pilots were sitting in their completely iced-up cockpits, half-blinded, to become an easy prey for the Thunderbolts. The appalling losses of this period were plainly due to the weather. The fact that, despite all objections, such forced actions of practically no value were demanded over and over again by the High Command shattered once more the confidence of the squadrons in the leadership.

Göring began to lay increasing blame on Fighter Command and the pilots, and as I felt I had earned the right to answer him back, we were soon at logger-heads. One meeting was particularly stormy. The *Reichsmarschall* had summoned a number of squadron leaders and pilots to discuss a raid against southern Germany in which the German fighters had scored very few victories. After some general remarks, he proceeded to comment on the Fighter Command's lack of spirit. He may have been exasperated by my replies to his previous questions; at all events, he got into such a state that he hurled reproaches and accusations at us, to the effect that we had been loaded with honours and decorations, but had proved ourselves unworthy of them, that Fighter Command had been a failure as early as the Battle of Britain, and that many pilots with the highest decorations had faked their reports to get Knight's Crosses over England.

As I listened to him I got more and more furious, until finally I tore my Knight's Cross off my collar and banged it on the table. The atmosphere was tense and still. The *Reichsmarschall* had literally lost the power of speech, and I looked him firmly in the eye, ready for anything. Nothing happened, and Göring quietly finished what he had to say. For six months after that I did not wear my war decorations.

Colonel Adolf Galland

Single Combat

. . . . In spring, 1944, I took part in a fighter operation of the Reich's defence together with the Inspector of the Day Fighters East, *Oberst* Trautloft. A "Fat Dog" was reported to be approaching the Dutch coast, and we were following it, as we always did, from my little control room in Hottengrund. I ordered two Focke-Wulfs to be warmed up on Staaken Airfield and invited Trautloft to accompany me. He sprinted across the fifty yards to the Fieseler-Storch which was waiting with the engine running, and ten minutes later we took off from Staaken. Course west—climb to twenty-five thousand feet.

On the Reich's Fighter Wavelength we received details of location, course, altitude and other important information concerning a major formation of about eight hundred B-17s and the other oddments which were flying in advance or safeguarding the flanks. We had just crossed the Elbe north of Magdeburg when we first caught sight of the enemy. We let the American formation pass at a respectful distance of from five to ten miles: eight hundred bombers went by, two thousand tons of death, destruction and fire inside their silver bodies, flying to their appointed targets in the heart of Germany. Something had to be done. Wave upon wave, endless formations of four-engined bombers, and right and left above them, with and without vapour trails, a vast pack of Mustang fighters. "The range of the enemy's fighter escort does not extend beyond the Elbe"—according to the

General Staff! They had stopped talking about the Ruhr long ago, but they still refused to see what was written in realistic letters in the German sky.

Where were our combat formations? Switching over to the other command wavelength, I found that part of our force was preparing to land after completing an attack and was preparing for a second take-off to catch the enemy on their way back. The bomber formation did not look at all as if it had just been through a battle. No wonder, with such masses of bombers and their protective escort.

Further German combat formations were being assembled between Berlin and Magdeburg. I had to watch them in action. One of the last formations had just passed by, and my fingers itched. Should I be passively watching this parade? I had just banked to the left and closed in on the formation when I saw a B-17 straggler trying to join another formation to the left. "Hannes," I called. "Going in! We'll grab this one!"

There was nothing heroic in the decision. We should have headed right into a complete formation and shot down the leading aircraft, but we should have been shot down for certain. Now, with this straggler, we had to act very quickly before he joined the next formation.

I was a hundred yards behind on his tail. The B-17 fired and took desperate avoiding action. The only thing that existed in the whole world was this American bomber, fighting for its life, and myself. As my cannons blazed away, pieces of metal flew off, smoke poured from the engines, and they jettisoned the entire bomb-load. One tank in the wings had caught fire. The crew was baling out. Trautloft's voice cried over the radio: "*Achtung*, Adolf! Mustangs! I'm beating it! Guns jammed!"

And then—with the first bursts from four Mustangs—I sobered up. There was no mistake about the B-17; she was finished, but I was not. I simply fled.

Colonel Adolf Galland

Bomber Hit

The explosion kicked my mind back a quarter of a century. Down. Down. We're going down. I can feel the rush of air. We are going so very fast—200, 300, 400 miles an hour. I don't know, but who in earth would? Alice in Wonderland didn't, did she? She only knew she was going down. Why do my eyes hurt so much? God, I can't see! Everything is black, black as a rook. No, raven, of course. Yes, raven, not rook. I must be blind. I've always wanted to know what it's like to be blind, and now I know. The funny thing is that it doesn't really seem any different, except merely that I can't see: there must be more to it than that. I suppose it's just that I've not got used to it yet! No! Good lord, how stupid I am! I'm not blind at all! It's that terrible flash. Yes, I'm beginning to remember now. Just in front of me. A terrible bright yellow flash. It seemed to split my eyes right open, right round to the back of my head. . . .

And the noise. Yes, what a noise! It felt as though it broke every bone in my body. But I don't think it can have; I feel more or less all right. A bit peculiar, that's all. What is it? I know, I feel sick. More at heart than anything, but it's in my stomach. We've got to jump. Jump? Yes, jump. I've never jumped in my life. I've often wanted to, but I never have. Now I've got to. It's not quite the same, though. If I was going to jump I wanted to do it in my own good time, not in Jerry's time.

. . . . God knows where my parachute is now. I hurled it somewhere in the nose when I got in, but I haven't seen it since. There were one or two there some time ago, but goodness only knows if any of them were mine. Yes, I've thought about all that from time to time, but I've always said, "Oh, well, you won't think anything to it, because if the situation arises where you've got to jump, you'll be so bloody glad to get out you won't give a damn about anything else," but now I know how foolish I was. The thought of jumping is worse than anything. I'd rather stay here and hope for the best.

"Have you dropped the bombs?"

What on earth made me say that? I wasn't thinking of bombs or anything like them. I didn't even mean to say it: it just slipped out. Nobody seems to answer: I don't suppose anybody's left alive. Anyway, as far as the bombs go, it doesn't matter very much. If we're going to crash the bombs may as well stay with us, and if we aren't going to crash we may as well drop them some place. What's making me cough? I haven't got a cold, have I? No, I'm sure I haven't. . . . My eyes are smarting, too. What a foul smell! Bitter, like that day in the shelter when they bombed the aerodrome. If it goes on much longer I won't be able to breathe. I need a towel soaked in water. "Desmond, get me a towel." No, of course, Desmond isn't there. I wonder what's happened to him. Oxygen mask! That's the thing: oxygen mask. Where is it? Hanging from my neck somewhere, but where? Good, I've got it. Quick man, quick, before it's too late.

". . . . Have you dropped the bombs yet?"

Nobody seems to answer. Funny, that; surely there must be someone there. Desmond wouldn't have gone off without saying cheerio. No, I'm wrong; somebody's speaking. What's he saying? I can't quite make it out. Yes, I can.

"I've been hit. I've been hit."

I wonder who it is. I can't recognize the voice and he doesn't say his name. It must be coming from the front, not the back. Something awful has happened at the back. I don't quite know what, but most of the explosion seemed to come from behind. First of all it was in front, that terrible bright flash. And then almost immediately afterwards a much bigger explosion from behind my back. There can't possibly be anyone left alive there: so it must be coming from the nose.

. . . . The smoke cleared, and like a ray of sunshine my eyesight came back. I blinked once or twice, perhaps; I don't know. Anyway, I could see quite well. I looked at the altimeter: five thousand feet. Plenty of height, much more than I would have thought possible. Somehow we seemed to have been diving for ages and ages, and we were still diving now. The instruments were all haywire; they did not make sense however you looked at them. They must have been shot away behind the panel. Awkward. But when we levelled out and ceased diving they began slowly to come back to normal, so probably they were intact, after all. I rubbed my forehead between my eyes, and started to take stock of the damage. First of all, the engines and the wings. Perhaps a few pieces of twisted burned metal: not more. They must have borne the brunt of the explosion. I looked out, and, like the man who saw the table slide slowly of its own accord across the floor, sat frozen to my seat. They were running; both of them. Running as they've always run before.

. . . . Something was stirring. I looked up and saw there was a figure standing in the well, staring at me. The lights had fused. In the half darkness of the moon it was a grotesque figure, leaning drunkenly on an enormous pair of arms, and a pair of wide, gaping eyes, and face and shoulders streaming with blood. Who or what it was, God only knows. I didn't. I tried to work things out, but somehow had to give up. The only association I could make was with the voice that said, "I've been hit. I've been hit." And all the time we were staring into each other's eyes. Suddenly he looked away, down the fuselage, and uttered a strangled cry:

"Fire! The tank's on fire!"

"Well, put it out then."

At last, thank God, I regained my senses. I don't think the figure in the well heard what I said: before I had finished speaking he had disappeared on his hands and knees down the fuselage, where the petrol tank was. And then for a long while I was left in solitude.

We were flying straight and level, at least more or less so, but something, somewhere, was radically wrong. The aircraft was wallowing and flopping around like a small boat on a gentle swell, and the controls felt as though they had come unstuck. I looked out at the engines with a song in my heart, and then back at the instruments. It was incredible, but nowhere on any of the gauges was there a sign of trouble. I could hardly believe my eyes. The compass, I noticed, was steady; so were the rest of the flying instruments. They couldn't have been damaged, then, after all. I set about synchronizing the gyro with the compass, for it was hopelessly out, and only then did I realize the truth. What a fool! What an incredible, bloody fool! We were flying almost due east, back into Germany, and down an eighty-mile-an-hour wind at that! Of all the times to forget an elementary principle! Without thinking what I was doing, I pulled the stick hard over, and again I cursed myself for being a fool. The port wing dropped, the nose reared up, and only just in time I stopped her spinning. From then on I treated the controls as though they were made of putty, and it was three minutes before we were back on a westerly course.

The thought of what I had done made me sweat, and that was comforting, because if I was capable of sweat there could not be overmuch wrong. But this comfort did not last long, and the smile came off my face. I began to notice the sweat was all on my back and not my front. What's more, my back was getting hotter and hotter all the time. By this time I was prepared to believe anything, but this was definitely not normal. I screwed my head round, and what I saw forced a quiet, unwanted curse from my lips. Thick, black, oily smoke, pouring out from beneath the petrol tank, and in the background red gashes of fire.

I did not stay looking long, for on the port and ahead of us a barrage of shells came up. They were bursting in bunches of twenty or thirty, like that Saturday over the Ruhr, only this time they seemed to make more noise, because the hatch above my head was missing and all around the perspex was torn. Instinctively I started to take evasive action, but remembered just in time. If only I knew what was wrong with the controls it would make it easier. It felt as though the cables were hanging on by a thread, but I could not be certain. Anyway, it was better to take the shells than settle everything by pulling the

controls off. So I flew straight and level. A searchlight
picked us up, then a lot more, and almost immediately a
rattle of splinters came through the fuselage somewhere
behind me. I switched on the microphone and started
speaking, but no one answered. The heat seemed no
worse, but I did not look round any more. Somehow, I
could not take my eyes off the shells. On the floor beside
me was a parachute. It was not mine. In the nose there
were two others, and there was no one except me this side
of the petrol tank. What if they could not put the fire out?
They would never get past the tank again. I found I was
clutching the control column like a drowning man at a
straw, and cursed myself. Tried to fix my mind on things
that mattered, but it was elusive. I could not hold it down.
Curious visions again. Damn them: it's as bad as being
drunk. A grotesque figure in the well. Who on earth was
it? I'm sure it can't have been the voice that said "I've
been hit", because the intercom in the front was u/s.
Good Lord, he's come back! I'll fix him this time. In fact
I'll ask him straight who he is. I looked up at his face, but
I did not have to ask him his name.

"Can you keep her in the air?"

"What do you think?"

"That's all I wanted to know."

"What about the fire?"

"If you can keep her going another five minutes, we'll
have it under control."

They were long, those five minutes, very long, but they
got the fire out. Taffy was the first to come back: bleeding
and glistening, but grinning all over his face.

. . . . Taffy came back and disappeared into the front
turret. The shells were still as fierce as ever, but now that
there had been diversion it was not quite so bad. Someone
flopped down beside me. I looked up. He was squatting on
the step, his head down below his knees and his arms
covering his face. I leant across and pulled him gently
back. Pray God I may never see such a sight again.
Instead of a face, a black, crusted mask streaked with
blood, and instead of eyes, two vivid, scarlet pools.

"I'm going blind, sir; I'm going blind!"

I didn't say anything: I could not have if I had wanted to. He was still speaking, but too softly for me to hear what it was. I leaned right across so as better to hear. The plane gave a lurch, and I fell almost on top of him. He cried out and once more buried his face below his knees. Because I could not stand it, I sat forward over the instruments and tried to think of something else, but it was not much good. Then suddenly he struggled to his knees and said:

"I haven't let you down, have I, sir? I haven't let you down, have I? I must get back to the wireless. I've got to get back. You want a fix, don't you, sir? Will you put the light on, please, so that I can see?"

So it was Davy. Davy: his very first trip. Someone came forward and very gently picked him up. Then came Desmond. He sat down beside me and held out his hand. I took it in both of mine and looked deep into his smiling blue eyes.

"Everything's under control."

"God bless you, Desmond." Never have I said anything with such feeling. "What about Davy? Is he going to die?"

"He's O.K. Revs is looking after him."

"Thank God. Tell me the worst. What's the damage?"

"Pretty bad."

"Will she hold?"

"I don't know. About evens, I should say. The whole of the port fuselage is torn: there's only the starboard holding."

"How about the controls?"

"I don't know. They look all right, but it's difficult to tell. Shall I go and look more carefully?"

"No, it makes no odds. We're going to make a break for it however bad they are. If they're damaged, I think I'd rather not know. If this ack-ack doesn't stop soon I shall lose control of myself, Desmond. I can stand all the rest, but this I can't. They've got us stone cold. We can't turn, and we can't dive, and we can't alter speed, and it's only their bad shooting that will——"

A staccato crack, and Desmond covered his face.

"Desmond, Desmond! Are you all right?"

"Yes, sure."

"You're bleeding."

"That's nothing. A bit of perspex, probably: the splinter missed me. Taffy's signalling. Have you still got the bombs or something?"

"Yes. Which way?"

"Right. Hard right. Go on, much farther."

"Tell him to shut up. What the hell does he think this is? A Spitfire?"

We went on like this for some time. Turning all the time, very gently, but none the less turning, and always to the right. Then at last the bombs went. I felt the kick as they left the aircraft. Desmond stood up and went back to Revs and Davy.

"Where was it?"

"Cologne."

Group-Captain Leonard Cheshire

Dresden

Dresden was still considered safe, possibly owing to the architectural fame of the town and the great pictures which drew people from all over the world. But in the end Dresden also received its share of bombing. There were two hundred thousand refugees in Dresden when, on the night of 13 February 1945, the fire-storms fell on the town. There are no figures of the numbers who perished that night in Dresden, for the simple fact that the chaos was so complete no one knew who was in the town and who was not. Identification being impossible, and a decent burial out of the question, petrol was poured over the corpses, and all of them were set alight. Officially it was reported by the German authorities that the casualties were four hundred thousand. The British gave the numbers as two hundred and fifty thousand. No one will ever know the truth. Most of our news about Dresden came from Evelyn, who was working there in a hospital.

Gerhart Hauptmann, the famous German poet, saw Dresden's end from one of the surrounding hills. He watched it burning for five whole days. He saw it in ruins. He had a stroke. After his recovery he wrote an appeal to the world in which he said, "He who has forgotten how to weep, learns again at Dresden's ruin. I know that in England and America there are enough good people to whom such glories as the Sistine Madonna were well known. I am at the end of my life, and I envy my dead friends who have been saved this terrible sight. I weep, and I am not ashamed of my tears. The great heroes of old were not ashamed of tears, were they? I am nearly eighty-three years old and I am standing before God beseeching him with my whole heart to show us His love more clearly, to show mankind how to purify ourselves, to show us how to reach our salvation."

Else Wendel

"Come on," he said aloud, and slid down from the hill of rubble. The narrow street was not blocked. The ruins on both sides were like filigree, with the sky glimmering through. Tangles of wires hung down from above and stretched across the street. He worked his way between them, careful not to be caught in them in the dark. Ahead of him was the main-street crossing. When he got that far, he must see the open space of the Pirna Platz on the left, and the wide Johann-Georgen-Allee a few yards farther on. Just in front of him he heard the sound of falling masonry and human voices shouting. That must be the fire brigade, busy clearing the main street. People! So he wasn't alone.

When he reached the corner of the street he saw that there were a lot of houses still blazing here. The main street itself was empty and, for as far as he could see, covered with stones, charred beams, and iron bars, as though there had been a barricade battle. There was no sign of fire-service parties. A dead human body lay flat on the tramway lines. That must have been a delusion, thinking he heard voices. The only things to be heard were the crackling and sighing of the fires and from time to time the rumble of walls collapsing.

He climbed over the debris. Showers of sparks and ashes prickled hot on his face. He inhaled the smell of burnt flesh and saw a house-front ahead of him swaying to and fro like a piece of blazing scenery on a stage. He tried to run past under, but his ski boots and the suitcase caught in the wires. The wall was coming down slowly straight in front of him. He threw himself to the ground, flattening himself close behind stone blocks lying about there. There came a short thundering roar, as of big waves breaking, followed by a long-drawn-out hissing. The blast and the heat swept over him. The dust cloud got into his nose, he fought for air, and during a long fit of coughing he realized that he was apparently unhurt. The burning houses to the right and left of him now all seemed to be swaying like gigantic loose back-drops. He tore himself free again, went running and jumping over the flames that shot up out of the ground, and as he reached the open square, behind him in the street he had just left walls crashed and a yellowish, white-hot lake spread out, with fetid smoke going up from it.

. . . . He walked towards the Grosse Garten. He felt rain trickling out of the sky, thin and cold, and heard the hum of aircraft engines. There were no more air-raid signals in this city. There was no hand to work them. He stumbled over the pieces of clothing in the roadway. If he went diagonally across the park, he could be in Blasewitz by three in the morning. In front of him the bare trees towered up, a broad front. He crossed a wide street where a great many things lay scattered about. The footpath leading into the park was also littered with clothes, pieces of luggage, shreds of material and books. Two bodies glimmered where they lay sideways across the path. They seemed to be children, one lying crosswise over the other. He walked round to them, but an instant later stumbled on something soft and shapeless which gave under his feet. It was better to go across the lawn and through the trees to the other side. A wan grey light showed the vague outlines of a clearing. He fell over a smashed tree-top lying on the ground. Now he could see quite clearly that there were corpses lying about among the trees, too. They lay scattered, this way and that, at brief intervals, like huge autumn leaves blown down from the branches. There must be hundreds of them, a boundless field of the dead disappearing into the dim darkness. He decided to turn back. Suddenly he noticed how violently his right arm was aching, and the smell of burning rose into his consciousness again, and the nauseating, choking taste of it lay on his tongue. He walked a few paces back towards the street, saw close in front of him a woman's red skirt edged with black rep, and felt the blood draining out of his head. Shutting his eyes, he leaned against a thick tree trunk, slid down it, and sat on the wet, cold earth, with the feeling that now he himself was a dead man among thousands of the dead.

If he had been there twenty-four hours earlier, he would have seen them die.

Adjoining the park was a hospital centre, in which wounded soldiers lay in white cots. It was a hospital for the blind and those who had lost limbs. When the fire started to rain through the trees, they let themselves drop out of the windows of the burning structure. The fireworks were noisy and colourful, and in the midst of it hopped the one-legged in their blue-and-white striped hospital smocks, dragging along by their arms those that had lost both legs.

The fire-engine that was on its way to the hospital came to a halt in the city. The motor was still running, but the firemen had suffocated. Their uniforms crumbled in the baking air and they sat naked on their seats, lined up against the metal ladder, with straps round their brown bodies and helmets on their yellow skulls.

Here in the hospital the soldiers rolled in strange antics on their stumps and tried to escape the vicinity of the glowing buildings. But they did not have the key to the gate in the high iron fence which separated them from the garden, and so they built human pyramids supported by

the blind. Whoever reached the top let himself fall to the
other side of the high fence. The striped smocks hopped
bare-footed in the hissing embers, supporting themselves
with crutches, spades and bars, and they limped or rolled,
screaming and in flames, among the trees, whose old
trunks split apart under the impact of the bombs. The air
grew thinner and thinner, and the striped ones fell
unconscious in the wet, smouldering leaves. It was a
gorgeous spectacle, glittering in violet, lemon-yellow,
emerald-green and raspberry-red colours, and filled with
whimpers and screams, roaring and howling, as never
heard before. Outside the fence stood women in
smouldering skirts trying to catch those who hurled
themselves from the top of the towering fence.

                                                              Bruno E. Werner

Where is the Luftwaffe?

On my arrival in Berlin, I asked for the latest figures of
the fighter reserve. They had increased to nearly eight
hundred, but with this good news I received orders from
O.K.L. to send the total fighter reserve immediately into
the defence battle in the west. That was absolutely
irresponsible! They were bound to get into the stream of
the retreat and be overrun, and they could no longer do
anything to change the critical situation of the Army, even
had there been a ground organization to receive them. One
cannot throw fighter groups into gaps like infantry
regiments! These squadrons, which consisted of eighty per
cent inexperienced pilots, could have gained their
experience with tolerable losses in the defence of the
Reich. The order to protect the German war industry from
total destruction would have justified their action in the
defence of the Reich and would have made it worthwhile!
But in the west they were doomed to be destroyed in the
air or on the ground without achieving any operational
effect.

My objection, which I raised with the Luftwaffe staff,
only received the answer: "The Führer's orders!" I could

not speak to Göring, who had retired because he was "not well". The real reason was probably his collapse under the continuous reproaches which were levelled against him and the Luftwaffe. Until the last moment he had tried to keep the real situation hidden from those above, but now there was no longer anything to hide or to falsify. The naked facts of the war in the air spoke realistically and inexorably.

As I could no longer count on Göring, I turned to the Minister for Armaments, Speer. Even in this desperate situation he remained sober and as strictly realistic as ever. He asked for information as to what the fighter arm could undertake against strategic day bombing; the key industries and transport had been hit so severely that things could not go on like this for more than a week. I reported to him that the Führer had irrevocably ordered the last fighter reserves to be transferred to the retreat in the west, which was now beginning.

Speer said, "If the *Reichsmarschall* does not act, then it is my duty to act. Please come with me immediately to the Ministry. We will fly and see the Führer at the 'Wolf's Redoubt'. This order must be cancelled." Four hours later we landed at Rastenberg, and soon afterwards were standing in the Führer's bunker. Hitler gave me the impression of being very irritable, overworked and physically and mentally overwrought. Speer explained briefly and precisely the situation of transport and the armament industry, which had become more acute through the increase of the American mass attacks. As usual, he accompanied his *exposé* with actual figures. Hitler listened with increasing irritation. When Speer requested a strengthening of the fighter forces in the Reich, even if necessary at the expense of the situation on the Western Front, and that the fighters which had just been ordered to France should be used for the defence of the Reich, he could not complete his sentence. He had just started, "Galland has just arrived from the west, and can give you, my Führer . . ." when Hitler interrupted him like a maniac, and Speer was given a slating which was particularly embarrassing because it was quite unjustified. The Führer forbade any interference with his operational measures and said, "Please look after the war industry!" Then, as an aside to me: "See that my orders are immediately executed!" And to both of us: "I have no time for you any more!"

We were thrown out.

Colonel Adolf Galland

A Letter to Russia

How can I write to you when there are a thousand British bombers overhead? We feel so wretched and depressed. Hans, it is high time you finished in the East, so that at least the Luftwaffe can be sent back. For if the Tommies are allowed to go on bombing us like this, soon there will be nothing left of Western Germany.

Anon.

Nothing Left

During March* the American and British raids increased, delivering an almost continuous shower of bombs. Night after night, day after day, death and destruction descended upon the ever-diminishing area of the Reich. Hardly a town remained untouched. On 12 March the largest weight of bombs ever dropped during a night raid on a German town was registered: 4,899 tons on Dortmund. The last week in March is entered as a record in the statistics of the R.A.F., the total weight of bombs dropped being 67,365 tons. On 6 April Harris stated that there were no worthwhile targets left for his strategic bomber fleet in Germany, and a day later large-scale R.A.F. air raids stopped. The bombing commission which functioned in London under the code name Jockey telegraphed to Allied Headquarters: "Jockey has unsaddled." Three days later, on 10 April, American four-

* 1945 (Ed.)

engined bombers raided Berlin for the last time. A fortnight later 8 A.A.F. was transferred to Okinawa in order to bomb Japan in conjunction with 20 A.A.F., which was already stationed in the Far East, until she was ripe for capitulation.

V1—V2

The German people had been clamouring for revenge against England, and in the summer of 1944 their leaders and scientists gave them what they asked for—the V1 jet-propelled flying bomb and the V2 rocket. A week after D Day the first V1 crossed the English coast, and in the following three months about eight thousand were launched against London. Then the longer-range V2s began to fall out of the sky, to the total number of about a thousand. In all, about two thousand four hundred V1s got through the defences, killing and injuring ten times as many people, mostly in London. The rest were brought down. Five hundred V2s hit London, causing nearly ten thousand casualties, but Hitler's weapons of revenge had come too late to affect the course of the war.

. . . . There was a lot of talk about the wonder weapons. We learned that our scientists had developed entirely new types of planes with four to five times the present speed, and these were now ready waiting for the Führer to give the order to go into action. And the real "wonder" weapons had shown during their trials that their power of destruction was so immense that anything we had developed before was a joke in comparison. That was why we were almost crazy with joy when we heard that the first secret weapon, the V1, was at last being used against Britain. There was panic in London, the town was in flames, and we saw again how the Führer had kept his word. It was now only a matter of his wonderful intuition when the final onslaught was going to take place to force the proud British on to their knees and make a vast desert out of their country.

Fritz Muehlebach, Storm Trooper

Dive-bombing V-Weapon Sites

. . . . On our return from the Orkneys it was decided to equip some Spitfires with 500 lb. bombs and make them dive-bomb the flying-bomb sites. 602 and 132 Squadrons were to be the guinea-pigs in this experiment.

On 13 March we left with our Spitfire IXs, which we had recovered, for Llanbedr, on the North Wales coast, for the first trials.

Dive-bombing with Spitfires is a technique on its own, as the bomb is fixed under the belly of the machine, in the place of the auxiliary tank. If you bomb vertically the propeller is torn off by the bomb. If you bomb at forty-five degrees, aiming is very difficult. After various attempts Maxie evolved the following method:

The twelve aircraft of the squadron made for the objective at twelve thousand feet in close reversed échelon formation. As soon as the leader saw the target appear under the trailing edge of his wings he dived, followed by the remainder, at seventy-five degrees. Each pilot took the objective individually in his sights and everyone came down to three thousand feet at full throttle. At that point you began to straighten out, counted three and let go your bomb. It was rather rudimentary, but after a fortnight the squadron was landing its bombs inside a hundred-and-fifty-yard circle.

During the three weeks we spent at Llanbedr we were the object of visits from every V.I.P. from Inter-Allied G.H.Q.; each time we staged a demonstration. They had their money's worth. At the first visit Dumbrell's bomb landed plumb on Fox at 450 m.p.h. and the poor blighter had to bale out *in extremis*. At the second visit one bomb, McConachie's, hung up. He decided to land with it and made a run over the airfield to warn them. As he passed the bomb came free at last and exploded bang in the middle of the airfield, covering the dismayed visitors with earth and mud.

Really, apart from Max and Remlinger, who were always eager beavers and dreamt of nothing but blood and thunder, nobody was very keen on this brand of sport. We preferred to await the first results against an objective well defended by flak before making up our minds.

. . . . After the first bombardments, in the course of which 16,432 tons of high explosive had been dropped on the launching sites in four months, the Germans had evolved a new type of much simplified installation. They were erecting more than fifty a month, very well camouflaged and hard to detect. The total German layout consisted of nine sectors, four directed against London and the other five against Southampton, Portsmouth, Plymouth, Brighton and the harbours of Dover and Newhaven respectively.

According to the latest information the flying bomb, or V1, was a jet-propelled device capable of carrying about a ton of explosive a distance of two hundred and fifty miles at roughly 425 m.p.h., and highly accurate, i.e. to within a thousand yards.

We returned to Detling on 8 April and we waited without exaggerated impatience for our first dive-bombing trip.

13 April 1944

The day before, for the first time, Spitfires had dive-bombed the Continent. 602 and 132 had attacked the flying-bomb installation at Bouillancourt, twelve miles south of Le Tréport.

Although our objective was in an area crammed with flak, the Germans had been so surprised at the sight of twenty-four Spitfires, each carrying a 500 lb. bomb, that they had opened fire only after we were out of range.

16 April 1944

We were going to repeat the prank on a big scale. We were to bomb Ligercourt, by the forest of Crécy. It was much less funny this time, as in a radius of two thousand yards round the target there were nine 88 mm. guns and twenty-four 20 and 37 mm.—not to mention the fact that we should be within range of Abbeville's formidable defences.

We took off at 12.25 hours. We were to attack first, followed by an Australian squadron (453), while 132 covered us against possible enemy fighter reaction. We passed the French coast at ten thousand feet and Sutherland put us into our attacking positions: "Max aircraft, echelon port, go!"

I was the tenth of the twelve and didn't feel at all happy.

"Max aircraft, target two o'clock below."

I could see Ligercourt woods just under my wing and I recognized the target—another flying-bomb site cleverly camouflaged among the trees—from the photos we had been shown at briefing.

We were now immediately above it. With a turn of the hand I depressed the switch that fused the bomb and removed the safety catch of the release mechanism.

"Max, going down."

Like a fan spreading out, all the Spitfires turned on their backs one after the other and dived straight down. This time the flak opened fire straightaway. Clusters of tracer began to come up towards us. Shells burst to left and right, and just above our heads a ring of fine white puffs from the 20 mm. guns began to form, scarcely visible against the streaky cirrus clouds. Our acceleration, with that heavy bomb, was terrific: in a few seconds we were doing well over 400 m.p.h. I had only just begun to get the target in my sights when the first bombs were already exploding on the ground—a quick flash followed by a cloud of dust and fragments.

Max and Skittles Flights were already climbing again, vertically, jinking hard, stubbornly followed by the flak.

My altimeter showed three thousand feet and I concentrated on my aim. I pulled the stick gently back to let the target slip under my Spitfire's nose, following our technique—a tough job at that height. I counted aloud—one, two, three—and pressed the release button.

For the next few seconds, as a result of the effect of the violent centrifugal force, I was only dimly aware of what was going on. I recovered to find myself hanging on the propeller, at full throttle, at eight thousand feet. The flak seemed to have given us up. A turn left soon showed me why. 453 were beginning their dive. The aircraft went over like a waterfall and were soon only tiny indistinct patches against the ground.

The flak redoubled. Suddenly there was a flash and a Spitfire turned over, leaving a trail of burning glycol, and crashed into the middle of the target. A horrifying sight, which I couldn't get out of my mind.

A bitter blow, one of the dead pilot's friends told me back at the airfield. It was Bob Yarra, brother of the famous "Slim" of Malta, also brought down by flak the year before. Bob had got a direct hit from a 37 mm. between the radiators as he was diving at well over 400 m.p.h. The two wings of his Spitfire had immediately folded up and come off, tearing off the tailplane on the way and spattering with debris the aircraft behind, which had to take violent avoiding action. Three seconds later the plane crashed into the ground and exploded. Not the ghost of a chance of baling out.

Pierre Clostermann

The Guards' Chapel

Sunday, 18 June 1944. I have good reason to remember that date: it was the last day on which I walked.

I came out of the Tube station in the Strand to find Pauline waiting for me. She was always first at our meeting places but smilingly recognized the fact that service life tended to make one unpunctual.

"Where shall we go? What shall we do?" The usual questions had to be settled. On this particular day it didn't take us long to make up our minds. I don't know who suggested it, but we were in full agreement that, as it was

early and as it was Sunday, a good way of starting a long
day would be a divine service at the Guards' Chapel,
Wellington Barracks—not far to walk, and a place loved
by us both, and visited by us in other, pre-war days.

"It would be peaceful there for you," Pauline said,
"after your sleepless night as orderly officer."

. . . . We sauntered through St. James's Park. What did
we talk about? I don't know; we nearly always talked at
the same time when we met—there was so much to say.
We came from the same home town, so I imagine we
talked a lot of home. I wish now, for her mother's sake,
that I could remember something of what Pauline said to
me. But it's no use, I can't.

I do remember that we argued a bit about where we
should lunch after the service, and that the siren sounded
while we were arguing. After five years, its blood-curdling
wail no longer had much effect on us. We sat down on a
bench opposite the Barracks for a few minutes, and
watched the Guards drilling on the square. When we got
up to cross to the chapel, I wondered a little nervously if I
should be able to return the sentry's salute as smartly as
he was sure to give it.

. . . . We sat near the back of the chapel and watched
the people come in. This part of the day is clearer than the
earlier part, and I do remember some of the people I saw,
in particular a young Canadian lieutenant who eagerly
surveyed his surroundings as if to memorize the details
that he might write them down in his next letter home. . . .
Then there was an elderly colonel with his wife and
daughters, and a section of A.T.S. girls, possibly those
stationed at the Barracks. In the gallery . . . a band of
Guardsmen began to play; the band, instead of an organ,
was one of the special charms of this charming chapel.
Military atmosphere here was very strong, and yet in some
curious way it never seemed to war with the peace of God.

We sang the opening hymn. I probably enjoyed that, for
my Welsh blood ensures a fondness for hymn singing. My
mind must have wandered during the reading of the first
lesson—it usually does. I daresay I was thinking about my

forthcoming leave or of what chance I had of getting my third pip.

"Here endeth the first lesson," the Guards' colonel who had been reading it must have said.

The congregation rose to its feet.

. . . . This is the clearest part of all. I can see what happened as clearly as I can see the last of the roses outside my window at this moment; I can hear what happened as loudly as I can hear a late thrush singing in the hawthorn tree in the lane.

In the distance hummed faintly the engine of a flying bomb.

"We praise thee, O God: we acknowledge Thee to be the Lord," we, the congregation, sang.

The dull burr became a roar, through which our voices could now only faintly be heard.

"All the earth doth worship Thee: the Father everlasting."

The roar stopped abruptly as the engine cut out. We were none of us then as familiar as later all London and the south was to become with Hitler's new weapon, to recognize this ominous sign. The *Te Deum* soared again into the silence.

"To Thee all Angels cry aloud: the Heavens, and all the Powers therein."

Then there was a noise so loud it was as if all the waters and the winds in the world had come together in mighty conflict, and the Guards' Chapel collapsed upon us in a bellow of bricks and mortar.

There was no time for panic, no time to stretch out a hand to Pauline for comfort. One moment I was singing the *Te Deum*, and the next I lay in dust and blackness, aware of one thing only—that I had to go on breathing.

I have often been asked since of what I thought during those hours when I lay buried. Did I think I was going to die? And if so did my past life parade its characters and scenes before me as is said to happen to a drowning person? All I can say is that I didn't think of anything, and yet I know that I was conscious. I felt no pain, I was

scarcely aware of the chunks of massed grey concrete that
had piled on top of me, nor did I realize that this was why
breathing was so difficult. My whole being was
concentrated in the one tremendous effort of taking in
long struggling breaths and then letting them struggle out
again.

It may have been an hour later, perhaps two or three or
more, that greater consciousness came to me. I was
suddenly aware that somewhere far above me, above the
black emptiness, there were people, living helpful people
whose voices reached me, dim and disembodied as in a
dream.

"Please, please, I'm here," I said, and I went on saying
it until my voice was hoarse and my throat ached with the
dust that poured down it. To this day I can sometimes
smell that acrid dust in my nostrils—I don't know what it
is that reminds me of it—and when I do smell it I
sometimes find my fingers curling as they did then in a
vain endeavour to scrape my way out of my living tomb.

The blessed relief of light and air! Someone frantically
scraped away the rubble from around my head; I learnt
later that it had been difficult for rescuers to find their
way into the chapel; walls and roof shut in the dead and
wounded, and there seemed at first to be no entrance at all
until at last one was found behind the altar.

I had until now felt no terror, but as soon as my eyes
were able to take in the ghastly scene around me my ears
began to do their part. Somewhere not far away from me
someone was screaming, screaming, screaming, like an
animal caught in a trap—and with the pain of that
dreadful sound ringing in my ears came realization of the
awfulness of what had happened. I could not fully take in
the scene of desolation around me, but my eyes rested
with horror on a blood-stained body that, had my hands
been free, I could have reached out and touched. It was
the body of a young soldier whose eyes stared unseeingly
at the sky. The Canada flash on the shoulder nearest me
glittered.

. . . . Although I was still pinned down by debris, rescue

work was progressing fast and it was with wonder that I gazed idly at a leg that had been uncovered and lay in front of me. It was dressed in a khaki silk stocking and shod with a brown brogue shoe. It looked lifeless. For a moment I thought of Pauline, but no, what would she be doing with *khaki* stockings? I looked again. . . . That was *my* stocking, *my* shoe, *my* leg. And yet it was no part of me. I could not move it, I could not feel it. I tried to wriggle my toes. Nothing happened. Engulfed now with fear, I tried to convince myself that, yes, this was truly a nightmare, one from which I was bound soon to wake up. I think I must have been given a morphia injection for I still felt no pain, but I did begin to have an inkling that I was badly injured. I turned my freed head towards a Guardsman who was helping with the rescue work, and hysterically I cried:

"How do I look? Tell me how I look!"

"Madam," he said, "you look wonderful to me!"

Elisabeth Sheppard-Jones

7

THE WAR AT SEA,
1941-1945

Throughout the war, in spite of the growing menace of air power and submarines, the capital ships of both sides played a vital part. In the Mediterranean and in the Atlantic their presence protected or threatened destruction for the convoys of both sides. While full-scale naval warfare between the British and Italian fleets was a feature of the fighting in the Mediterranean, the threat of German battleships sitting in their protected harbours was sufficient to tie up most of Britain's remaining large warships on the Atlantic seaboard. British command of home waters suffered a severe reverse in 1942 when the Scharnhorst and Gneisenau successfully broke out of Brest and escaped to northern ports. Sometimes a German battleship would sally out into the Atlantic and wreak havoc among the convoys before it slipped back to its home port or, in the case of Bismarck and later Scharnhorst, was destroyed.

However, even in their ports battleships were not invulnerable, as the "human torpedoes" and midget submarines employed successfully by the Italians and British proved.

Matapan

On 27 March 1941 a British battle fleet under Admiral Cunningham sailed from Alexandria to protect British convoys bound for Greece against the Italian fleet. It consisted of three battleships, Warspite, Barham *and* Valiant, *the aircraft carrier* Formidable *and nine destroyers. In support were Vice-Admiral Pridham-Wippell's squadron of four cruisers and four destroyers. On the morning of the 28th the latter located the Italian battleship* Vittorio Veneto *and a considerable number of other enemy warships. The whole British fleet gave chase, damaging the Italian battleship and endeavouring to overhaul her. The cruiser* Pola *was also hit and stopped. Night fell.*

Admiral Angelo Iachino was in command of the Italian fleet with his flag in the *Vittorio Veneto*. I have read his account of the operation and the night battle, and there is no doubt that he was badly served by his air reconnaissance. This is surprising to us who know how efficient the Italian reconnaissance had been on many other occasions. However, as Admiral Iachino says, the Italian naval co-operation with the air in the tactical field was very imperfect.

It appears that they were relying upon German aircraft reports before the battle, and as the weather was by no means unfavourable it is not easy to understand why their reconnaissance failed. At 9 a.m. on 28 March German aircraft from the Aegean had actually reported one aircraft carrier, two battleships, nine cruisers and fourteen destroyers in such and such a position at 7.45. This actually was our fleet, which up to that time Admiral Iachino had thought was still safely at Alexandria. However, on plotting the position given, the Admiral convinced himself that his Aegean reconnaissance had mistaken the British fleet for his own, and signalled to

Rhodes to this effect. He does not seem to have become aware that the British battle-fleet was at sea until later.

On the evening of the 28th, when the *Pola* was damaged by our air attack, Admiral Iachino's information led him to believe that the nearest British battleship was ninety miles astern of him, something over four hours' steaming. With this in mind his decision to detach the *Zara* and the *Fiume* to help the crippled *Pola* cannot be questioned. He was originally urged to send destroyers; but finally decided that only a Flag Officer, Rear-Admiral Carlo Cateneo in the *Zara*, who did not survive, could take the responsibility of deciding whether the *Pola* should be taken in tow, or abandoned and sunk.

Instead of being ninety miles astern, the British battle-fleet was roughly half that distance.

.... At 9.11 we received Pridham-Wippell's report that an unknown ship lying stopped five miles to port of him had been located by radar. We went on after the enemy's fleet and altered course slightly to port to close the stopped ship. The *Warspite* was not fitted with radar; but at 10.10 the *Valiant* reported that her instruments had picked up what was apparently the same ship six miles on her port bow. She was a large ship. The *Valiant* gave her length as more than six hundred feet.

Our hopes ran high. This might be the *Vittorio Veneto*. The course of the battle-fleet was altered forty degrees to port together to close. We were already at action stations with our main armament ready. Our guns were trained on the correct bearing.

Rear-Admiral Willis was not out with us. Commodore Edelsten, the new Chief of Staff, had come to gain experience. And a quarter of an hour later, at 10.25, when he was searching the horizon on the starboard bow with his glasses, he calmly reported that he saw two large cruisers with a smaller one ahead of them crossing the bows of the battle-fleet from starboard to port. I looked through my glasses, and there they were. Commander Power, an ex-submarine officer and an abnormal expert at recognizing the silhouettes of enemy warships at a glance, pronounced them to be two *Zara* class 8-inch gun cruisers with a smaller cruiser ahead.

Using short-range wireless the battle-fleet was turned back into line ahead. With Edelsten and the staff I had gone to the upper bridge, the captain's, where I had a clear all-round view. I shall never forget the next few minutes. In the dead silence, a silence that could almost be felt, one heard only the voices of the gun control personnel putting the guns on to the new target. One heard the orders repeated in the director tower behind and above the bridge. Looking forward, one saw the turrets swing and steady when the 15-inch guns pointed at the enemy cruisers. Never in the whole of my life have I experienced a more thrilling moment than when I heard a calm voice from the director tower—"Director layer sees the target"; sure sign that the guns were ready and that his finger was itching on the trigger. The enemy was at a range of no more than three thousand eight hundred yards—point-blank.

It must have been the Fleet Gunnery Officer, Commander Geoffrey Barnard, who gave the final order to open fire. One heard the "ting-ting-ting" of the firing gongs. Then came the great orange flash and the violent shudder as the six big guns bearing were fired simultaneously. At the very same instant the destroyer *Greyhound*, on the screen, switched her searchlight on to one of the enemy cruisers, showing her momentarily up as a silvery-blue shape in the darkness. Our searchlights shone out with the first salvo, and provided full illumination for what was a ghastly sight. Full in the beam I saw our six great projectiles flying through the air. Five out of the six hit a few feet below the level of the cruiser's upper deck and burst with splashes of brilliant flame. The Italians were quite unprepared. Their guns were trained fore and aft. They were helplessly shattered before they could put up any resistance. In the midst of all this there was one milder diversion. Captain Douglas Fisher, the Captain of the *Warspite*, was a gunnery officer of note. When he saw the first salvo hit he was heard to say in a voice of wondering surprise: "Good Lord! We've hit her!"

The *Valiant*, astern of us, had opened fire at the same time. She also had found her target, and when the *Warspite* shifted to the other cruiser I watched the *Valiant* pounding her ship to bits. Her rapidity of fire astonished me. Never would I have believed it possible with these heavy guns. The *Formidable* had hauled out of the line to starboard; but astern of the *Valiant* the *Barham* was also heavily engaged.

The plight of the Italian cruisers was indescribable. One saw whole turrets and masses of other heavy debris whirling through the air and splashing into the sea, and in a short time the ships themselves were nothing but glowing torches and on fire from stem to stern. The whole action lasted no more than a few minutes.

Our searchlights were still on, and just after 10.30 three Italian destroyers, which had apparently been following their cruisers, were seen coming in on our port bow. They turned, and one was seen to fire torpedoes, so the battle-fleet was turned ninety degrees together to starboard to avoid them. Our destroyers were engaging, and the whole party was inextricably mixed up. The *Warspite* fired both 15-inch and 6-inch at the enemy. To my horror I saw one of our destroyers, the *Havock*, straddled by our fire, and in my mind wrote her off as a loss. The *Formidable* also had an escape. When action was joined she hauled out to starboard at full speed, a night battle being no place for a carrier. When she was about five miles away she was caught in the beam of the *Warspite*'s searchlight sweeping on the disengaged side in case further enemy ships were present. We heard the 6-inch control officer of the starboard battery get his guns on to her, and were only just in time to stop him from opening fire.

The four destroyers, *Stuart*, Captain H. M. L. Waller, Royal Australian Navy; *Greyhound*, Commander W. R. Marshal-A'Deane; *Havock*, Lieutenant G. R. G. Watkins; and *Griffin*, Lieutenant-Commander J. Lee-Barber, in company with the battle-fleet, were then ordered to finish off the enemy cruisers, while the battle-fleet collected the

Formidable and withdrew to the northward to keep out of their way. According to their own reports the destroyers' movements were difficult to follow; but they had a wild night and sank at least one other enemy destroyer.

At 10.45 we saw very heavy gunfire, with star-shell and tracer, to the south-westward. Since none of our ships was on that bearing it seemed to us that either the Italians were engaging each other, or that the destroyers of our striking force might be going in to attack. Just after 11 p.m. I made a signal ordering all forces not engaged in sinking the enemy to withdraw to the north-eastward. The objects of what I now consider to have been an ill-considered signal were to give our destroyers who were mopping up a free hand to attack any sizeable ship they saw, and to facilitate the assembly of the fleet next morning. The message was qualified by an order to Captain Mack, and his eight destroyers of the striking force, now some twenty miles ahead, not to withdraw until he had attacked. However, it had the unfortunate effect of causing Vice-Admiral Pridham-Wippell to cease his efforts to gain touch with the *Vittorio Veneto*.

Just after midnight the *Havock*, after torpedoing a destroyer and finishing her off by gunfire, reported herself in contact with a battleship near the position where we had been in action. The battleship was Captain Mack's main objective, and the *Havock*'s report brought Mack's destroyer striking force back hot-foot from their position nearly sixty miles to the westward. An hour later, however, the *Havock* amended her report to say that it was not a battleship she had sighted, but an 8-inch cruiser. Soon after 3 a.m. she sent a further message reporting herself close to the *Pola*, and, as all her torpedoes had been fired, Watkins asked whether "to board or blow off her stern with depth-charges".

The *Havock* had already been joined by the *Greyhound* and *Griffin*, and when Captain Mack arrived he took the *Jervis* alongside the *Pola*. That ship was in a state of indescribable confusion. Panic-stricken men were leaping over the side. On the crowded quarterdeck, littered with

clothing, personal belongings and bottles, many of the
sailors were drunk. There was no order or discipline of
any sort and the officers were powerless to enforce it.
Having taken off the crew, Mack sank the ship with
torpedoes. The *Pola*, of course, was the vessel reported by
Pridham-Wippell and the *Valiant* between nine and ten
the night before as lying stopped on the port side of our
fleet's line of advance. She had not been under gunfire or
fired a gun; but had been torpedoed and completely
crippled by one of the aircraft from the *Formidable* during
the dusk attack.

Her sinking at 4.10 a.m. was the final act of the night's
proceedings.

Reconnaissance at dawn by the *Formidable*'s aircraft,
with others from Greece and Crete, failed to discover any
trace of the enemy to the westward. As we discovered
afterwards, the *Vittorio Veneto* had been able to increase
speed and get clear away during the night.

As daylight came on 29 March our cruisers and
destroyers were in sight making for the rendezvous with
the battle-fleet. Feeling fairly certain in our minds that the
Warspite had sunk a destroyer in the mêlée the night
before, we eagerly counted them. To our inexpressible
relief all twelve destroyers were present. My heart was
glad again.

It was a fine morning. We steamed back to the scene of
the battle to find the calm sea covered with a film of oil,
and strewn with boats, rafts and wreckage, with many
floating corpses. All the destroyers we could spare were
detached to save what life was possible. In all, counting
the men from the *Pola*, British ships rescued nine
hundred, though some died later. In the midst of this work
of mercy, however, the attentions of some German JU88s
pointed the fact that it was unwise to dally in an area
where we were exposed to heavy air attack. So we were
compelled to proceed to the eastward, leaving some
hundreds of Italians unrescued. We did the best we could
for them by signalling their exact position to the Italian
Admiralty. They sent out the hospital ship *Gradisca*,

which eventually saved another hundred and sixty.

. . . . Although the *Vittorio Veneto* had escaped, we
had sunk the three ten-thousand-ton, 8-inch cruisers *Zara*,
Pola and *Fiume*, together with the fifteen-hundred-ton
destroyers *Alfieri* and *Carducci*. The Italian loss in
personnel was about two thousand four hundred officers
and men, most of them being caused by our devastating
bombardment at close range. The *Fiume* received two 15-
inch broadsides from the *Warspite* and one from the
Valiant; the *Zara* four from the *Warspite*, five from the
Valiant, and five from the *Barham*. The effect of those
six- or eight-gun salvoes of shell, each weighing nearly a
ton, cannot be described.

Admiral Cunningham

The End of the *Bismarck*

On 24 May 1941, the Bismarck *and* Prince Eugen,
*raiding in the North Atlantic, were intercepted off
Greenland and brought to action. The British battleship*
Hood *was sunk by the* Bismarck. *The latter was damaged
and was pursued by a powerful British force, which scored
several hits with torpedoes. On the 26th the* Bismarck *was
stopped four hundred miles west of her base at Brest.*

Winston Churchill at the Admiralty

On this Monday night I went to the Admiralty and
watched the scene on the charts in the War Room, where
the news streamed in every few minutes. "What are you
doing here?" I said to the Controller, Admiral Fraser. "I
am waiting to see what I have got to repair," he said. Four
hours passed quickly away, and when I left I could see
that Admiral Pound and his select company of experts
were sure the *Bismarck* was doomed.

The German commander, Admiral Lutjens, had no
illusions. Shortly before midnight he reported, "Ship
unmanoeuvrable. We shall fight to the last shell. Long live
the Führer!" The *Bismarck* was still four hundred miles

from Brest, and no longer even able to steer thither. Strong German bomber forces were now sent to the rescue, and U-boats hastened to the scene, one of which, *having already expended her torpedoes*, reported that the *Ark Royal* had passed her within easy striking distance. Meanwhile the *King George V* and the *Rodney* were drawing near. Fuel was a grave anxiety, and Admiral Tovey had decided that unless the *Bismarck*'s speed could be greatly reduced he would have to abandon the chase at midnight. I suggested to the First Sea Lord, and he signalled accordingly, that he should be towed home if necessary, but by then it was known that the *Bismarck* was actually steaming in the wrong direction. Her main armament was uninjured, and Admiral Tovey had decided to bring her to battle in the morning.

A north-westerly gale was blowing when daylight came on the 27th. The *Rodney* opened fire at 8.47 a.m., followed a minute later by the *King George V*. The British ships quickly began to hit, and after a pause the *Bismarck* too opened fire. For a short time her shooting was good, although the crew, after four gruelling days, were utterly exhausted and falling asleep at their posts. With her third salvo she straddled the *Rodney*, but thereafter the weight of the British attack was overwhelming, and within half an hour most of her guns were silent. A fire was blazing amidships, and she had a heavy list to port. The *Rodney* now turned across her bow, pouring in a heavy fire from a range of no more than four thousand yards. By 10.15 all the *Bismarck*'s guns were silent and her mast was shot away. The ship lay wallowing in the heavy seas, a flaming and smoking ruin; yet even then she did not sink.

At eleven o'clock I had to report to the House of Commons, meeting in the Church House, both about the battle in Crete and the drama of the *Bismarck*. "This morning," I said, "shortly after daylight the *Bismarck*, virtually at a standstill, far from help, was attacked by the British pursuing battleships. I do not know what were the results of the bombardment. It appears, however, that the *Bismarck* was not sunk by gunfire, and she will now be dispatched by torpedo. It is thought that this is now proceeding, and it is also thought that there cannot be any lengthy delay in disposing of this vessel. Great as is our loss in the *Hood*, the *Bismarck* must be regarded as the most powerful, as she is the newest battleship in the world." I had just sat down when a slip of paper was passed to me which led me to rise again. I asked the indulgence of the House and said, "I have just received news that the *Bismarck* is sunk." They seemed content.

It was the cruiser *Dorsetshire* that delivered the final blow with torpedoes, and at 10.40 the great ship turned over and foundered. With her perished nearly two thousand Germans and their Fleet Commander, Admiral Lutjens. One hundred and ten survivors, exhausted but sullen, were rescued by us. The work of mercy was interrupted by the appearance of a U-boat and the British ships were compelled to withdraw. Five other Germans were picked up by a U-boat and a ship engaged in weather reporting, but the Spanish cruiser *Canarias*, which arrived on the scene later, found only floating bodies.

This episode brings into relief many important points relating to sea warfare, and illustrates both the enormous structural strength of the German ship and the immense difficulties and dangers with which her sortie had confronted our very numerous forces. Had she escaped the moral effects of her continuing existence as much as the material damage she might have inflicted on our shipping would have been calamitous. Many misgivings would have arisen regarding our capacity to control the oceans, and these would have been trumpeted round the world to our great detriment and discomfort. All branches rightly claimed their share in the successful outcome. The pursuit began with the cruisers, which led to the first disastrous action. Then when the enemy was lost it was aircraft that found him and guided the cruisers back to the chase. Therefore it was a cruiser which directed the sea-borne aircraft who struck the decisive blows, and finally it was the destroyers who harassed and held him through a long night and led the battleships to the last scene of

destruction. While credit is due to all, we must not forget
that the long-drawn battle turned on the first injury
inflicted on the *Bismarck* by the guns of the *Prince of
Wales*. Thus the battleship and the gun were dominant
both at the beginning and at the end.

The traffic in the Atlantic continued unmolested.
To the President I telegraphed on the 28th:

> I will send you later the inside story of the fighting
> with the *Bismarck*. She was a terrific ship, and a
> masterpiece of naval construction. Her removal eases
> our battleship situation, as we should have had to keep
> *King George V*, *Prince of Wales*, and the two *Nelsons*
> practically tied to Scapa Flow to guard against a sortie
> of *Bismarck* and *Tirpitz*, as they could choose their
> moment and we should have to allow for one of our
> ships refitting. Now it is a different story. The effect
> upon the Japanese will be highly beneficial. I expect
> they are doing all their sums again.
>
> Winston Churchill

The Channel Dash: 11-12 February 1942

With American and British interest shifting to the
Pacific and East Indies, Raeder began to consider using
the German surface fleet in the Atlantic again. The
German ships *Scharnhorst*, *Gneisenau* and *Prinz Eugen*
had been stationed at Brest ever since the *Bismarck* had
been sunk. They had been heavily attacked by the R.A.F.,
and Raeder suggested to Hitler, who had himself pointed
out that the protection of these ships from air attack was
proving too difficult, that the Brest Group should be sent
into the Atlantic against Allied convoys.

But, besides being deterred by the precedent of the
Bismarck, Hitler had suddenly decided that the Allies
were about to land in Norway.

For these reasons Hitler had refused to allow Raeder to
send the surface fleet into the Atlantic, and had ordered

him instead to send the Brest Group north to protect the Norwegian coast and to operate against the Russian convoys.

Raeder protested strongly; he pointed out the difficulties—the Brest Group had only two alternative routes, either by a long voyage round the British Isles, when they would almost certainly be attacked by the Home Fleet from Scapa Flow, or by the shorter but equally hazardous route through the English Channel, where they would be attacked by the R.A.F. as well as by the Home Fleet. The crews of the German ships were untrained and enervated by their long stay at Brest, and there was no question of their being able to fight a sustained action such as the *Bismarck* had encountered.

Hitler insisted that the threat to Norway was extremely serious and that the ships must be moved. He left it to Raeder to decide how, but he showed himself strongly in favour of the Channel route.

The Naval Staff set to and produced rough plans for operation "Cerberus", the code word for the movement of the Brest ships. In view of the state of training of the crews, unfitting them for a long voyage, they decided that the ships should go through the Straits of Dover.

In the second week of January, when the plans were completed, Hitler summoned a general conference to discuss the operation.

Ciliax* . . . explained that he had decided that the ships should leave Brest under cover of darkness, making the actual passage of the Straits of Dover in daylight, since they would thereby be able to have the maximum air cover. Lieutenant-General Jeschonnek, Göring's Chief of Staff, doubted whether the necessary aircraft would be available, but Hitler ordered him to see to it that they were. Hitler finally summed up:

"In view of past experience I do not believe the British are capable of making and carrying out lightning decisions. I do not believe that they will be as swift as the

* Vice-Admiral Ciliax, in command of the operation (Ed.)

Naval Staff and Vice-Admiral Ciliax assumed in transferring their bomber and fighter aircraft to the south-eastern part of England for an attack on our ships in the Dover Straits. Picture what would happen if the situation were reversed, i.e. if a surprise report came in that British battleships had appeared in the Thames estuary and were heading for the Straits of Dover. Even we would hardly be able to bring up fighters and bombers swiftly and methodically. The situation of the Brest Group is like that of a patient with cancer who is doomed unless he submits to an operation. An operation, on the other hand, even though it may have to be drastic, will at least offer some hope that the patient's life may yet be saved. The passage of our ships through the Channel is such an operation. It must therefore be attempted. . . .

"There is nothing to be gained by leaving the ships at Brest; their 'flypaper' effect, that is their ability to tie up enemy air forces, may not continue for long. Only as long as the ships remain in battleworthy condition will the enemy feel obliged to attack. But the moment they are seriously damaged—and this may happen any day—the enemy will discontinue his attacks. Such a development will nullify the one and only advantage derived from leaving the ships at Brest. The operation is to be prepared as proposed by the C-in-C., Navy."

On the evening of 11 February, the *Scharnhorst*, *Gneisenau* and *Prinz Eugen*, accompanied by destroyers and E-boats, left Brest, and, at full speed, began their dash up the English Channel.

Running the Gauntlet

It was planned that the squadron should keep an average speed of twenty-six knots, and in the beginning, with favourable tides, they were actually making about thirty knots. After rounding Ushant to the west of Brittany, the formation set course for the Channel at 1.13 a.m. As total radio silence was observed, reports of

position came only from our radar stations along the
French coast, which picked up the warships at intervals.
Each time this was a pleasant surprise. After the loss of
two valuable hours, I was fairly certain that at dawn I
should have to transfer the fighter forces standing by from
the Pas de Calais down to the Le Havre-Caen-Cherbourg
sector. Allowance had been made for such a case in the
plan, but it would have meant an additional strain on
everyone concerned. Each new report showed that the
warships were catching up on their initial delay until, early
in the morning, it was clear that they would make up their
time and, with the first light of day, would be in the
prearranged position exactly to the minute.

. . . . At 6.30 a.m. decks were cleared for action on
board the battleships, which were travelling at high speed
through the darkness towards the Channel. Off Cherbourg
a flotilla of torpedo boats joined them to strengthen the
outer safety belt which so far had only been formed by
destroyers. The whole unit consisted now of the two
battleships, the cruiser, seven destroyers and eight to
fifteen E-boats, the latter relieved from sector to sector.

The weather was cloudy, with a fifteen hundred-foot
ceiling and relatively good visibility. At 8.14 a.m. the first
night-fighters took off in complete darkness and were over
the fleet at 8.50 a.m. From now onwards, during the
whole day, fighter forces kept in continuous and direct
contact with the ships. The air umbrella—a small one, of
course—was opened. Our destroyer fighters were flying
only a few feet above the water in order not to be detected
by the English radar stations. All radio communications
were, of course, silenced. At 8.54 a.m. the dawn broke.
The units were off the Cotentin peninsula.

The first dramatic note crept into the operation when
naval security forces discovered a previously unnoticed
minefield off Dieppe only a few hours before the ships
were due, and although a channel was swiftly swept by an
all-out effort of four minesweepers, the decision to pass
through this barely cleared path was a very risky one. But

there was no alternative bar returning and calling the whole operation off. The unit passed through without incident.

The night-fighters, which flew mainly on the port side of the warships, the side towards the enemy, had been joined in the meantime by day-fighters. The operation ran according to plan. Discovery by the enemy, which, luckily, had not yet occurred, had to be avoided for as long as possible. In briefing the pilots, each commander had therefore stressed to the utmost the orders: fly at the lowest possible level and with radio silence. Those who knew the general lack of radio discipline in the Luftwaffe, and particularly among fighter pilots, can imagine how worried I now was in this respect.

. . . . At eleven o'clock Middle European Time (ten o'clock British time) an alerting radio message from a British fighter was intercepted by our listening service. It said nothing except that a large German naval formation consisting of three capital ships and about twenty warships was steaming at high speed towards the Straits of Dover, present position about fifty miles off the mouth of the Somme. The secret was out.

. . . . The German high-frequency experts took a large share in creating the obvious confusion of the British command. Usually we gave little heed to these contraptions, which always remain a mystery to the uninitiated, and indeed to quite a few laymen in the high command of the German Luftwaffe, including its C.-in-C., who once said to me that his understanding of such things was already overtaxed when operating a radio set. One should value all the more the activities of these experts, who often have to struggle against stupidity, unintelligence and even ill-will! They had created strong interference with the British radar stations by a series of installations and by different methods. They had also directed interference transmissions against the British fighter intercoms, and by special instruments in bombers had simulated radar signals giving false reports of approaching large formations, against which the British actually sent strong fighter forces. The confusion created in this way continued even when the German warships were clearly located and when practical deception was no longer possible.

At this moment [15.30 hours] the flagship *Scharnhorst* was heavily shaken; the lights failed, and the wireless went dead. She had struck a mine, and, leaving a trail of oil behind her, now came to a standstill. The leading destroyer, Z29, was ordered alongside to take aboard the Commander and the fighter liaison. At the same time the weather was deteriorating rapidly with a cloud ceiling of five to six hundred feet, visibility half to one mile, and rain. The naval formation proceeded with *Prinz Eugen* and *Gneisenau* as well as the bulk of the destroyers and torpedo boats, the enemy concentrating on the *Scharnhorst* and the destroyer Z29. It was 3.50 p.m. Near *Prinz Eugen* an M.T.B. approached. Change of course, detonation of the torpedo a thousand yards aft. With the stopping of the *Scharnhorst* the naval formation split up. *Prinz Eugen* and *Gneisenau* proceeded with the main destroyer and torpedo-boat force, while *Scharnhorst* stayed behind.

. . . . Meanwhile, ill luck still dogged the C.-in-C. of the battleships. Since his flagship had been damaged by the mine he had been aboard the destroyer Z29, which now developed engine trouble in the port engine. Again the C.-in-C. and the fighter liaison, with a limited staff, had to be transferred. The destroyer *Hermann Schömann* was ordered to stand by, and the transfer was effected by means of a cutter, under continuous attacks by British aircraft and in a rough sea. At 6.45 p.m., while the Admiral was still bobbing up and down in the cutter, the *Scharnhorst*, which had been brought under way again, went off at full speed, trying to catch up with the flotilla. This must have been a great personal disappointment, mitigated, however, by the satisfaction of knowing that the *Scharnhorst* was now able to continue towards her destination.

Towards 7 p.m. it was getting dark. Day- and night-fighters were battling with the last Wellington bombers, which attacked incessantly and with tenacity. *Gneisenau*, *Prinz Eugen* and *Hermann Schömann* reported kills by fighters and A.A. fire. At 7.35 hours it was quite dark, and fighter action was ended for the day. Successes and losses could not yet be assessed, but one thing was clear: we had completed our task to form and maintain an air umbrella over the German warships while they were breaking through.

. . . . During the night the R.A.F. was very active. Besides intensive air reconnaissance, they were mainly busy with mine-laying operations, in order to mine the whole route right up to the German Bight and the Elbe Estuary. Our night-fighters kept in contact with the enemy, but there were no major actions.

The British mines still did some damage that night. Shortly after 9 p.m. the *Gneisenau* shook under an explosion and all her engines stopped. She had hit a mine! Yet the damage was only superficial, and after a short time she was under way again, making twenty-five knots. An hour and a half later the *Scharnhorst* hit another mine. She too could soon continue, although at first only at ten, later at fifteen knots.

It was still dark when the *Gneisenau* and *Prinz Eugen* reached the mouth of the Elbe and cast anchor. At that time the German Bight was still outside the range of British fighters. After their heavy defeat in their attack on Wilhelmshaven on 4 September and 18 December 1939, the British bombers no longer ventured during daytime into this area, which was well covered by radar stations.

. . . . The remarkable thing about Churchill's description is it shows that Hitler in his planning judged the suspected reaction of the British command absolutely correctly. Faced with the German surprise, they showed amazingly little ability to improvise. Hitler had been right in his statement that the British would not make any lightning decisions, and this was the only possible explanation which all those who took part in the venture could find for the unbelievable fact that the formation was not attacked before noon, when it had already nearly reached the narrowest point of the Channel. This was the key to our success.

. . . . The British Prime Minister describes in detail the failure of the radar organization during the operation. Until after the war, opinion in Britain was that it had been an unaccountable episode, a national misfortune. Only after the war was it discovered that the reason for this inexplicable failure was no less than a clever trick of the chief of German radio communication, Martini. Unfortunately, the German command did not draw the necessary conclusions from this victory in the radar war and did not start a rapid development of this weapon. The British learned from their defeat and developed radar interference to a perfection which later on during the bombing war became fatal for the Reich.

Colonel Adolf Galland,
commanding Luftwaffe fighter cover

"Vice-Admiral Ciliax," wrote *The Times*, "has succeeded where the Duke of Medina Sidonia failed. . . . Nothing more mortifying to the pride of sea power has happened in Home Waters since the seventeenth century."

The Small Killers

The Italian Navy, having been worsted in surface action in the Mediterranean, still had a trump card to play. On the night of 17 December 1941 the Italian submarine Scire *lay outside Alexandria harbour. She carried several "pigs"—torpedo-shaped craft on which two men, sitting astride, could penetrate protected harbours undetected and plant limpet mines on shipping inside them.*

Alexandria: 18 December 1941

The plan of operations provided for the arrival of the *Scire* on a certain evening, a few thousand metres from the entrance to Alexandria harbour; as it was assumed that everything would be in darkness (owing to the black-out), it had been arranged that, in order to facilitate the submarine's landfall, the coast being low-lying and without conspicuous features, and allow her to identify the harbour (for the success of the operators' raid would depend largely on the precision with which the point of their release was determined) on the evening before, and also on the one of the action, our aircraft would bomb the harbour. The submarine would then release the operators. The latter, proceeding on courses laid down beforehand, as soon as they arrived in front of the harbour, would have to overcome the obstructions and attack the targets previously assigned to them by the commander of the *Scire*, who would base his orders on the latest data transmitted to him by radio. After attaching the charges to the hulls of the targets, the operators were to lay a certain number of floating incendiary bombs with which they had been supplied. These bombs would go off about an hour after the warheads had exploded and were intended to set alight the oil which would by then have spread from the ships which had been attacked; it was expected that this would cause fire to break out in the harbour, affecting all the vessels therein, together with the floating docks, the harbour installations and the warehouses . . . thus putting the chief enemy naval base in the Eastern Mediterranean utterly out of action.

The sea was very calm, the night dark. Lights in the harbour permitted the pilots to determine their position, which they found to be precisely as planned. They went ahead so coolly that at one point, as de la Penne relates in his report, "as we were ahead of schedule, we opened our ration tins and had a meal. We were then five hundred metres from the Ras el Tin Lighthouse."

At last they reached the net defences at the harbour's entrance.

"We saw some people at the end of the pier and heard them talking; one of them was walking about with a lighted oil-lamp.

"We also saw a large motor-boat cruising in silence off

the pier and dropping depth-charges. These charges were
rather a nuisance to us."

While the six heads, only just above the water, were
looking, with all the concentrated attention of which they
were capable, for a gap in the net, three British destroyers
suddenly appeared at the entrance to the harbour, waiting
to go in: guide lights were switched on to show them the
way and the net gates were thrown wide open. Without a
second's hesitation our three assault craft slipped into the
harbour with the British destroyers: they were in! They
had lost sight of one another during this manoeuvre, but
they were now close to their targets. The latter had been
distributed as follows: de la Penne was to take the
battleship *Valiant*, Marceglia the battleship *Queen
Elizabeth*, and Martellotta was to look for the aircraft
carrier; if she were not in harbour, he was to attack a
loaded tanker in the hope that the oil or petrol which
would issue from it would spread over the water and thus
furnish excellent fuel for the floating incendiary bombs the
operators were to scatter before abandoning their "pigs".

Inside the harbour, after passing the interned French
warships, the presence of which was well known, de la
Penne sighted, at the presumed anchorage, the huge dark
mass of the target assigned to him, the thirty-two-
thousand-ton battleship *Valiant*. As he approached her, he
encountered the anti-torpedo net barrier: he got through it
surfaced, "in order to lose as little time as possible, for I
found that my physical condition, owing to the cold,
would be unlikely to let me hold out much longer." (His
diver's suit had been leaking ever since he had left the
submarine.) He had no difficulty with negotiation of the
net: he was now thirty metres from the *Valiant*; it was
nineteen minutes past two. He touched the hull, giving it a
slight bump; in performing the evolution necessary to get
beneath the hull, his "pig" seemed to take on extra weight
and went to the bottom in seventeen metres of water; de la
Penne dived after it and discovered to his amazement that
there was no sign of his second pilot. He rose to the
surface to look for him, but could not see him; everything

was quiet aboard the battleship; no alarm had been given.
De la Penne left Bianchi to his fate, returned to the
bottom and tried to start the engine of his craft to get it
underneath the hull, as it had meanwhile moved some
distance away. But the engine would not start; a rapid
check-over soon showed what the trouble was: a steel
wire had got entangled in the propeller.

What was to be done? All alone, with his craft
immobilized on the sea-bed a few metres from the target,
de la Penne resolved to try the only possible expedient:
this was to drag the "pig" by main force, finding his
direction from the compass, beneath the battleship. Speed
was essential, for he feared that at any moment the British
might pick up his second pilot, who had probably fainted
and would be floating about close by. . . . The alarm
would be given, depth-charges would be dropped, his
operation and those of his companions would be doomed
to certain failure, for they would be at work only a few
hundred metres away. With all his strength, panting and
sweating, he dragged at the craft; his goggles became
obscured and the mud he was stirring up prevented his
reading the compass, his breath began to come in great
gasps and it became difficult to breathe at all through the
mask, but he stuck to it and made progress; he could hear,
close above him, the noises made aboard the ship,
especially the sound of an alternating pump, which he
used to find his direction. After forty minutes of
superhuman effort, making a few inches at every pull, he
at last bumped his head against the hull. He made a
cursory survey of the position: he seemed to be at about
the middle of the ship, an excellent spot for causing
maximum damage. He was now almost exhausted; but he
used the last vestiges of his strength to set the time fuses;
in accordance with the orders he had received he regulated
them so as to cause the explosion at five o'clock precisely
(Italian time, corresponding with six o'clock local time).
He did not release his incendiary bombs, for when they
rose to the surface they would reveal the presence and the
position of the threat now established under the hull with

the fuses in action. He left his craft on the sea-bed under
the vessel and swam to the surface. The moment he got
his head above water he removed his mask and sank it;
the fresh, pure air revived him; he began to swim slowly
away from the ship. But someone called out to him, a
searchlight picked him out, a burst of machine-gun fire
brought him to a halt. He swam back towards the vessel
and climbed out of the water on to the mooring-buoy at
the bows of the *Valiant*. He found there his second pilot
Bianchi, who, after fainting, had risen to the surface like a
balloon and on regaining consciousness had hidden
himself on the buoy so as not risk causing an alarm which
would have disturbed the work of his leader. "Aboard
they were making facetious remarks, believing that our
operation had failed; they were talking contemptuously
about Italians. I called Bianchi's attention to the
probability that in a few hours they would have changed
their minds about the Italians." It was then about 3.30. At
last a motorboat turned up and the two "shipwrecked"
men were picked up by it and taken aboard the battleship.
A British officer asked who they were, where they had
come from and expressed ironical sympathy with their
lack of success. The two operators, who were now
prisoners of war, made clear who they were, by handing
over their military identity cards. They refused to answer
any other questions. They were taken in the motor-boat,
separated from each other, to a hut ashore, near the Ras
el Tin Lighthouse. Bianchi was the first to be cross-
examined; on leaving the hut he made a sign to de la
Penne indicating that he had said nothing. It was then the
latter's turn: naturally, he held his tongue; the Britisher,
who had a revolver in his hand, seemed to be an excitable
sort of fellow, "I'll soon find a way to make you talk," he
said in excellent Italian. The men were taken back aboard
the *Valiant*: it was then four o'clock.

They were received by the commanding officer, Captain
Morgan, who asked them where the charge was located.
On their refusing to answer the two men, accompanied by
the officer of the watch and escorted by an armed picket,

were placed in one of the holds forward, between the two gun-turrets, not very far from the point at which the charge would explode.

We will now let de la Penne take up the tale.

"Our escort were rather white about the gills and behaved very nicely to us; they gave me rum to drink and offered cigarettes; they also tried to make us talk. Bianchi sat down and went to sleep. I perceived from the ribbons on the sailors' caps that we were aboard the battleship *Valiant*. When there were about ten minutes left before the explosion, I asked if I could speak to the commanding officer. I was taken aft, into his presence. I told him that in a few minutes his ship would blow up, that there was nothing he could do about it and that, if he wished, he could still get his crew into a place of safety. He again asked me where I had placed the charge, and as I did not reply had me escorted back to the hold. As we went along I heard the loudspeakers giving orders to abandon ship, as the vessel had been attacked by Italians, and saw people running aft. When I was again in the hold I said to Bianchi, as I came down the ladder, that things had turned out badly and that it was all up with us, but that we could be content, since we had succeeded, in spite of everything, in bringing the operation to a successful conclusion. Bianchi, however, did not answer me. I looked for him and could not find him. I supposed that the British, believing that I had confessed, had removed him. A few minutes passed (they were infernal ones for me: would the explosion take place?) and then it came. The vessel reared, with extreme violence. All the lights went out and the hold became filled with smoke. I was surrounded by shackles which had been hanging from the ceiling and had now fallen. I was unhurt, except for pain in a knee, which had been grazed by one of the shackles in its fall. The vessel was listing to port. I opened one of the port-holes very near sea level, hoping to be able to get through it and escape. This proved to be impossible as the port-hole was too small, and I gave up the idea: but I left the port open, hoping that through it more water would enter. I waited

for a few moments. The hold was now illuminated by the
light which entered through the port. I concluded that it
would be rash to stay there any longer, noticing that the
vessel was now lying on the bottom and continuing slowly
to list to port. I climbed up the ladder and, finding the
hatchway open, began to walk aft; there was no one
about. But there were still many of the crew at the stern.
They got up as I passed them; I went on till I reached the
Captain. At that moment he was engaged in giving orders
for salvaging his ship. I asked him what he had done with
my diver. He did not reply and the officer of the watch
told me to be silent. The ship had now listed through four
or five degrees and come to a standstill. I saw from a
clock that it was a quarter-past six. I went farther aft,
where a number of officers were standing, and began to
watch the battleship *Queen Elizabeth* which lay about five
hundred metres astern of us.

"The crew of that battleship were standing in her bows.
A few seconds passed and then the *Queen Elizabeth*, too,
blew up. She rose a few inches out of the water and
fragments of iron and other objects flew out of her funnel,
mixed with oil which even reached the deck of the
Valiant, splashing everyone of us standing on her stern.
An officer came up and asked me to tell him on my word
of honour if there were any other charges under the ship. I
made no reply and was then again taken back to the hold.
After about a quarter of an hour I was escorted up to the
officers' mess, where at last I could sit down, and where I
found Bianchi. Shortly afterwards I was put aboard a
motor-boat, which took me back to Ras el Tin.

"I noticed that the anchor, which had been hanging at
the bows, was now underwater. During transit an officer
asked me whether we had got in through the gaps in the
mole. At Ras el Tin we were locked in two cells and kept
there until towards evening. I asked whether I could be
given a little sunlight, as I was very cold. A soldier came,
felt my pulse and told me that I was perfectly all right.

"Towards evening we were put into a small lorry
and transported therein to a prisoner-of-war camp in

Alexandria. I found some Italians in the camp who had heard the explosions that morning. We lay down on the ground without having had any food, and, though we were soaked through, we slept till the following morning. I was taken to the infirmary for treatment of my knee injury and some Italian orderlies gave me an excellent dish of macaroni. The next morning I was removed to Cairo."

In 1944 after de la Penne and Bianchi had come back to Italy from prison, they were awarded the gold medal for gallantry in war. And he who pinned the medal on the chest of de la Penne was none other than Admiral Morgan, formerly commanding officer of the *Valiant* and at that time chief of the Allied Naval Mission in Italy.

J. Valerio Borghese

Two could play at this game.

Please report what is being done to emulate the exploits of the Italians in Alexandria Harbour and similar methods of this kind.

At the beginning of the war Colonel Jefferis had a number of bright ideas on this subject, which received very little encouragement. Is there any reason why we should be incapable of the same kind of scientific aggressive action that the Italians have shown? One would have thought we should have been in the lead.

Please state the exact position.

Winston Churchill to General Ismay, 18 January 1942

Mr. Churchill had realized that the enemy's employment of a manned torpedo was a mode of warfare particularly suited to the capabilities and needs of Britain in the dark days of 1942. Heavy capital units of the German and Italian navies were constituting a serious menace to our lines of communication and compelling large-scale strategic positioning of our own capital ships, merely by remaining safely for months on end in strongly defended anchorages.

The Navy had not been blind to this situation and

was already in the process of producing a midget
submarine—the X craft—to be manned by three or four
men.

*The British planned an attack with midget submarines
on Kaafjord on the coast of Norway, where the* Tirpitz,
Scharnhorst *and* Lützow *lay.*

22 September 1943

Next morning the entrance of Kaafjord began; X.7 left
the lee of the Brattholm islands shortly after midnight,
and X.6 followed an hour later. Within three hours Place
had taken his craft successfully through the first obstacle,
the anti-submarine net at the entrance to the fjord. With
Cameron, however, things were a little more difficult. The
periscope flooded soon after they left the billet and
continued to flood and reflood time and time again. It was
a mystery how he conned them throughout the rest of the
attack, for he could hardly see anything. But luck was
with them. They surfaced in the wake of a small coaster
and followed her through the nets in broad daylight.
Cameron had acted in the coolest manner. They must
have been invisible.

Meanwhile life in Kaafjord in general and in *Tirpitz* in
particular pursued its normal course, as the following
extract from the battleship's deck-log shows:

05.00-22 Called the hands.
Set normal anti-aircraft and anti-sabotage watch ashore
and afloat. Boat-gate in anti-torpedo nets opened for
boat and tug traffic. Hydrophone listening office closed
down.

Once his craft had entered Kaafjord, Cameron went to
sixty feet and proceeded by dead reckoning, taking the
opportunity to strip the periscope, but without managing
to effect a permanent repair. To add to the difficulties the
periscope hoisting-motor brake burnt out, resulting in

manual control of the brake being necessary when raising
or lowering the very dimly-lensed "stick". It is no wonder
that twice they only just avoided collisions by a coat of
paint. "Once," wrote Lorimer, "we passed under the bows
of a destroyer, between her stem and her mooring buoy."
A few minutes later they were so close to the tanker
Nordmark, lying half a mile from *Tirpitz*, that a periscope
sight came just in time for another mooring buoy to be
avoided by a very sharp alteration of course. E.R.A.
Goddard was kept busy on the wheel.

By 07.05 X.6 had closed the anti-torpedo shore-net
defence of *Tirpitz* and was through the boat-entrance and
within striking distance of her target.

After entering the fjord at four o'clock X.7 had her first
piece of bad luck when she was forced deep by a
patrolling motor-launch. While she was thus temporarily
"blind" she got caught in the unoccupied square of A/T
nets, once used to house the *Lützow*, but by then empty.
They spent a busy, if cautious, hour or more in getting
free. Place had no wish to put a diver out unless it was
really necessary, especially as this was a case of getting
free from a net as opposed to getting through one. After
much pumping and blowing the craft shook herself free
and shot up to the surface. Luckily she was not spotted
during her brief moments before she dived again. All this
violent action seemed to have put the gyro-compass "off
the board", as Place wrote, and the trim-pump was also
out of action. Then the craft was "hooked" again, this
time by a lone wire across the periscope standard. But by
six o'clock she was free once more, and although, without
a trim-pump, her trim at periscope-depth was somewhat
precarious, she was soon headed down the fjord for her
target.

At 07.10, Place having decided in favour of passing
under *Tirpitz*'s A/T net defences, X.7 endeavoured to do
this at seventy-five feet (which should have been well
below the maximum depth of such nets) and was
surprisingly caught. Up to this point no suspicions had
been aroused in *Tirpitz*, and normal harbour routine was

in progress. That the two craft should have reached the
innermost defences of the battleship after so long a
journey and through so many hazards to arrive within five
minutes of each other was a supreme credit to careful and
intelligent planning and to able and determined execution.

X.6 made her way through the boat-gate, following
close behind a picket-boat. Once the latter was through
the gate was closed, which fact Cameron was able to
discern on his periscope and report to his crew.

"So we've had it now as far as changing our mind,"
joked Goddard.

The water was very calm, and it was unfortunate that
the craft should run aground on the north shore of the
netted enclosure. As she was at remarkably shallow depth
when this occurred it was impossible for her to be freed
without just breaking surface for a few moments. This
surfacing was observed in *Tirpitz* but, although reported
as a "long black submarine-like object", there was a five-
minute delay in passing the information on to higher
authority as it was thought that the object sighted might be
a porpoise. So X.6 was enabled, by some German's fear of
ridicule, to close inside the range of *Tirpitz*'s main and
subsidiary armament. Five minutes later their luck,
hitherto so good, deserted them again. They hit a
submerged rock and were pushed to the surface.

Lorimer took her down immediately, and from her
position some eighty yards abeam of the battleship her
head was again turned to close. But this time she had been
clearly sighted and correctly identified. The gyro had been
put out of action by the grounding and by the subsequent
acute angles that the craft had taken, and the periscope
was almost completely flooded, with the result that
progress in the target's direction was blind. Indeed,
Cameron was hoping to fix their position by the shadow of
the battleship.

After another five minutes X.6 got caught in an
obstruction which she took to be the A/T net on the far
(starboard) side of *Tirpitz*, but which was probably
something hanging down either from the battleship or

from one of the small vessels alongside. She surfaced
where she was, close on *Tirpitz*'s port bow, to be greeted
with a brisk fire from small arms and hand-grenades from
the deck that loomed above her. Don Cameron realized
that escape was hopeless, so, directing the crew to destroy
the most secret equipment, he had the craft go astern until
the hydroplane guard was scraping *Tirpitz*'s hull abreast
"B" turret. There he released the charges, both of which
had been set earlier to detonate one hour after release, and
scuttled the craft. It was 7.17 a.m.

"Bail out!" came the order.

"This we did," wrote Lorimer subsequently, "and we
were very sad to see X.6 go. She went down on top of the
charges, under 'B' turret. It was the end of an old friend."

They were picked out of the water by *Tirpitz*'s picket-
boat, which also made unsuccessful attempts to secure a
tow to the X-craft before it sank.

On board *Tirpitz* and in Kaafjord the alarm had now
been properly raised and it is clear from entries in the
battleship's log-book that complete surprise had been
achieved. "Action stations" was sounded in the battleship,
steam was ordered, and the ship prepared for sea, in order
to get her outside the nets. This order was apparently not
given until all the watertight doors were closed, twenty
minutes after the crew of X.6 had been embarked. It is
not clear why there was this delay, nor why the Germans
initially took the four of them for Russians, unless
because of their unshavenness, or because of their
presence in such northerly waters, or both. The four of
them—Cameron, Lorimer, Goddard and Sub-Lieutenant
"Dick" Kendall—were huddled together in a group while
orders were shouted and divers put down over the side.
Their interrogation was being left until later, but an
attempt was made to warm them up after their "dip" with
generous amounts of hot coffee and schnapps. They all
recall that as the time neared 8.15 there was a certain
amount of anxious and surreptitious looking at watches,
mingled with speculation as to what effect the charges
would have, and connected, in Lorimer's mind at least,

with the knowledge that the divers were still under the ship. These unfortunate men had been given the unpleasant task of examining the hull for limpet mines, although it appears that some form of charge dropped under the ship was also expected, as the extract from the log recording the preparations for sea reads: "In order to leave the net enclosure if possible before the time-fused mines detonate."

The interrogation was just starting when the charges went off—at 08.12.

"I was thrown off my feet with the force of the explosion," Lorimer recalls, "and we all ended up on the deck. I could not help thinking that the two divers must have come up much more quickly than they went down—with the aid of what I knew would be at least four tons of amatol and which I now know to have been eight."

"There was panic on board the *Tirpitz* as our charges went off," wrote Kendall after his return from Germany. "The German gun-crew shot up a number of their own tankers and small boats and also wiped out a gun position inboard with uncontrolled firing. Everybody seemed to be waving pistols and threatening us to find out the number of midgets on the job. The Germans lost about a hundred men all told, mostly due to their own lack of discipline."

Place had been disappointed to see *Tirpitz* still on the surface following the explosion. The fact that she survived at all was largely due to the limited evasive action she was able to take after the sinking of X.6. This was achieved by heaving in on the starboard cable and veering port to take the ship as far away as possible from the position in which the craft had gone down. The battleship's log records at 08.12 "two heavy consecutive detonations to port at one-tenth of a second interval". The first explosion was abreast "X" turret about six to eight yards from the ship, the other fifty to sixty yards off the bow in X.6's last position. The latter explosion was almost certainly composed of three charges going up together, for a subsequent examination of the sea-bed failed to discover any of the charges, or even fragments.

With the explosions the giant ship was heaved five or six feet upward, and a large column of water was flung into the air on the port side. Members of the ship's company on deck were hurled off their feet and several casualties resulted. The ship took on an immediate list to port of about five degrees. All the lights failed. Oil-fuel started to leak out from amidships. From the damage reports compiled in *Tirpitz* during the morning after the attack the following items of the battleship's structure and equipment were put out of action: all three main engines; one generator room; all lighting equipment; all electrical equipment; wireless telegraphy rooms; hydrophone station; "A" and "C" turrets; anti-aircraft control positions; range-finding gear; port rudder.

One person was killed and about forty wounded by the explosion, in addition to those killed and injured by the Germans' own gunfire, and five hundred tons of water were taken aboard. In all, the final effect of the attack was completely satisfactory. Even though the *Tirpitz* was still afloat, and even though many of the minor disablements she suffered were only temporary, she was certainly immobilized as far as undertaking any sea-action was concerned. On 22 November, two months after the attack, the German *Marinegruppenkommando Nord* reported to the German Naval War Staff that "as a result of the successful midget-submarine attack the battle cruiser *Tirpitz* had been put out of action for months". It was, indeed, considered by the War Staff that the forty-thousand-ton ship might never regain complete operational efficiency. The truth of the estimates was borne out by the fact that it was not until April of the following year that *Tirpitz* was able to limp from her anchorage, only to be further damaged and finally destroyed by air attack.

Grudge Fight

The men who fought the war at sea were not always fighting the enemy. . . .

I was interviewing request-men one morning and had reached the last man.

"Next request is by Able Seaman Morris, sir," said the Coxswain; then he shouted—"Able Seaman Morris . . . 'hun. Able Seaman Morris . . . three paces forward . . . *march.*" He looked down to consult the request book. "Able Seaman Morris requests to see the First Lieutenant through Divisional Officer for permission to have a grudge fight with Ordinary Seaman Sweeney."

The Coxswain completed the formal introduction. "Able Seaman Morris, sir." Having satisfied himself that I was fully aware of the identity of the requestman before me he stood back to see how I would deal with this somewhat extraordinary request.

Able Seaman Morris saluted and got his eyes focused on a point on the bulkhead behind my left shoulder.

"Well, Morris," I started, "what's all this about?"

Morris spoke with suppressed emotion—" 'e pinched the end orf me banger, sir."

"He did what?" I cried, thoroughly startled.

"Pinched the end orf me banger, sir," repeated Morris stolidly, not shifting his sphinx-like gaze. "Ordinary Seaman Sweeney did, sir."

I was nonplussed. Banger, of course, was a sausage, but how one pinched the end off one, or what excuse that was for a grudge fight was beyond me. I turned to the Coxswain for enlightenment.

"Do you know anything about this, Coxswain?" I asked.

Of course he did. Coxswains know everything.

"It appears, sir," he said, "that number five mess —that's Able Seaman Morris's mess—don't go much for Pusser's sausages, sir, so they got some from Naafi. Naafi bangers—sausages, sir—have skins and sometimes when they're cooked the skins burst at the ends and the innards come out. Well, sir, it seems that Able Seaman Morris arranges with the cook to have a couple of bangers—beg pardon, sir, sausages—with the ends sticking out where the skin's burst. It appears Able Seaman Morris likes these end bits. . . ."

"Very partial I am, sir, to the ends of Naafi bangers, sir," interjected Able Seaman Morris. The Coxswain silenced him with a frown and continued. "But when he gets his ban—er—sausages down to the mess, sir, and turns his back for a minute, he finds the ends gone and Ordinary Seaman Sweeney eating them. So he wants to fight Sweeney, sir."

I turned back to Morris. "Anything further to add?" I queried.

"I jest goes ter get me knife, sir, and when I turns around I finds the ends gorn—nipped orf, sir, as yer might say. The best part, too. I'm very partial to the ends, sir."

"Quite," I said. "So you want to fight Ordinary Seaman Sweeney?"

"Yessir. I wants me revenge, sir," answered Morris grimly.

"What about Sweeney?" I asked. "Does he want to fight too?"

"Yes, sir," said the Coxswain.

"Right, request granted. Fourteen hundred to-morrow on the upper deck," I said.

"Thank yer, sir," said Morris.

"Request granted. Fourteenhundredtomorrowupperdeck-aboutturndoublemarch," echoed the Coxswain.

As Morris doubled away I reflected that he must indeed like the "ends orf bangers" to be prepared to suffer physical pain for their sake.

That he would suffer physical pain I had no doubt, for Ordinary Seaman Sweeney was young, active and aggressive, while Morris was one of the pillars of the Royal Navy—a three-badge Able Seaman. Aged about forty-eight, he had, either through lack of ambition, or reluctance to shoulder responsibility, never bothered to pass professionally for Leading Seaman.

There are many such "stripeys" in the Navy. They are reliable, tolerant, staid and conservative and know all the tricks of the trade from sailmakers to 16-inch guns; from the Persian Gulf to Pompey Hard. In wartime they are invaluable in a crew to balance the younger, inexperienced ratings. Morris was a typical "stripey".

At fourteen hundred the next afternoon I went on the upper deck with the boxing-gloves. Quite a crowd had gathered and in the centre, but standing ostentatiously apart, were Morris and Sweeney, clad in singlets and shorts.

"Now you both know the rules," I said as the gloves were laced on; "carry on fighting until one of you has had enough. And after it's over shake hands, and no more quarrelling or you'll be run in."

They nodded and took up their varied ideas of a fighting stance.

"Go to it," I shouted.

It was obvious from the start that Morris was going to get a good hiding. Sweeney made rings round him and was altogether too fast for the stripey's main advantage—weight—to be put to any use. However, he stuck it for nearly ten minutes before he raised his hand in surrender. He was not in the least disgruntled; he had had his grudge fight, which was all that counted. He hadn't even expected to win.

So I put the gloves away and regarded the matter as closed. Alas, I didn't know my sailor.

Four days later I was again holding request-men and Morris was the first in the line. He didn't wait for a proper introduction, but, at the first syllable of the Coxswain's order "Able Seaman Morris . . . 'hun," he bounded forward to the request table, saluted and blurted out—" 'e done it agen . . . 'e pinched the end orf me banger agen. So 'elp me, sir, I jest turns me back and that there young . . . hrrrrrmph . . . was stuffin' it in 'is marf. Sneaked up behind me 'e did, and nicked it right orf me plate . . . standin' there larfin' at me. . . . I wants ter fight 'im agen, sir. I wants another grudge fight. . . ." Morris was absolutely chattering with rage, the veins stood out on his forehead and he was rolling his eyes like a man possessed.

The Coxswain took advantage of his breathlessness to get in his little speech. "Able Seaman Morris, sir, requests to have second grudge fight with Ordinary Seaman Sweeney."

"Now, Morris," I said, in what I hoped was a pacifying manner, for I could see he was smouldering and would shortly erupt into impassioned outburst, "now, Morris, before you started the last fight you understood the rules. I should charge both you and Sweeney with needless, frivolous quarrelling and. . . ."

"Needless . . . ? Frivolous . . . ?" stuttered Morris, "but 'e 'alf-'inched me end agen, sir, right under me nose. Cor stone the. . . ." The Coxswain silenced him with an upraised hand.

I thought for a moment. Strictly speaking, I should run both of them in as defaulters, but I was thinking ahead to the problems of making out the charge sheets and giving the reasons for the quarrel. I couldn't see the representatives of Their Lordships looking with any favour at all on a charge reading, "Did commit an act to the prejudice of Good Order and Naval Discipline in that he did sneak the end off a N.A.A.F.I. sausage, the property of J. Morris, Able Seaman, C/JX 113037."

"Granted. Fourteen hundred, upper deck, to-morrow," I said.

"Granted . . . brrp . . . brrp . . . brrp . . . aboutturndoublemarch," said the Coxswain.

At fourteen ten the following afternoon Morris wearily picked himself up off the deck and signified his surrender. There was a triumphant grin on his bloodied face. Honour was satisfied; he had had his grudge fight.

And there the matter rests for the moment. But I am uneasy. I feel as if I am living on the top of an active volcano. I'm sure that at any moment Ordinary Seaman Sweeney will succumb to the temptation and pinch another of Morris's ends. I know he'll do it again. Shall I implore N.A.A.F.I. to make their sausages without skins, or should I draft both Sweeney and Morris away for a gunnery course?

I don't know . . . I can't think. Who'd be a First Lieutenant?

Alan Vale

8

THE END IN AFRICA

After the battle of El Alamein, Rommel was driven in precipitate retreat westwards for the last time, his army in ruins. Thanks to halts in the pursuit occasioned by breaks in the weather, the Eighth Army out-running its transport and supplies, and its commander's skill in delaying tactics, the Afrika Korps escaped encirclement and annihilation. By the end of November 1942 the British stood once more at El Agheila.

Rommel Retreats

WITH the Afrika Korps broken through between 15 and 21 Panzer Divisions and no more reserves left, I gave orders—with a heavy heart, because of the German and Italian formations still on the march—for the withdrawal to Mersa Matruh.

When the orders were out, we too, moved off. It was a wild helter-skelter drive through another pitch-black night. Occasional Arab villages loomed up and dropped behind us in the darkness, and several vehicles lost contact with the head of the column. Finally, we halted in a small valley to wait for daylight. At that time it was still a matter of doubt as to whether we would be able to get even the remnants of the army away to the west. Our fighting power was very low. The bulk of the Italian infantry had been lost. Of XXI Corps, part had been destroyed after a stiff resistance against the over-whelmingly superior British, and part had been over-taken in its retreat and taken prisoner; the vehicles which we had repeatedly demanded for them from the Italian Supply H.Q. had not arrived. X Italian Corps was on the march south-east of Fuka, short of water and ammunition, and, to be quite frank, with no hope of escaping to the west. Of the formations only the transport échelons were on the coast road, choking it with their traffic as they slowly trickled west. There was little we could do to get order into the columns; it would have taken time and all we had to do was to get the move over as quickly as possible.

. . . . Conditions on the road were indescribable. Columns in complete disorder—partly of German, partly of Italian vehicles—choked the road between the minefields. Rarely was there any movement forward and then everything soon jammed up again. Many vehicles were on tow and there was an acute shortage of petrol, for the retreat had considerably increased consumption.

Meanwhile, our columns were steadily streaming westwards and were now approaching Sollum. In the afternoon the Italian General Gandin appeared on behalf of Marshal Cavallero to enquire about our situation and plans. This suited me very well. I gave him a detailed account of the battle, laying particular stress on the effects of the supply crisis and the Führer's and Duce's order. I told him point-blank that with the present balance of forces there was not a chance of our making a stand anywhere, and that the British could keep on going right through to Tripolitania, if they chose to. We could never accept battle, but would have to confine ourselves to trying to delay the British long enough to allow our columns, in which the utmost confusion reigned, to get across the Libyan frontier. There could be no attempt to restore any semblance of order until they arrived in Libya, because so long as they were this side of the frontier they were in constant danger of being cut off. Speed, therefore, was the one thing that mattered. We could attempt no operation with our remaining armour and motorized forces because of the petrol shortage; every drop that reached us had to be used for getting our troops out. Gandin left my H.Q. visibly shaken.

During that day*, we succeeded in forming a fairly firm front and beat off all enemy attacks. Although the enemy must have been aware of our weakness, he still continued to operate with great caution. All German troops everywhere, and some of the Italian units, made a very disciplined and good impression and appeared to be firmly in the hands of their officers. It was a personal blow to every man to have to give up all this territory we had conquered with such high hopes during the summer.

Rommel

Pursuit

Reveille would be at 5.30 a.m.; at six would come the order "Prepare to Move"; five minutes later, "Move". A dim red light glowed on the Navigator's vehicle, and the rest would follow it. Soon there would be a little light; at 7.15 a.m. the chilly sun would pop into the sky; then there would be a halt, and the order "Brew up!" A hundred little petrol fires would spring into being, and there would be a delicious breakfast of sausages, bacon, biscuits, marmalade and tea. While it was preparing, everyone would wash and shave in a mugful of water each. Off again, faster now with the advantages of daylight, the morning still crisp like a woodcock day at home, the Battalion's vehicles fanning out wide, now that they could see each other; halt and brew-up at noon, halt and brew-

* 6 November (Ed.)

up again just before dark; and then five miles on a slightly different course, in case the enemy might make an intelligent guess at the location of the laager. Then the Navigator would flash "Halt!" on his red light, the convoy would pull up, everyone would climb stiffly from his place, his face rigid with its mask of dust; and each would dig his slit trench. By half-past eight, all would be asleep except for the sentries.

Bernard Fergusson

November

General Montgomery to General Sir Alan Brooke: 10 November

What saved him from complete annihilation was the rain; I had nearly reached Matruh and was getting in behind all his transport when torrential rain turned the desert into a bog, and I had two armoured divisions . . . bogged and unable to move.

Mines

Nightly and gingerly our line was advanced, until the original No Man's Land of five thousand yards had shrunk by more than half.

It was here that the British made their first acquaintance with a new and nauseating type of anti-personnel mine—the "S" mine. The Germans had little expected defeat at Alamein, but when it had come upon them they realized that the door at Agheila must be not only shut but bolted against the inevitable pursuit. That pursuit had developed quickly; and elaborate mining was the quickest means of putting the Agheila position into a state of defence. They used mines as standing patrols; to deny the use of observation posts; and to make all movement difficult and costly. The whole area was a minefield, with "S" mines everywhere. This pestilent device leaped six feet in the air when it was set off, flinging a shower of metal in all directions, and causing casualties many feet away.

They had been laid with cunning and imagination. One night a truck-load of Middlesex hit an anti-tank mine at a point in the road where there was a deep crater. The survivors, jumping clear, found themselves in an "S" minefield, and were killed. During the night some Camerons sent out a patrol to bring in the bodies; they were fired on, they took cover in the crater, they found it full of mines and six of them were killed. Once more the Camerons tried, but this time the Germans had attached "S" mines to the bodies, and three more lives were lost. That particular spot is said to have cost thirty-six lives before it was finally cleared.

Bernard Fergusson

TORCH

While in early November the Eighth Army was beginning its drive to victory, a vast Anglo-American armada had set sail from Gibraltar, bound for the North African coast. "Operation Torch", under the command of General Eisenhower, was designed to win the whole of North-west Africa from French Morocco to Tunisia, as yet occupied only by the Vichy French. Thus the Allies would obtain control of the southern Mediterranean shore, which could be a jumping-off point for future operations against Southern Europe, and also take Rommel on two sides.

It was hoped that the French in North Africa would be led peacefully into the Allied camp by General Giraud.

Because of the earnest belief held in both London and Washington that General Giraud could lead the French of North Africa into the Allied camp, we had started negotiations in October, through Mr. Murphy, to rescue the General from virtual imprisonment in southern

France. An elaborate plan was devised by some of our French friends and Mr. Murphy, who had returned to Africa after his visit to London. General Giraud was kept informed of developments through trusted intermediaries and at the appointed time reached the coastline in spite of the watchfulness of the Germans and the Vichyites. There he embarked in a small boat, in the dark of night, to keep a rendezvous with one of our submarines, lying just offshore. A British submarine, commanded for this one trip by Captain Jerauld Wright of the United States Navy, made a most difficult contact with General Giraud and put out to sea. At another appointed place the submarine met one of our flying boats, and the General, with but three personal aides and staff officers, flew to my headquarters during the afternoon of 7 November. The incident, related thus briefly, was an exciting story of extraordinary daring and resolution.

General Giraud, though dressed in civilian clothes, looked very much a soldier. He was well over six feet, erect, almost stiff in carriage, and abrupt in speech and mannerisms. He was a gallant, if bedraggled figure, and his experiences of the war, including a long term of imprisonment and a dramatic escape, had not daunted his fighting spirit.

It was quickly apparent that he had come out of France labouring under the grave misapprehension that he was immediately to assume command of the whole Allied expedition. Upon entering my dungeon, he offered himself to me in that capacity. I could not accept his services in such a role. I wanted him to proceed to Africa, as soon as we could guarantee his safety, and there take over command of such French forces as would voluntarily rally to him. Above all things, we were anxious to have him on our side because of the constant fear at the back of our minds of becoming engaged in a prolonged and serious battle against Frenchmen, not only to our own sorrow and loss, but to the detriment of our campaign against the Germans.

General Giraud was adamant; he believed that the

honour of himself and his country was involved and that he could not possibly accept any position in the venture lower than that of complete command. This, on the face of it, was impossible. The naming of an Allied Commander-in-Chief is an involved process, requiring the co-ordinated agreement of military and political leaders of the responsible Governments. No subordinate commander in the expedition could legally have accepted an order from General Giraud. Moreover, at that moment there was not a single Frenchman in the Allied Command; on the contrary, the enemy, if any, was French.

All this was laboriously explained to the general. He was shaken, disappointed, and after many hours of conference felt it necessary to decline to have any part in the scheme. He said, "General Giraud cannot accept a subordinate position in this command; his countrymen would not understand and his honour as a soldier would be tarnished." It was pitiful, because he had left his whole family in France as potential hostages to German fury and had himself undergone great personal risks in order to join up with us.

. . . . The conversation with General Giraud lasted, intermittently, until after midnight. Though I could understand General Giraud's French fairly well, I insisted on using an interpreter, to avoid any chance of misunderstanding. When we had worn out more expert ones, General Clark volunteered to act in this capacity, and though he is far from fluent in the language, we made out fairly well. One reason for this was that after the first hour of talk each of us merely repeated, over and over again, the arguments he had first presented. When, finally, General Giraud went off to bed there was no sign of his modifying, in any degree, his original demands. His good-night statement was: "Giraud will be a spectator in this affair." He agreed, however, to meet me at the Governor's house the next morning. The political faces in our headquarters that night were long.

Fortunately a night's sleep did something to change General Giraud's mind, and at the next morning's meeting

Navy, in charge of all coastal defences, are going all out.

"It is fantastic, but there it is," the French captain said.

"And the German Armistice Commission?" Colonel Ratay asked.

"The Fedala contingent, fifteen of them, have been quartered at the hotel for some months. *Assez correctes, mais de sales types au fond.*"

Colonel Charles Codman

Confusion

Swell had been increasing during the day, and we landed about 15.00 in a pounding surf. My jeep was embedded in heavy sand within a few yards of the water's edge, and there it was to remain all night. There was much confusion on the beach, for craft destined for Green Beach were also landing on Blue. The soft, powdery sand, much worse than we had anticipated, was causing trouble. The wire netting and burlap roadways on the sand across dunes were already ruined by traffic, but the engineers were building others and reconnoitring for better routes. The landing craft had broached to in the surf and had been abandoned by their crews. Some weapons and equipment had been dumped into the surf, but everywhere were working.

The beach command post, marked only by a staff bearing the Blue Beach flag and lantern and the voice of the beachmaster's radio, little was known of the situation inland and nothing of the situation on other beaches. There were rumours of heavy fighting inland, and a non-commissioned officer from McCarley's was somewhere on the beach looking for tanks. We could barely see the transports at sea. They were out of range of the beachmaster's signal lamps and radio. However, I wrote a message to be sent off to and the Commodore when it might be and went inland to learn how things were going.

In a half-track, we followed the trace of the 1st bringing two light tanks and a tank destroyer on

he decided to participate on the basis we desired. I promised that if he were successful in winning French support I would deal with him as the administrator of that region, pending eventual opportunity for civil authorities to determine the will of the population.

General Eisenhower

On 8 November the Allied landings began; at Casablanca in French Morocco, and at Oran and Algiers. There were British units among the forces going ashore at Algiers, but the Americans played a predominant part in "Torch", and it was they who were mainly involved in the heavy fighting which took place with the French at Oran and Casablanca. Unlike their comrades in the Pacific, these men had never seen battle before, but they were to be blooded and were to vindicate themselves on the battlefields of Africa and Europe. General George S. Patton was in command of the forces landing around Casablanca.

First Battlefield

In Africa, for the first time I saw the loneliest and most ominous of all landscapes, a battlefield. And I knew for the first time that strange exhilaration that grips a man when he knows that somewhere out there in the distance hostile eyes are watching him and that at any moment a bullet he may never hear, fired by an enemy he cannot see, may strike him.

General Matthew B. Ridgway

Our first battle contact report was disappointing. The U.S.S. *Thomas Stone*, proceeding in convoy towards Algiers and carrying a reinforced battalion of American troops, was torpedoed on 7 November, only a hundred and fifty miles from its destination. Details were lacking and there existed the possibility of a very considerable loss of life. Though our good fortune to this point had been amazing, this did not lessen our anxiety for the men aboard. We could get no further information of her fate that evening, but later we learned that the incident had a happy outcome so far as the honour of American arms was concerned. Casualties were few and the ship itself was not badly damaged. There was no danger of sinking. Yet officers and men, unwilling to wait quietly until the ship could be towed to a convenient port, cheered the decision of the commander to take to the boats in an attempt to reach, on time, the assault beach to which they were assigned. Heavy weather, making up during the afternoon, foiled their gallant purpose and they had to be taken aboard destroyers and other escort vessels, but they were finally placed ashore some twelve hours behind schedule. Fortunately the absence of these troops had no appreciable effect upon our plans.

General Eisenhower

CASABLANCA: 7 NOVEMBER

Fedala

Midnight. The stars are out, but it's dark as hell on deck. The *Ancon*'s engines are down to a slow throb. According to the timetable we should be easing into the transport area preparatory to going over the side. Elements of 3 Division are lining up at their deck stations adjacent to the disembarkation nets. All very orderly. They seem to know where to go and what to do. They are going over the side now. The technique seems to be to step up on a stanchion and back-climb over the rail. Weighted down with sixty-five pounds of equipment exclusive of steel helmet and tommy-gun, it is something of a trick. A landing net is a mean piece of equipment. With the outward roll of the ship it swings clear. That is fine. You can get your hands and feet into the rungs. The inboard roll is something else again. The net flattens hard against the ship's side, reducing finger and toe holds to next to nothing.

. . . . A steel helmet well heated by the subtropical sun, a slippery tommy-gun, a saturated uniform, trench coat, and full infantry pack are not conducive to speed, but it didn't take us long to scramble up the dune to the crest tufted with coarse grass. Beyond and behind its comforting protection stretched a wide field. It presented a curious appearance. Standing and sitting in small groups, the French officers and coal-black enlisted men of the Fedala garrison. Their rifles were stacked in neat array and most of them were smoking *jaunes*.

"What outfit is this?" we asked a French captain.

"102nd Company of the Sixth R.T.C." (*Régiment de Tirailleurs Sénégalais*.) "We came over to your side rig[ht] after H-hour," he said pleasantly.

"Is the whole garrison here?"

"No, some of them have gone back to the barra[cks]" He pointed to a row of low wooden buildings at th[e] of the town.

"Fedala is yours," said the French captain.

"In that case, what is all the shooting for?"

"Doubtless the Marine battery of seventy-f[ives] the end of Cap Fedala. It's a pity, but you[r] is——" he shrugged—"our Navy has a[ ] comprehension than the Army."

Two small Arab boys loped up. Smili[ng] palms, they had not yet acquired the [ ] gum refrain. It was still early.

The French captain shooed them [ ] co-operative, but he didn't really[ ] landing, he said, had been a comp[lete surprise.] Senegalese garrison, the only F[rench] itself were three or four Re[ ] Lieutenant Lefèvre, whose [ ] right place. He had, the [ ] assault wave as it landed [ ] alarm by at least an [ ] Resident-General in [ ] order to resist, and [ ] arriving from Rabat and M[ ]

the way, we took them along. One of the tank gunners almost ended my career right then and there. When I told them to load and to follow me, one of the gunners fired an accidental burst from a machine-gun that missed my head by a hair's breadth. On the ridge just east of the southern end of the lagoon, we found McCarley's rear command post with his executive officer, Major Otto Koch, in charge. There, also, was part of Company A and part of the Regimental anti-tank company, which had established the road blocks along the Rabat Road to protect the flank. There had been fighting along the Rabat Road during the afternoon—French infantry and tanks had overrun our road blocks. Some few men had straggled in, but the company commander was missing. However, most of the company were there and in position with anti-tank guns, and Major Koch had sent to the beach for tanks. I left the two light tanks and the tank destroyer with him, and set off to find McCarley.

Leaving Bond and Netterbald with the command half-track struggling to establish radio communication with the ship and with the other battalions, Conway, Southworth and I set off on foot along McCarley's telephone line. After an hour's rugged going through the dense woods along the ridge east of the lagoon, with naval gunfire cracking overhead and the distant crash of bursting shells and clatter of machine-guns to keep us company, we found McCarley. He had not reached the south end of the lagoon until 11.00, and his progress northward had been slow. He had been held up by machine-gun fire from along the road to the east, and had only located the source a short while before. A skirmish was in progress in that direction, and artillery shells were crashing in the woods beyond.

McCarley had not yet made contact with the 2nd Battalion, but we could hear sounds of firing along the ridge to the north not more than a mile distant. It was now almost six o'clock and the day was nearly done. I told McCarley to make contact with the 2nd Battalion during the night and to advance at daylight the next morning on the airfield. Company A would have to remain where it was to protect the south flank until I could get Semmes and his armour there, but I would send the Provisional Assault Company up to him during the night so that he would have some reserve at least. McCarley and others whom I had encountered were all in good spirits even though our plans were behind schedule.

It was nearly dark when we had retraced our steps and reached the staff car. Our radio had not been able to contact anyone. French infantry and tanks were still in the woods along the Rabat Road, and I was fearful of an attack from that direction. Stopping only to send the Provisional Assault Company to join McCarley, and to warn Major Koch of the danger, we went on to the beach. Our half-track could not negotiate the steep slope of the sand dunes in the darkness. Leaving it with Bond in charge, Conway, Netterbald and I set off on foot once more.

At the beach command post, all was dark and silent. There was only a sleepy operator listening for radio signals which he could not hear. No officers were about, but all around men were sleeping the profound sleep of exhaustion. Figures were stumbling about the beach and sand dunes in the darkness. There, shouts and oaths and calls of "George" and "Patton". And there was roaring surf. But I had to find Semmes and his tanks. Sending Conway to the north and Netterbald to the south to find him, I sat down on the sand dune to wait.

When their figures disappeared into the gloom it came to me that even with hundreds all around me I was utterly alone. And I had to stay just where I was, or they would never find me when they returned with Semmes. Out to sea, much closer than when we had come ashore, signal lamps were flashing among the ships. As far as I could see along the beach, there was chaos. Landing craft were beaching in the pounding surf, broaching to the waves, and spilling men and equipment into the water. Men wandered about aimlessly, hopelessly lost, calling to each other and for their units, swearing at each other and at nothing. There was no beach party or shore party anywhere in sight. And I was chilled. Not a light could I see on shore except the dim blue lantern under which I sat. I was lonely. More than anything else right then I wanted a cigarette. There had been no enemy aircraft since early morning. A cigarette on shore could be no more dangerous than those flashing lights at sea. I lit one. In a matter of moments I was glad when other glows appeared as other lonely and uncertain men sought the comfort of tobacco. They would have been surprised to know that the Commanding General had been the first to violate the blackout order.

I was sitting there with my cigarette half smoked wondering what I was going to do next and how, when out of the gloom from the shore appeared a strange-looking figure, approaching with uncertain steps, and peering nervously from side to side. He stopped in front of me and in alien accents addressed me: "Heyyuh, gimme a cigarette." I handed him one from the package I held. He spoke again: "Goddam. All wet. Gimme a light too." I extended the lighted end of my cigarette. As he put it to his face, Conway appeared on one side, Semmes the other, both thrust tommy-guns into his midriff, and Conway challenged "George". And the response was instantaneous: "George? George, hell. Me no George. My name Lee, Cook, Company C, 540th Engineers."

General L. K. Truscott

First Sight of Patton

Near the embankment an infantryman, his tommy-gun beside him, lay face downward on the sand. With a speed surprising in so large a man, the tall figure raced to the recumbent soldier, snatched up his tommy-gun, and leaning over him, shouted, "Yea-a-h."

The soldier half turned over, shielding his face with his arms. "Go 'way and lemme sleep," he said.

"Yea-a-h."

The barrel of his own tommy-gun was boring insistently

into the pit of his stomach as the soldier decided to open his eyes. His glance climbed slowly up the cavalry boots, the wet trouser leg, the pearl-handled revolver, the deep-chested torso. Behind the butt of the tommy-gun, grey eyes blazing from an inexorable face surmounted by the dripping helmet with its two stars.

"Jesus," he said simply.

Stepping back, General Patton examined the lock of the tommy-gun. O.K.

"Get up, boy," he said gently.

The soldier scrambled to his feet, swaying uncertainly.

"Are you hurt?" the General said.

"No, sir."

"I know you're tired," the General said. "We're all tired. That makes no difference."

He put his hand on the man's shoulder. "The next beach you land on will be defended by Germans. I don't want one of them coming up behind you and hitting you over the head with a sockful of silt." Only that was not quite the word he used.

The man grinned.

"Here's your gun." The sharpness returned to the General's voice. "Now, get going."

General Giraud's attempts to rally the French to the Allied cause had been a complete failure, but by chance, Admiral Darlan, Commander-in-Chief of all the Vichy French fighting forces, was present in Algiers at the moment of the invasion. Every Frenchman in North Africa obeyed him, as the representative of Marshal Pétain. He was won over, and the problem of French co-operation was solved. Darlan ordered a cease-fire, and on 13 November an armistice was concluded. The sequel both for him and for his Government was unfortunate, for he was assassinated eleven days later, and the infuriated Germans occupied Vichy France. But in North Africa, the armed forces of France joined the Allies.

Capitulation at Casablanca

General Keyes looks at his watch. His face is impassive, but around his eyes there are lines of strain.

The hum of engines. Louder. Streaking across the sky directly overhead a squadron of fighter planes. Colonel Lauris Norstad's P-40s from Port Lyautey. Out at sea a glint of wings—the Navy bombers taking off from the *Ranger*. Twelve miles distant the sleeping city of Casablanca, under whose white roofs half a million souls lie mercifully unconscious of the terrible engines of destruction closing in on them from the land, the sea, and the air.

Colonel Hammond's walkie-talkie comes to life. "3 Division C.P.?" "Yes. Just a minute." He hands the receiver to General Keyes.

"That you, Geoff?" The sharp, incisive voice of General Patton.

"Yes, sir."

"Call it off. The French Navy has capitulated. Ratay has just been here. You are still in touch with Hewitt?"

"Yes, sir."

"Good, but you'll have to work fast."

At General Patton's first words a vigorous nod from General Keyes to Hammond, and a second radio set is already crackling its message across the water. Aboard the *Augusta* Admiral Hewitt and his staff get busy. Very busy indeed.

Outside the Casa breakwater the covering group, big guns elevated, is now plainly visible. Over the city the Navy bombers circle and circle and circle. The seconds and minutes tick off. No one speaks. Without warning the leading bomber banks and peels off. The next, the next, as the circle dissolves into a long serpentine line headed for the open sea, where the *Ranger* is poking up into the wind to receive them. Once again the roar of engines over our heads as our P-40s hit the trail for home, dipping their wings to show they have understood.

General Keyes lowers his field-glasses and with his

handkerchief carefully wipes the lenses. Before starting
down the stairs from the roof, he takes a last look in the
direction of Casablanca.

"Thank God," he says.

. . . . Shortly before three o'clock General Patton
ordered a guard of honour drawn up before the hotel
entrance. At the prescribed hour a black limousine with
motor-cycle outrider swept up the drive. Out of it got
General Noguès, trim, erect, ascetic, rather Spanish in
appearance. He walked smartly up the steps, followed by
General Lascroux, the compact, stoutish Commander of
the Ground Forces, and General Lahoulle, Chief of the
French Air Forces, whose genial, forthright aspect made
an immediately favourable impression.

At the top of the steps they were met by General Keyes,
who escorted them to the smoking-room, where General
Patton received them.

A preliminary conference attended by Admirals Hewitt
and Hall had taken place with the French Admirals,
Michelier and Ronarch. Matters concerning the ports had
been discussed. Michelier had been *pincé* and difficult, but
thawed out more or less when Admiral Hewitt offered to
shake hands.

General Patton now opened the full *séance* by
expressing his admiration for the courage and skill shown
by the French armed forces during the three days of
battle.

"We are now met to come to terms," he said. "Here
they are."

As the conditions of Treaty C were read aloud and the
full import of their stringency began to sink in, the faces
of the French grew more and more sombre. At the end
there was a strained silence, then General Noguès arose.
"Permit me to point out," he said, "that if these terms are
enforced it means the end of the French Protectorate in
Morocco."

In the discussion which followed it became apparent
that while Treaty C as drawn might reasonably be applied
to a civilian set-up such as exists in Algeria, its literal

enforcement here would virtually cancel the responsibility of the French Military Protectorate to maintain law and order in Morocco. If, as provided by the treaty, the French forces are disarmed and disbanded, to us will fall the entire task not only of preserving order among seven million Arabs and Berbers, but of securing the Spanish Zone frontier, the port of Casablanca, and the long and vulnerable lines of communication to far off Tunisia—now our immediate goal. Communications with General Eisenhower in Gibraltar and with General Clark in Algiers are nil. General Patton is on his own.

It did not take him long to decide. Rising to his full height, he picked up the familiar typescript of Treaty C and tore it into small strips.

"Gentlemen," he said, "I had the pleasure of serving with your armed forces throughout two years of World War One. Needless to say, I have implicit faith in the word of honour of a French officer. If each of you in this room gives me his word of honour that there will be no further firing on American troops and ships, you may retain your arms and carry on as before—but under my orders. You will do thus and so. We will do this and that. Agreed?"

It was.

"There is, however, an additional condition upon which I must insist."

The faces of the French delegation, which had brightened considerably, lengthened.

"It is this," General Patton said, signalling one of his aides, "that you join me in a glass of champagne."

Colonel Charles Codman

THE RACE FOR TUNIS

Meanwhile the Germans, fully alive to the dangers to them inherent in "Torch", were unwilling to cut their losses. They began desperately to feed troops and equipment into Tunisia, as yet unoccupied by Allied

*forces, beginning only one day after the latters' landings
farther west. The race for control of Tunisia was on, but
the British 1 Army, under General Anderson, struggling
eastwards towards the ports of Tunis and Bizerta,
possession of which would strangle Rommel, was
hampered by small numbers, appalling communications
and constant, heavy German air attacks. First contact
with German troops was made on 17 November, and on
the 28th the British were in sight of Tunis, but they were
too late and too weak. By the end of November the
Germans had fifteen thousand men in Tunisia; a force
which was trebled a month later. On 1 December they
were able to repulse the British advance, and further
Allied attacks bogged down in the mud of winter. The
force of their blow was spent, and Tunisia was held for
the Axis.*

Rommel Meets Hitler: November

There was a noticeable chill in the atmosphere from the
outset. I described all the difficulties which the army had
had to face during both the battle and the retreat. It was
all noted and the execution of the operation was described
as faultless and unique.

Unfortunately, I then came too abruptly to the point
and said that, since experience indicated that no
improvement in the shipping situation could now be
expected, the abandonment of the African theatre of war
should be accepted as a long-term policy. There should be
no illusions about the situation and all planning should be
directed towards what was attainable. If the army
remained in North Africa, it would be destroyed.

I had expected a rational discussion of my arguments
and intended to develop them in a great deal more detail.
But I did not get as far, for the mere mention of the
strategic question worked like a spark in a powder barrel.
The Führer flew into a fury and directed a stream of
completely unfounded attacks upon us. Most of the
F.H.Q. staff officers present, the majority of whom had

never heard a shot fired in anger, appeared to agree with every word the Führer said. In illustration of our difficulties I mentioned the fact that only five thousand of the fifteen thousand fighting troops of the Afrika Korps and 90 Light Division had weapons, the remainder being completely unarmed. This provoked a violent outburst in which we were accused, among other things, of having thrown our arms away. I protested strongly against charges of this kind, and said in straight terms that it was impossible to judge the weight of the battle from here in Europe. Our weapons had simply been battered to pieces by the British bombers, tanks and artillery and it was nothing short of a miracle that we had been able to escape with all the German motorized forces, especially in view of the desperate petrol shortage, which had allowed us to retreat at a rate of only tens of kilometres a day. I stated that all other armies would suffer the same fate if the Americans ever succeeded in setting foot on the Continent.

But there was no attempt at discussion. The Führer said that his decision to hold the eastern front in the winter of 1941-42 had saved Russia and that there, too, he had upheld his orders ruthlessly. I began to realize that Adolf Hitler simply did not want to see the situation as it was, and that he reacted emotionally against what his intelligence must have told him was right. He said that it was a political necessity to continue to hold a major bridgehead in Africa and there would, therefore, be no withdrawal from the Mersa el Brega* line. He would do everything possible to get supplies to me.

Rommel

Allied Supply Difficulties

Supply was the absorbing problem in every head-quarters in North Africa. There was still a dearth of service troops and transportation. Few units in North

* Before El Agheila (Ed.)

Africa yet had their full scale of motor transportation. The single rail line eastward from Oran and Algiers had suffered from neglect, and there was a shortage of locomotives and rolling stock. The two principal roads east from Algiers, one along the coast and the principal highway farther inland, although paved, were not in good repair; and both traversed rugged, mountainous terrain with steep grades and turns and many bridges. British supplies and equipment destined for Tunisia came for the most part from Algiers and the small ports of Bone and Philippeville. Oran was the principal American port and base. French supplies and equipment came in part from local sources, the remainder from British and American stocks. So critical was the problem of supply that the loss of a single truck was almost a tragedy, the destruction of a bridge or locomotive a catastrophe of concern even to the high command. And the Germans were employing agents already in the country and others dropped by parachute to sabotage this tenuous line of communications.

Reinforcements in men and material were arriving as rapidly as shipping permitted, but the only troops immediately available to reinforce the front were the American 1 Armoured and 1 and 34 Infantry Divisions. Both of the latter were for the most part scattered in small detachments protecting airfields and critical points on the line of communications.

General Truscott

The Race Lost

Clark and I found Anderson beyond Souk-Ahras, and forward of that place we entered a zone where all around us was evidence of incessant and hard fighting. Every conversation along the roadside brought out astounding exaggerations. "Beja has been bombed to rubble." "No one can live on this next stretch of road." "Our troops will surely have to retreat: humans cannot exist in these conditions." Yet on the whole morale was good. The exaggerations were nothing more than the desire of the individual to convey the thought that he had been through the ultimate in terror and destruction—he had no thought of clearing out himself.

Troops and commanders were not experienced, but the boldness, courage, and stamina of General Anderson's forces could not have been exceeded by the most battle-wise veterans. Physical conditions were almost unendurable. The mud deepened daily, confining all operations to the roads, long stretches of which practically disintegrated. Winter cold was already descending upon the Tunisian highlands. The bringing up of supplies and ammunition was a Herculean task. In spite of all this, and in spite of Anderson's lack of strength—his whole force numbered only about three brigades of infantry and a brigade of obsolescent tanks—he pushed on through Souk-el-Khemis, Beja, and finally reached a point from which he could look down into the outskirts of Tunis.

. . . . Courage, resourcefulness and endurance, though daily displayed in overwhelming measure, could not completely overcome the combination of enemy, weather and terrain. In early December the enemy was strong enough in mechanized units to begin local but sharp counter-attacks and we were forced back from our most forward positions in front of Tunis.

As soon as we ceased attacking, the situation in northern Tunisia turned bleak for us, even from a defensive standpoint. Through a blunder during a local withdrawal we had lost the bulk of the equipment of Combat Command B, of 1 Armoured Division. The 18th Infantry of the U.S. 1 Infantry Division took severe losses, and practically an entire battalion of a fine British regiment was wiped out. General Anderson soon thought he would have to give up Medjez-el-Bab, a road centre and a junction point with the French forces on his right. Since this spot was the key to our resumption of the offensive when we should get the necessary strength, I forbade this move—assuming personal responsibility for the fate of its garrison and the effect of its possible capture upon the safety of the command.

We were still attempting to mount an attack of our own. Work continued twenty-four hours a day to build up the strength that we believed would, with some temporary improvement in the weather, give us a good fighting chance to capture north-eastern Tunisia before all operations were hopelessly bogged down. 24 December was chosen as the date for our final and most ambitious attack. Our great hope for success lay in our temporary advantage in artillery, which was relatively great. But reports from the Tunisian front were discouraging; the weather, instead of improving, continued to deteriorate. Prospects for mounting another attack grew darker.

I was determined not to give up unless personally convinced that the attack was an impossibility. Weather prohibited flying and I started forward by automobile on 22 December, encountering miserable road conditions from the moment we left Algiers. Travelling almost incessantly, I met General Anderson at his headquarters in the early morning of 24 December, and with him proceeded at once to Souk-el-Khemsi. At that point was located the headquarters of the British V Corps, which was to make the attack and which was commanded by Major-General C. W. Allfrey of the British Army. The preliminary moves of the attack had already been made by small detachments, attempting to secure critical points before the beginning of the major manoeuvre, scheduled for the following night.

The rain fell constantly. We went out personally to inspect the countryside over which the troops would have to advance, and while doing so I observed an incident which, as much as anything else, I think, convinced me of the hopelessness of an attack. About thirty feet off the road, in a field that appeared to be covered with winter wheat, a motor-cycle had become stuck in the mud. Four soldiers were struggling to extricate it, but in spite of their most strenuous efforts succeeded only in getting themselves mired into the sticky clay. They finally had to give up the attempt and left the motor-cycle more deeply bogged down than when they started.

We went back to headquarters and I directed that the attack be indefinitely postponed.

General Eisenhower

After a pause on the Eighth Army front, Rommel was dislodged from El Agheila on 13 December and was again in full retreat to the west. Tripoli fell on 23 January 1943.

After the capture of the El Agheila position, a staff officer from Eighth Army Headquarters was visiting Benghazi. Here he met a high personage from Cairo. They started talking about the future. The staff officer said, "The Army Commander hopes to be in Tripoli in five weeks' time." The reply he got was: "Oh! that's impossible, we have just approved a Joint Planners' paper which says that a two or three months' pause is required to ensure a safe maintenance situation."

Major-General Sir Francis de Guingand

The Poor Relations

We had still received no strategic decision from the supreme German and Italian authorities on the future of the African theatre of war. They did not look at things realistically—indeed, they refused to do so. What we found really astonishing was to see the amount of material that they were suddenly able to ship to Tunisia, quantities out of all proportion to anything we had received in the past. The urgency of the danger had at last percolated through to Rome. But the British and Americans had meanwhile multiplied their supply shipments many times over and were steadily increasing their strategic command over sea and air. One Axis ship after the other was going down beneath the waters of the Mediterranean, and it was becoming obvious that even the greatest effort could no longer hope to effect any decisive improvement in the supply situation; we were up to our necks in the mud and no longer had the strength to pull ourselves out.

The mismanagement, the operational blunders, the

prejudices, the everlasting search for scapegoats, these were now to reach the acute stage. And the man who paid the price was the ordinary German and Italian soldier.

Rommel

Small Success

During January, a number of our A.A. gunners succeeded in surprising a British column of the Long-Range Desert Group in Tunisia and captured the commander of 1st S.A.S. Regiment, Lieutenant-Colonel David Stirling. Insufficiently guarded, he managed to escape and made his way to some Arabs, to whom he offered a reward if they would get him back to the British lines. But his bid must have been too small, for the Arabs, with their usual eye to business, offered him to us for eleven pounds of tea—a bargain which we soon clinched. Thus the British lost the very able and adaptable commander of the desert group which had caused us more damage than any other British unit of equal strength.

Rommel

28 December 1942

Dearest Lu,

Our fate is gradually working itself out. Supplies have been very short and it would need a miracle for us to hold on much longer. What is to happen now lies in God's hands. We'll go on fighting as long as it's at all possible. I saw this coming when we were last together and discussed the most important things with you.

Rommel

Free French

There was one other formation that was in touch with the enemy—General Leclerc's force. This fine Frenchman had moved his troops from Lake Chad across the desert and gained contact with Eighth Army about the time we

arrived at Tripoli. It was a real mixture—a bit of
everything. He had Frenchmen and native soldiers, some
artillery of various types, an armoured car or two,
machine-guns, some oddly assorted transport which by
some miracle had made the journey, and even some
aircraft. They were short of most things, food, clothes and
material; but a wonderful spirit went a long way towards
surmounting the deficiencies. I remember my first meeting
with Leclerc. I was sitting in my caravan outside Tripoli
when he arrived to report. At first I thought one of the
characters of Wren's *Beau Geste* had come along to pay a
call. His appearance personified the hardened French
colonial soldier. He was thin and drawn, but intensely
alert. His clothes had long since seen their day. Thin drill
uniform with threadbare breeches, and old but shapely
riding boots. A French *képi* completed the picture. He told
me who he was and from whence he came. He said this
just as you might say you had dropped over from the next
village to tea. I took him along to the Army Commander,
who shook hands and looked him up and down. Leclerc
said, "I place myself and my troops under your
command." Montgomery then said he accepted the offer,
and told me to discuss with the French General details of
his co-operation and matters affecting material and
supplies. Later Montgomery told me, "I can make use of
that chap."

                         Major-General Sir Francis de Guingand

THE CASABLANCA CONFERENCE

*In the middle of January 1943 Winston Churchill and
President Roosevelt met at Casablanca to discuss further
strategy. It was agreed that after Tunisia had been won,
the next Allied blow should fall on Europe itself: Sicily
was to be invaded. The date of the cross-Channel invasion
of Western Eruope was fixed for 1944. At the same
conference, unconditional surrender of the Axis powers*

was proclaimed as the war aim of the Allies; a declaration
which was used by the Germans as propaganda to stiffen
the resistance of their armies.

Unconditional Surrender

We propose to draw up a statement of the work of the
conference for communication to the Press at the proper
time. I should be glad to know what the War Cabinet
would think of our including in this statement a
declaration of the firm intention of the United States and
the British Empire to continue the war relentlessly until
we have brought about the "unconditional surrender" of
Germany and Japan. The omission of Italy would be to
encourage a break-up there. The President liked this idea,
and it would stimulate our friends in every country.

Winston Churchill, 20 January

We, the United Nations, demand from the Nazi, Fascist
and Japanese tyrannies unconditional surrender. By this
we mean that their willpower to resist must be completely
broken, and that they must yield themselves absolutely to
our justice and mercy. It also means that we must take all
those far-sighted measures which are necessary to prevent
the world from being again convulsed, wrecked and
blackened by their calculated plots and ferocious
aggressions. It does not mean, and it never can mean, that
we are to stain our victorious arms by inhumanity or by
mere lust of vengeance, or that we do not plan a world in
which all branches of the human family may look forward
to what the American Declaration of Independence finely
calls "life, liberty, and the pursuit of happiness".

Winston Churchill, 30 June 1943

The Allied demand for unconditional surrender and the
persistent claim by the Allies that Germany must be
destroyed (shades of the earlier cry, *"Delenda est*
Cartago!" during the war between Rome and Carthage)

reinforced the will of the German people to fight to the
bitter end. The Allies offered no alternative.

General Hasso von Manteuffel

Another Meeting: 4 February 1943

Local note: Fast car driven by nicely turned-out
Moroccan in European clothes is stopped by American
M.P. on the main road.
"Pull over to the kerb. Where's the fire?"
The Moroccan takes it calmly.
M.P.: "Your name?"
Moroccan: "Sidi Mohammed ben Youssef."
M.P.: "Your profession?"
Moroccan: *Fonctionnaire.*"
M.P.: "What function?"
Moroccan: "Sultan of Morocco."
Tableau.

THE BATTLE FOR TUNISIA

*In Tunisia both sides reinforced for the coming final
battle for Africa, strong American forces and some
French units moving in to support 1 Army. In spite of
losing a large proportion of his men and supplies to Allied
air and naval forces in the Mediterranean, Rommel, now
in command of all Axis forces in Tunisia, struck first and
struck hard. On 14 February he launched a powerful
assault on the Americans in the south, his veterans driving
back their gallant but unseasoned opponents through the
Kasserine Pass, taking Kasserine, Feriana and Sbeitla, and
threatening Tebessa.*

Kasserine: 14 February

About half-past ten that night, I telephoned the Corps
G-3 to ask if there was any further information about the

tank battle which had been reported as imminent shortly
before dark. I was told that it had apparently been only a
reconnaissance as the German tanks had withdrawn to the
east.

All seemed relative quiet, so I turned in about half-past
eleven. But I was not to sleep for long. At one o'clock in
the morning, General Fredendall telephoned, and my
records show:

Fredendall reported that German tanks were fighting on
edge of Sbeitla; estimates gave them eighty-nine
tanks—eighty Mark IVs and nine Mark VIs. Apparently
had pierced covering position five kilometres east of
Sbeitla, which had been established along the line: Djebel
Koumin (?)—south slope Djebel Mrhila, and had
attacked in the moonlight. Considered situation extremely
grave, and uncertain of ability to hold. If kicked off
Sbeitla, the Thelepte-Feriana position exposed as well as
valley towards Maktar. Said he had talked to McNabb
earlier and had asked to be allowed to withdraw to high
ground but had been refused. Said he had not reported
present situation to McNabb yet.

Directed him to report situation to McNabb and let me
know result.

Said Ward had just reported situation in person. Ward
considered situation grave—but was doing best he could.

I had barely finished talking with General Fredendall
when a message from Carleton reported that tanks were
fighting in the moonlight in Sbeitla, and were all around
Ward's command post. Ward was determined to fight it
out there. He was uncertain of the outcome, but could not
withdraw then if he wanted to do so.

At half-past one General Fredendall telephoned again:

Fredendall reported that McNabb had authorized him
to withdraw. Orders had been sent as follows:

To Colonel Moore at Kasserine with one battalion 26th
Infantry, four companies 19th Engineers, four 37 mm.
guns, two 75 mm. guns of Cannon Company, reinforced
by one company of medium tanks and 805th Tank
Destroyer Battalion (less company) from Stark's

command, to hold at all costs along the Oued east of Kasserine for a minimum of at least twelve hours. When forced to withdraw, to withdraw to the north and hold Kasserine Pass.

Armoured Division to move north through Kasserine Pass in direction of Thala.

Stark to pull in covering force to hold main ridge line at Feriana, leave covering force of one company infantry, one battery artillery, one company light tanks. Take remainder of command including French to ridge north of Thelepte airdrome.

Williams (Air Support Commander) informed of situation, making arrangements to remove aircraft from Thelepte at daylight.

Ward reported tank battle east edge of Sbeitla himself. Uncertain of ability to hold. Was not breaking off battle at Sbeitla because he could not if he would. He fears we have lost 1 Armoured Division.

Fredendall feels that 1 Army has not given credit to his reports as to gravity of situation.

Towards morning, there was another message from Carleton. The German attack had apparently been beaten off at Sbeitla, but there was still firing. He would report when he could find what the situation actually was.

And a message from Conway at Feriana. His radio operator had roused him from sleep to inform him that everyone had pulled out of Feriana. The headquarters was gone. He would follow and report when he could find it.

Just at daylight another message from Conway reported that our people on the airfield at Thelepte were destroying airplanes and burning fuel and other supplies. Roads were crowded with vehicles but the troops were establishing themselves on the ridge north of the airfield.

Those early hours of 17 February had been anxious hours at the Advanced C.P.—and elsewhere.

By now it was obvious even to General Anderson that this was the German offensive which intelligence officers had been so certain was to come through the passes around Fondouk farther to the north. We knew that some of Rommel's Panzer divisions were involved, and there had still been no action anywhere else on the front.

At half-past nine the morning of 17 February, Brigadier McNabb telephoned to say that one brigade of the British 6 Armoured Division with artillery and anti-tank guns had been ordered from the northern sector to Thala, and that 34 Infantry Division on the right of what had been the French sector was to hold the high ground east of Sbiba.

At 10.45, General Fredendall called to report that our troops had withdrawn from Feriana to the ridge north of the airfield at Thelepte, and that our forces were already withdrawing through Kasserine Pass. Ward was to start west at 11.00 to come through Kasserine Pass and take position south of Tebessa. McQuillin was to start at 11.00 but was to delay en route and reach Sbiba at nightfall in order to ensure protection of Ryder's (34 Infantry Division) south flank. Fredendall said, "There is some confusion, but we are getting along pretty well. We are acting offensively in the air and have air cover over them."

Fredendall had had another big argument with General Anderson. He said, "He wanted me to hold all day at Sbeitla, but if I had, it (the armoured division) would have been tangled up in another dogfight. Finally I got him to agree to let me go ahead. They not only want to tell you what to do, but how to do it. Anyway, I think we are going to get our tail out of the door all right."

Fredendall wanted a battalion of the 18th Field Artillery to replace the one that had lost its guns at Sidi bou Zid and all but some three hundred of its personnel. In answer to my question as to what else he would need, he replied that he was going to survey the situation and take inventory and would let me know. He had already asked for a battalion of tanks. Then he added, "We are going to have to write Drake and his battalion off. I am going to get a plane over him and tell him to give in. There is no out. He is completely surrounded. He had two days' ammunition and two days' rations. He had been out for twenty-four hours. There is no use prolonging the agony. We have got to write him off."

That was bitter news.

I sent messages to Carleton to report General Ward's plan in full, and to A.F.H.Q. reporting the situation and the sad news about Drake's battalion. More of General Alexander's 18 Army Group were to inform themselves of the situation. And about noon, a staff officer called from Tebessa to say:

"Hello, General Truscott. This is Colonel Arnold. Got a little point. The French railroad people in Tebessa are packing up and evacuating—apparently on orders from their higher headquarters. I wonder if something could be done to cancel this and make them stay here. They are sort of panicking the population here."

I was hard put to answer that one. I telephoned Whitely at A.F.H.Q. He said he would find someone in authority there to deal with it, and suggested that I get after the line of communications people, both British and French, in Constantine, which I did. Then I reported the matter to Brigadier McNabb at 1 Army, and he replied:

"Yes, we have heard the rumour. I think it is fairly a rumour. I am sorry to say that I think it was started by the British Town Major in the place. I am not quite sure about the French civil. The whole thing has been started by some blasted rumour. I am after the bloke who did it. I think we have got it in hand, but I will make sure again."

General Eisenhower had A.F.H.Q. actually scraping the bottom of the barrel, but there was little there which would help our hard-pressed troops in the battles then in progress.

General Fredendall telephoned again at half-past one that afternoon (17 February) to appeal for another regimental combat team. As he expressed it:

"I am holding a lot of mountain passes against armour with three and one-half battalions of infantry. If they get together any place a couple of infantry battalions, they might smoke me out. . . . I haven't got a damn bit of reserve. I need a combat team of infantry worse than hell. All I have got are three and one-half battalions of infantry. They are not enough. And we just got a little dope from 1 Army that indications are the enemy is going to continue the attack from Feriana with the objective of taking Tebessa."

I explained to General Fredendall that the artillery and cannon companies of 9 Infantry Division were on their way, but that even they could not be expected for several days. The rest of the Division was moving, although it would be some time before any of its infantry regiments could reach the forward area. I suggested that he appeal to General Anderson again for infantry to help meet the emergency.

About mid-afternoon, Carleton reported heavy fighting at Sbeitla where our troops had just been attacked by twelve Me.109s. Our people were blowing up ammunition dumps and destroying supplies in preparation for withdrawing. And we had thought the withdrawal was already well under way!

. . . . As it turned out later, Ward had held Sbeitla until three o'clock in the afternoon to cover the withdrawal, and had then withdrawn through Kasserine Pass.

We did succeed in "getting our tail out of the door" during 17 February, and we were hopeful that the doors—Kasserine Pass and the Feriana Gap—were shut and barred so that we could lick our wounds and repair some of the damage.

On the morning of 18 February, General Fredendall telephoned to say that he wanted one hundred and twenty M-4 tanks, including the fifty-four diesels which were to come from the British, and which McNabb had already informed me the British had made arrangements to turn over to II Corps. Fredendall concluded:

"We are a little thin but if they will just reconnoitre for awhile, we'll be all set. The longer they let us alone, the better we'll be set. The air is working fine. 1 Armoured will not have its tail in until noon, so I am giving them air cover."

So far we could only guess at the extent of our losses and what would be needed to make them good. And I was becoming doubtful of obtaining any prompt or exact report from the Corps staff. Accordingly, I charged Carleton to check with every element of 1 Armoured Division to obtain an accurate account of the requirements. Carleton's report telephoned in the evening of 18 February, and confirmed in writing the following morning, summarized what defeat in battle can mean to an armoured division. He wrote:

"Since the start of the Sbeitla battle the morning of 15 February until its close at dark 17 February, 1 Armoured Division suffered the following losses:

Medium tanks	112
Light tanks (81 Recon. Sq.)	5
Half-tracks	80
Self-propelled 105s	11
Assault 75 mm. howitzer self propelled	5
Half-tracks 81 mm. mortar mounts	5
Scout cars	15
Wreckers	7
Tank destroyer 75 mm. self-propelled gun	10

"These losses are the best information available. Scattered portions of units were still putting in their appearance and vehicles of various types that had been abandoned on the field of battle and considered lost were appearing.

"Though the loss in personnel in the division had been considerable, it has in no way been commensurate with the losses in vehicles, and trained replacements are available and are being made promptly.

"The reverses suffered by this unit in the past few days and the magnification of losses in conversation between soldiers would normally indicate a decided lowering of morale and consequent effect upon efficiency. However in the case of this division, I do not believe this to be true. A very fine spirit still exists . . . and I am convinced that they can always carry more than their own weight against the Boche under any circumstances.

"There is a definite feeling in 1 Armoured Division which it is very difficult to argue against and which I have made every effort to explain logically—that our Allies are being given A-1 modern American equipment while they must be content to fight with obsolete Mark III tanks. I do not believe this has a detrimental effect upon the morale, as might appear in stating it; however, the feeling is there. The Mark III tank has a thirty-four-degree traverse of its only effective gun—the 75 mm. In a withdrawal, it is helpless. The tank crews and the officers who man the Mark III tanks have a definite inferiority complex when opposed to the German Mark IVs. . . ."

It is to be noted that Colonel Carleton's summary of losses applied only to 1 Armoured Division. It did not include the guns and half the personnel of the 2nd Battalion, 17th Field Artillery; all of one infantry battalion and most of another one lost on the Djebels at Sidi bou Zid; the numerous half-tracks mounting the light 75 mm. guns with which the tank destroyer battalions and companies had challenged the superior German armour and armament; nor any losses in 1 or 34 Infantry Divisions or among the Corps troops. There were plenty of holes in the dikes and all too few boys' fingers with which to plug them.

On 19 February, we were "getting set" as General Fredendall expressed it. Holding Kasserine Pass was Colonel Moore's force, the 19th Engineers, a battalion of the 39th Infantry, a chemical mortar company, a company of medium tanks, and the 805th Tank Destroyer Battalion (less one company). West of Kasserine, in the valley leading towards Tebessa, was Robinette with Combat Command B—one battalion and one company of medium tanks, 13th Armoured Regiment, the 27th Field Artillery Battalion, the 601st Tank Destroyer Battalion, and the 2nd Battalion, 6th Armoured Infantry Regiment. To the north around Thala was the remnant of Combat Command A, and in this area the "Nick Force"—so called from its British commander, Brigadier Nicholson, 6 Armoured Division—was gathering. Nick Force included an armoured brigade of 6 Armoured Division equipped with obsolete Crusader and Valentine tanks, a reconnaissance squadron, three batteries of artillery with twenty-four 25-pounder guns, several anti-tank detachments with forty-eight 6-pounder and eight 17-pounder anti-tank guns, a battalion of infantry, and the Cannon Company of the 39th U.S. Infantry. To the east, defending the Sbiba Gap, was 34 Infantry Division (less one regimental combat team and one infantry battalion) with the 18th Regimental Combat Team of 1 Infantry Division attached.

During the day, the Germans reconnoitred along the front from Feriana to Sbiba, and on 20 February, the German Panzer divisions struck through our poorly organized defences at Kasserine Pass. Infiltrating around the small infantry forces placed too far out in front, and on to the heights behind them, and avoiding the minefield and obstacles which had been carefully marked off with tape and flags to avoid casualties among our own troops during the withdrawal, Rommel's Panzer divisions struck through the pass and then fanned out in two columns: one of Germans and Italians heading west towards Tebessa, the other stronger column northward towards Thala and Maktar. During these hours we had little information at the Advanced C.P., and most of that discouraging. To us, it seemed almost touch and go. If we had not been able to hold the strong position at Kasserine Pass, how could we hope to hold the weaker ones of the wide front between Thala and Tebessa?

From all along the front and from the rear, every gun and tank which could be brought to bear upon the enemy was being rushed to the critical area. And the whole weight of Allied air power in North Africa, including the mighty B-17s, was brought in to support our hard-pressed troops. At nightfall, no one knew what would happen next.

That night the enemy was reported withdrawing, but he

was only regrouping himself for battle. At dawn on the 21st, he renewed the attacks. In the south, the Germans and Italians drove Combat Command B back to a point only eight miles from Tebessa, but a counter-attack by the 2nd Battalion, 6th Armoured Infantry, supported by a company of tanks, in the late afternoon regained all lost ground. In the north, the Germans were stopped just short of Thala by the fires of massed artillery and the pounding of the Allied air forces.

This was not the end of the Kasserine battle, but it was to be the high-water mark in the tide of the German storm.

. . . . 23 February brought an end to the Kasserine battle.

. . . . Rommel, pounded by our vastly superior air forces and confronted by superior strength in front, had actually begun his withdrawal the night of 22 February. Attacking troops on 23 February received only light artillery fire. On the 24th there was no opposition at all—the bird had flown. We reoccupied Feriana and Sbeitla and within a few days the Germans were back on the ground from which they had begun operations the morning of 14 February. Rommel had accomplished little in the way of gaining elbow room in Tunisia and he had sustained losses which could not be replaced. He had thrown a scare into every headquarters in North Africa, and he had taught us much. More than enough to pay the cost in men and material which had fallen so heavily upon the American troops of II Corps.

General Truscott

By 28 February Rommel was back in his original positions.

General Alexander Worries

Have just returned from three days on the American and French front lines. . . . Broadly speaking, Americans require experience and French require arms. . . . I am

frankly shocked at whole situation as I found it. . . . Hate
to disappoint you, but find victory in North Africa is not
just around the corner.

> General Alexander to Winston Churchill,
> 27 February 1943

Dr. Goebbels Worries

We have about seventy-five thousand men in North
Africa and the Italians about two hundred thousand. That
is quite a concentration of troops, but it lacks weapons,
fuel, and in some places even food. Only sixty per cent of
the supplies reach Tunis; forty per cent must be written
off as lost. What is being sent to the bottom of the ocean
in the way of equipment almost baffles description;
consequently we are short of these supplies at decisive
points on the Eastern Front. Nevertheless the Führer has
decided that Tunis must be held as long as possible and
has opposed every compromise proposal.

Rommel described in detail to the Führer his difficulties
with the Italians. Hearing his description, one can
understand why he fell ill. In North Africa actually almost
half a dozen different command points are functioning one
against the other—Rommel, Kesselring, Arnim, the
Commando Supremo in Rome, the local Italian
commander, etc. It is simply hopeless to try and wage war
with authority and jurisdiction in such a muddle.

. . . . If the Italians were also to lose Tunis, a very
serious crisis might conceivably ensue at this critical
moment.

> Dr. Goebbels, 17 March

Mareth

On 21 March, having repulsed a last attack by the
Afrika Korps near Medenine, the Eighth Army to the
south launched its own assault on the Mareth Line, the
last really formidable desert position their old enemies
could hold. The Mareth Line was a bristling system of

fortifications built before the war by the French against possible attack from Italian Tripolitania.

Medenine

February—we closed up to the Mareth Line, the last enemy barrier between us and the Allied armies to the north. On a cold, misty morning we moved north round Medenine and isolated the twin features of the Tadjera hills, the outposts to Mareth. Here on 6 March, Rommel, whose gambles had so frequently before been successful, tried one last throw against us.

. . . . It was a most unusual battle for us. All day Kinnaird and I sat in the A.C.V. as the reports came in from all parts of the front. I listened and marked the enemy moves on the map, and Kinnaird sat for most of the time silent, with his chin cupped in his hands. I did not know what thoughts were passing through his mind. For myself, when I had a moment to spare I could not help comparing this day with many in the past. After two and a half years of deadly struggle against an enemy who always seemed to have the power to come back, it was a new feeling to be utterly confident of the outcome of so vicious a battle. In character it was almost exactly the same as our successful defensive battle at Alam Halfa, against Rommel's final attack at Alamein. We waited, making no move, for the enemy to attack our fixed defences. But whereas the previous year, after so long a series of faults and disasters in the weary withdrawal to Alamein, we had not dared to hope that the tide had really turned and that we could in fact defeat the German tanks, now we were completely confident.

As the day passed we began to be sure, with an absolute certainty, that never again would we feel the sting of disaster, never again would the enemy be able to turn defeat to triumph. On that day we really began to know that the Germans had begun to crack. Throughout their long, skilfully conducted withdrawal it had not been very obvious, but now it showed in a number of things—some small, some big. It showed in the sterility of the German tactics—the same methods which, though they had succeeded often enough when we were out-gunned, out-armoured and unco-ordinated, had proved ineffective at Alam Halfa. It showed in the hesitation of the advance of their tanks, now cautious and indecisive, a pale shadow of what they had been in the past. It showed in the failure of the German artillery and infantry to take any part in the battle. And finally it showed most clearly and convincingly in their failure to withdraw or destroy some of their tanks which were only slightly damaged, but which they allowed to fall into our hands.

Kinnaird broke his silence towards evening when the battle was clearly won. "That's that, Tony. However long the war goes on for now, I don't believe we'll ever again have the trouble we first had with their Panzers. Come on, let's go and drink to the swiftest, shortest, surest victory I've ever seen."

Cyril Joly

Maoris at Mareth

On the Maori front there was trouble. The tanks were unable to climb Hill 209 and sheered off to go round it. An 88 mm., cleverly placed behind the hill, knocked out five in succession and the others drew back. The right of the battalion was pinned down by heavy fire from 209 but C Company on the left, under Peta Awatere, swung right and attacked in the most spirited fashion. A lower feature of 209, later called Hikurangi, was strongly held and a bitter fight ensued on its steep slopes. The barrage had gone over, the tanks in the vicinity had lost interest or were out of touch, and the Maoris had to fight it out themselves.

I went up in a Bren carrier just before dusk and found that C Company had at last forced the Germans off the top of Hikurangi on to the reverse slope, but they were unable to stay on the top themselves under the intense fire from 209. Awatere had been wounded and the remnants of the company under one of the platoon commanders, Ngarimu, were clinging to a position just under the lip of the hill. The Germans had closed up to within twenty yards and a furious grenade and stone-throwing fight was in progress.

Brigadier Kippenberger

Gurkhas

The Gurkhas from 4 Indian Division were given a sort of roving commission in the hills towards Hallouf. Their main task was to beat up any posts, destroy any large guns which were firing from that area, and generally cause alarm and despondency. They appeared to have had excellent sport. They got busy with their knives very quietly in the dark. I don't think the Germans quite liked it. I remember one particular Gurkha situation report which finished as follows:

". . . Enemy losses ten killed, ours nil. Ammunition expenditure nil."

Major-General Sir Francis de Guingand

DEBACLE

By 26 March the Mareth Line was broken and the Germans were once more in full flight; now northwards into Tunisia. On 7 April the Americans linked up with Montgomery's men: the two arms of the nutcracker had met, after five months. In the last days of April the Allied forces, closing in on all sides, delivered the first of a series of great assaults. Some of the Eighth Army's strength, tied up before Enfidaville, was switched to 1 Army to lend weight to the knock-out blow. After much hard fighting the final break-through came on 6 May; on the 7th both Tunis and Bizerta fell. The German front collapsed completely, and by the 13th all resistance was at an end. The large forces which the Germans had poured so recklessly into Tunisia were trapped and destroyed almost to a man.

Two British Armies Meet

May—and we were half-way over the mountains which separated us from 1 Army, facing the gates of Tunis. The call had been dramatic in its scope and suddenness. At midday the previous day we were facing still the enemy positions at Enfidaville—resigned to seeing the campaign concluded by others, impotent in face of the natural strength of the physical barrier that held our further advance. By nightfall the tanks were already loaded on to transporters, and as darkness closed in we moved off on a march of a hundred and seventy miles with the beckoning prospect of being in at the kill. Over wild, unmarked tracks, in places almost disappearing among a mass of tangled rocks and undergrowth, in wireless silence so that our move would not be detected, we drove until we reached the first signs of the new army which we were to join.

In two days we were together again, in an area a hundred and twenty miles west of Tunis. Here we were issued with new tanks and new vehicles to fill the gaps in the ranks of the sand-covered, battered columns of our units. We were given, too, a generous share of the delicacies of their canteens—food and drink which we had not tasted for three long years, whisky, English chocolate and beer, English cigarettes. Only when we saw them did we realize how atrocious had been the supplies on which we had existed so long—Egyptian beer, "V" cigarettes, chocolate tasting of straw.

We began to note and silently judge the Army among whom we had so abruptly arrived. They were smarter than we were, their equipment and uniforms new and glistening with paint and polish. Their methods were different, too. They relied to a great extent on written orders, whereas we had become accustomed to settling all but the smallest details by conference and discussion, swiftly convened and quickly over, the decisions just as complete and binding.

Perhaps it was most like the meeting between a mature, seasoned veteran and a young, brilliant, eager amateur. We had learnt too much from bitter experience to put much faith in the books and manuals; our new companions had thought and trained for so long that they were steeped in the exact theory of the conduct of operations. They had fought a hard, bitter war for each yard of their advance and were not so ready as we had learned to be for moves of more scope and speed.

Gradually we began to know each other, and some of the rough edges of our mutual suspicion wore away under the surge of the imminence of our next enormous task. We became less conscious of, and boasted less of, the length of our advance; we were less aware of the difference of our garb and the colouring of our equipment, still splashed with the dappled yellow and grey which had served to hide us among the ridges of the desert. We began to feel less guilty of our peculiar manners, our peculiar and barbaric phrases—all the hundred and one differences of manner, language, outlook which had grown from so long an isolation from home and been nurtured by the multiple character of the nations and races which formed our army.

"They look like novices, but they've done a good job," was a typical, somewhat patronizing remark. It was difficult for each side not to be patronizing—their "Of course you won't find it the same in the mountains" was no less offensive than our "After three years we ought to be able to do something."

Cyril Joly

The Last Days

During the final days of the Tunisian campaign two local battles in the north, one in the British sector and one in the American, gripped the interest of the entire theatre. Both positions were exceedingly strong naturally and fiercely defended, and both were essential to us in our

final drive for victory. The position in the British sector
was Longstop—the battle for its possession from the
beginning to the end of the African campaign probably
cost more lives than did the fighting for any other spot in
Tunisia. In the American sector the place was Hill 609,
eventually captured by 34 Division, to the intense
satisfaction, particularly, of the American high command.
This division had been denied opportunity for training to a
greater degree than any other, and its capture of the
formidable 609 was final proof that the American ground
forces had come fully of age.

Following immediately upon the break-through, Alexander sent armoured units of the British 1 Army
rapidly forward across the base of the Bon Peninsula,
where we believed the Germans might attempt to retreat
to make a last stand in the manner of Bataan. Alexander's
swift action, regardless of the many thousands of enemy
still fighting in confused pockets along the front of 1
Army, destroyed this last desperate hope of the enemy.
From then on the operations were of a mopping-up
variety. Some fighting continued until the twelfth but by
the following day, except for a few stragglers in the
mountains, the only living Germans left in Tunisia were
safely within prison cages. The number of prisoners during
the last week of the campaign alone reached two hundred
and forty thousand, of whom approximately 125,000 were
German. Included in these captures was all that was left of
the Afrika Korps and a number of other crack German
and Italian units.

Rommel himself escaped before the final débâcle,
apparently foreseeing the inevitable and earnestly desiring
to save his own skin. The myth of his and Nazi
invincibility had been completely destroyed. Von Arnim
surrendered the German troops, and Field-Marshal Messe,
in nominal command of the whole force, surrendered the
Italian contingent. When von Arnim was brought through
Algiers on his way to captivity, some members of my staff
felt that I should observe the custom of bygone days and
allow him to call on me.

The custom had its origin in the fact that mercenary soldiers of old had no real enmity towards their opponents. Both sides fought for the love of a fight, out of a sense of duty or, more probably, for money. A captured commander of the eighteenth century was likely to be, for weeks or months, the honoured guest of his captor. The tradition that all professional soldiers are really comrades in arms had, in tattered form, persisted to this day.

For me the second World War was far too personal a thing to entertain such feelings. Daily as it progressed there grew within me the conviction that as never before in a war between many nations the forces that stood for human good and men's rights were this time confronted by a completely evil conspiracy with which no compromise could be tolerated. Because only by the utter destruction of the Axis was a decent world possible, the war became for me a crusade in the traditional sense of that often misused word.

In this specific instance, I told my Intelligence officer, Brigadier Kenneth Strong, to get any information he possibly could out of the captured generals but that, so far as I was concerned, I was interested only in those who were not yet captured. None would be allowed to call on me. I pursued the same practice to the end of the war. Not until Field-Marshal Jodl signed the surrender terms at Rheims in 1945 did I ever speak to a German general, and even then my only words were that he would be held personally and completely responsible for the carrying out of the surrender terms.

The outcome of the Tunisian campaign was of course eminently satisfactory, but the high command was so busily engaged in preparation of the Sicilian attack that little opportunity was available for celebration. However, a Victory Parade was held in Tunis on the 20th to mark the end of the Axis Empire in Africa.

The very magnitude of our victory, at least of our captures, served to intensify our difficulties in preparing for the Sicilian affair. We had more than two hundred and fifty thousand prisoners corralled in Tunisia, where poor communications made feeding and guarding difficult and rapid evacuation impossible. But the end of the campaign did have the effect of freeing commanders and staffs from immediate operations and allowed them to turn their full attention to the matter in hand. Preparatory planning had been going on ever since February in a special group under General Alexander. This group was now absorbed completely in General Alexander's staff and the whole process of preparation was vastly speeded up.

The Tunisian victory was hailed with delight throughout the Allied nations. It clearly signified to friend and foe alike that the Allies were at last upon the march.

General Eisenhower

I am grateful to the British soldiers—to those small humble citizens who are capable of being the greatest soldiers. But they do not talk about their deeds; they do not boast; and as soon as the war ends they will modestly disappear into their homes and cease to be heroes. Therein lies their greatest glory.

President Masaryk of Czechoslovakia,
on the occasion of the Allied victory in Tunisia

Masaryk was speaking from Britain, which he knew so well. His gratitude extended to all who were striving in the cause which would liberate his country.

KEY TO THE SOURCES OF EXTRACTS

For an explanation of how to use this Key and the following section entitled *Sources*, see page xvi

SOURCES

The Editors wish to express their gratitude to all the publishers, authors, literary agents and others who so kindly granted permission for the reproduction of the extracts in this anthology.

1. *Above Us the Waves (The Midget Raiders)*, by C. E. T. Warren and James Benson. Harrap, 1953; Sloane, 1954.
2. *After the Battle*, by Boris Agapov. Hutchinson, 1943.
3. *Big Show, The*, by Pierre Clostermann. Chatto & Windus; Random, 1951.
4. *Black Watch and the King's Enemies, The*, by Bernard Fergusson. Collins; Crowell, 1950.
5. *Bomber Pilot*, by Group-Captain Leonard Cheshire. Hutchinson, 1943.
6. *Bridge to the Sun*, by Gwen Terasaki. Joseph, 1958; University of North Carolina Press, 1957.
7. *Camouflage Story, The*, by Geoffrey Barkas. Cassell, 1952.
8. *Canadian Army, 1939-45, The*, by Colonel C. P. Stacey. Department of Public Printing and Stationery, Ottawa, 1948.
9. *Colditz Story, The*, by P. R. Reid. Hodder & Stoughton; Lippincott, 1952.
10. *Command Missions*, by Lieutenant-General L. K. Truscott, Jr. Dutton, Copyright 1954 by Lieutenant-General L. K. Truscott.

11. *Commando,* by Brigadier John Durnford-Slater. Kimber, 1953.
12. *Crusade in Europe,* by Dwight D. Eisenhower. Heinemann; Doubleday, 1948.
13. *Day After Day,* by Odd Nansen. Putnam, 1949.
14. *Decisive Battles of the Western World, The,* Vol. 3, by Major-General J. F. C. Fuller. Eyre & Spottiswoode; Scribner, 1956.
15. *Defeat in the West,* by Milton Shulman. Secker & Warburg, 1947; Dutton, 1948.
16. *Dieppe at Dawn (At Whatever Cost),* by R. W. Thompson. Hutchinson, 1956; Coward, 1957.
17. *Dittybox, The,* No. 5. H.M.S.O., 1944.
18. *Drive: A Chronicle of Patton's Army,* by Charles Codman. Little, Brown, © 1957 by Theodora Duer Codman.
19. *Fatal Decisions, The,* by Werner Kreipe and others, edited by Seymour Freiden and William Richardson. Joseph; Sloane, 1956.
20. *First and the Last, The,* by Adolf Galland. Holt, 1954; Methuen, 1955.
21. *Follow My Leader,* by Louis Hagan. Wingate, 1951.
22. *Gauntlet to Overlord,* by Ross Munro. Macmillan, 1945.
23. *German Morale 1939-45,* by General Hasso von Manteuffel; *An Cosantóir: The Irish Defence Journal,* 1949.
24. *Goebbels Diaries, The,* by Louis P. Lochner. Doubleday, 1948.
25. *Going to the Wars,* by John Verney. Collins; Dodd, 1955.
26. *Goon in the Block,* by Eric Williams. Cape, 1945.
27. *Great Escape, The,* by Paul Brickhill. Norton, 1950; Faber, 1952.
28. *Green Beret, The,* by Hilary St. George Saunders. Joseph, 1949.
29. *Hausfrau at War,* by Else Wendel. Odhams, 1957.
30. *Hitler and His Admirals,* by Anthony Martienssen. Secker & Warburg, 1948; Dutton, 1949.

31. *Hitler Directs His War,* by Felix Gilbert. Oxford, 1950.

32. *Infantry Brigadier,* by Major-General Sir Howard Kippenberger. Oxford, 1949.

33. *In Their Shallow Graves (Road to Stalingrad),* by Benno Zieser. Elek, 1956; Ballantine, 1955.

34. *I Walk on Wheels,* by Elizabeth Sheppard-Jones. Bles, 1958.

35. *Last Letters From Stalingrad.* Coronet, 1955; Methuen, 1956.

36. *Lofoten Letter,* by Evan John. Heinemann, 1941.

37. *Look Down in Mercy,* by Walter Baxter. Putnam, 1952; Heinemann, 1953.

38. *Lost Victories,* by Field-Marshal Erich von Manstein. Methuen; Regnery, 1958.

39. *MacArthur, 1941-1951: Victory in the Pacific,* by Major-General Charles A. Willoughby and John Chamberlain. McGraw, 1954; Heinemann, 1956.

40. *Magnificent Mitscher, The,* by Theodore Taylor. Norton, copyright 1954 by Theodore Taylor.

41. *Memoirs of Field-Marshal the Viscount Montgomery of Alamein.* Collins; World, 1958.

42. *Midway: The Battle that Doomed Japan,* by Mitsuo Fuchida and Masataka Okumiya. U. S. Naval Institute, 1955; Hutchinson, 1957.

43. *One That Got Away, The,* by Kendal Burt and James Leasor. Collins and Joseph, 1956; Random, 1957.

44. *Operation Victory,* by Major-General Sir Francis de Guingand. Hodder; Scribner, 1947.

45. *Panzer Battles, 1939-1945,* by F. W. von Mellenthin. Cassell, 1955; U. of Okla. Press, 1956.

46. *Peter Moen's Diary.* Faber; Farrar, Straus & Cudahy, copyright 1941 by Creative Press, Inc.

47. *Privileged Nightmare, The,* by Giles Romilly and Michael Alexander. Weidenfeld, 1954.

48. *Rommel Papers, The,* edited by B. H. Liddell Hart. Collins; Harcourt, 1953.
49. *Royal Artillery Commemoration Book, 1939-1945, The.* Bell, 1950.
50. *Sailor's Odyssey, A,* by Admiral of the Fleet Viscount Cunningham of Hyndhope. Hutchinson; Dutton, 1951.
51. *Sea Devils,* by J. Valerio Borghese. Melrose, 1952; Henry Regnery, 1954.
52. *Second World War, The,* by Winston Churchill, Vol. 2. Houghton, 1949.
53. *Second World War, The,* by Winston Churchill, Vol. 3. Houghton, 1950.
54. *Second World War, The,* by Winston Churchill, Vol. 4. Houghton, 1950.
55. *Sergeant in the Snow, The,* by Mario Rigoni Stern. MacGibbon & Kee, 1954.
56. *Skorzeny's Special Missions,* by Otto Skorzeny. Hale; McGraw, 1957.
57. *Slave Ship, The,* by Bruno E. Werner. Pantheon, 1951; Heinemann, 1953.
58. *Soldier,* by General Matthew B. Ridgway. Harper, 1956.
59. *Stalingrad,* by Heinz Schroter. Joseph; Dutton, 1958.
60. *Sunk,* by Mochitsura Hashimoto. Cassell; Holt, 1954.
61. *Take These Men,* by Cyril Joly. Constable, 1955.
62. *Ten Summers: Poems,* by John Pudney. Bodley Head, 1944 (also in *Collected Poems,* Putnam, 1957; *Flight Above Cloud,* Harper, 1944).
63. *They Have Their Exits,* by Airey Neave. Hodder & Stoughton; Little, Brown, 1953.
64. *Thirty Seconds Over Tokyo,* by Captain T. W. Lawson. Hammond; Random, 1943.
65. *Three Came Home,* by Agnes Newton Keith. Little, Brown, 1947; Joseph, 1948.
66. *To Perish Never,* by Henry Archer and Edward Pine. Cassell, 1954.

67. *Trial of Joseph Kramer, The,* edited by Raymond Phillips. Hodge; British Book Centre, 1949.
68. *Trial of German Major War Criminals, The: Proceedings of the International Military Tribunal at Nuremburg, 1946.* H.M.S.O.
69. *Turn of the Tide, The,* by Sir Arthur Bryant. Collins; Doubleday, 1957.
70. *Twenty Thousand Thieves, The,* by Eric Lambert. Muller, 1952.
71. *Voices From Britain,* edited by Henning Krabbe. Allen & Unwin, 1947; Macmillan, 1948.
72. *Warrior Without Weapons,* by Marcel Junod. Cape; Macmillan, 1951.
73. *We Landed at Dawn,* by A. B. Austin, Gollancz; Harcourt, 1943.
74. *With Rommel in the Desert,* by Heinz Werner Schmidt. Harrap: British Book Centre, 1951.
75. *Year of Stalingrad, The,* by Alexander Werth. Hamilton, 1946; Knopf, 1947.

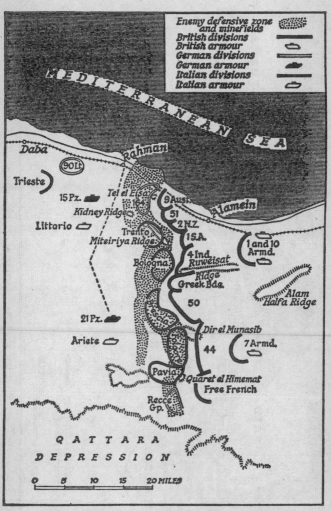

Legend:
- Enemy defensive zone and minefields
- British divisions
- British armour
- German divisions
- German armour
- Italian divisions
- Italian armour

MEDITERRANEAN SEA

Daba
Trieste
90 It.
15 Pz.
Kidney Ridge
Littorio
Rahman
Tel el Eisa
164
9 Aust.
51
2 N.Z.
Trento
Miteiriya Ridge
Bologna
4 Ind.
Ruweisat
Ridge
Greek Bde.
50
Alamein
1 and 10
Armd.
Alam
Halfa Ridge
21 Pz.
Ariete
Dir el Munasib
44
7 Armd.
Pavia
Quaret el Himemat
Free French
Recce
Gp.

QATTARA DEPRESSION

0 5 10 15 20 MILES

THE ALAMEIN FRONT: OCT. 23, 1942

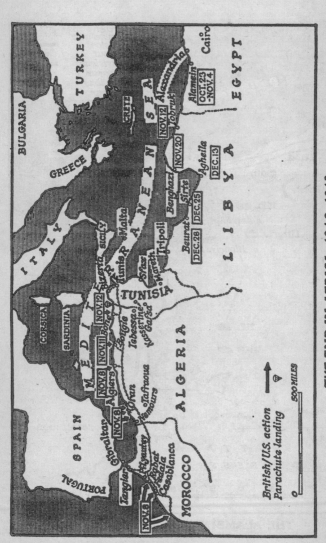

THE END IN AFRICA. 1942–1943

INDEX

THE TASTE OF COURAGE, THE WAR, 1939-1945
edited by Desmond Flower and James Reeves

A MAJOR FIVE-VOLUME SERIES ON
WORLD WAR II
FROM BERKLEY

The drama, the humor, the horror, and sometimes the tenderness of men and women confronting their greatest ordeal speak through this absorbing narrative of World War II, told in eyewitness accounts by soldiers, housewives, and journalists in the many countries involved.

VOLUME I:
  THE BLITZKRIEG   (Z1814-$1.25)

VOLUME II:
  THE AXIS TRIUMPHANT   (Z1976-$1.25)

VOLUME IV:
  THE ALLIES ADVANCE   (Z2008-$1.25)

VOLUME V:
  VICTORY AND DEFEAT   (Z2018-$1.25)

Send for a free list of all our books in print

These books are available at your local newsstand, or send price indicated plus 15¢ per copy to cover mailing costs to Berkley Publishing Corporation, 200 Madison Avenue, New York, N. Y. 10016.